D1207314

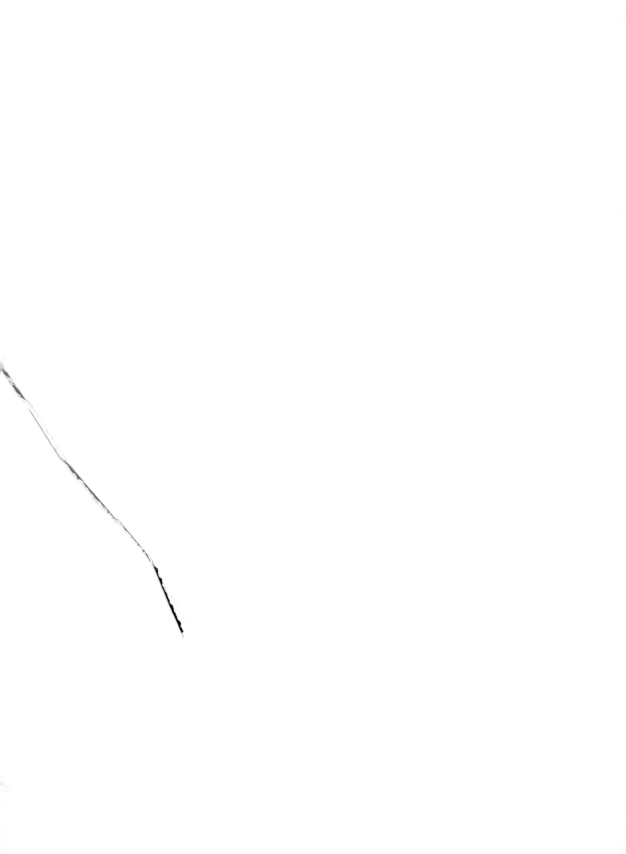

Warped Space

Warped Space

Art, Architecture, and Anxiety in Modern Culture

Anthony Vidler

The MIT Press   Cambridge, Massachusetts   London, England

This book was set Adobe Garamond by Graphic Composition, Inc. and was printed and bound in the United States of America.

Library of Congress Cataloging-in-Publication Data

Vidler, Anthony.
    Warped space : art, architecture, and anxiety in modern culture / Anthony Vidler.
        p. cm.
    Includes bibliographical references and index.
    ISBN 0-262-22061-X (hc : alk. paper)
    1. Space (Architecture)—Psychological aspects.   I. Title.

NA2765 .V53 2000
701´.8—dc21

00-026898

Contents

Preface

Folds, blobs, nets, skins, diagrams: all words that have been employed to describe theoretical and design procedures over the last decade, and that have rapidly replaced the cuts, rifts, faults, and negations associated with deconstruction, which had previously displaced the types, signs, structures, and morphologies of rationalism. The new vocabulary has something to do with contemporary interest in the *informe;* it seems to draw its energies from a rereading of Bataille and a new interest in Deleuze and Guattari; its movies of choice would perhaps be *Crash* before *Blade Runner, The Matrix* before *Brazil;* its favorite reading might take in Burroughs (but no longer Gibson), Žižek (but maybe not Derrida). The representative forms of this by now strong tendency are complex and curved, smooth and intersecting, polished and translucent, thin and diagrammatic. Both the new vocabulary and its materializations intersect with and take many of their techniques from digital technology; indeed many of the projected and built designs would be unrealizable, if not unimaginable, without it. They are words and forms conceived and manipulated in a virtual space, with, nevertheless, an intimate relationship to production techniques and the technology of materials. Such a relationship would be impossible without the digital interface that construes information, theoretical and practical, according to the same rules of representation and replication.

The terms and forms of this new tendency take their place, however, no matter how unprecedented they may seem, within a particular modernist genealogy, on which they draw for their imagery as well as their philosophy. A common concern for space albeit defined in an entirely different manner from that of the first avant-gardes, and a similarly shared registration of the aftereffects of psychology and psychoanalysis, provide a historical continuity with early twentieth-century developments. The intersection of spatial thought with psychoanalytical thought, of the nature of containment and the characteristics of the subject, has been a preoccupation of social and aesthetic discourse since the turn of the century; certain of the avant-garde movements of the 1920s and 1930s, among them expressionism, explored this intersection in terms of its representation; contemporary experimentation preserves these two terms, while distorting the traditional space of modernism and questioning the equally traditional fiction of the humanist subject. The results in each case, theoretically or in design, have been the production of a kind of warping, which I have called warped space.

In this book I am concerned with two apparently distinct but in fact closely related forms of spatial warping. The first is that produced by the psychological culture of modernism from the late nineteenth century to the present, with its emphasis on the nature of space as a projection of the subject, and thus as a harbinger and repository of all the neuroses and phobias of that subject. Space, in this ascription, is not empty, but full of disturbing objects and forms, among which the forms of architecture and the city take their place. The arts of representation, in their turn, are drawn to depict such subject/object disturbances, themselves distorting the conventional ways in which space has been described since the Renaissance.

The second kind of warping is that produced by the forced intersection of different media—film, photography, art, architecture—in a way that breaks the boundaries of genre and the separate arts in response to the need to depict space in new and unparalleled ways. Artists, rather than simply extending their terms of reference to the three-dimensional, take on the questions of architecture as an integral and critical part of their work in installations that seek to criticize the traditional terms of art. Architects, in a parallel way, are exploring the processes and forms of art, often on the terms set out by artists, in order to escape the rigid codes of functionalism and formalism. This intersection has engendered a kind of "intermediary art," comprised of objects that, while situated ostensibly in one practice, require the interpretive terms of another for their explication.

The relationship between these two kinds of warping, psychological and artistic, is established by the common ground of all artistic and architectural practice in modernity: the space of metropolis, in its different forms and cultural identifications, from the Vienna and Berlin of the late nineteenth century

to the Los Angeles of the late twentieth. This space, whether examined socio-
logically, psychologically, or aesthetically, has operated as the flux, so to speak,
in which subjects and objects have been forced to adjust their always uneasy relations. And whether architects or artists seek to solve the problems inherent in
metropolitan life with material or utopian solutions, or simply to represent
them in all their implicit horror and excitement, the need to develop new forms
of expression was and is the result. Without idealistic enthusiasm, but also with
no extreme dystopianism, I have examined a few of the examples of this process that, in all its ramifications, underlies the continuing experiment we call
modernism.

Anthony Vidler
Los Angeles, May 1999

Acknowledgments

The initial inspiration for my study of the cultural history of agoraphobia was provided by an invitation to present a paper at a symposium entitled "Siegfried Kracauer: The Critic in Exile," organized at the Goethe House, Columbia University, by Andreas Huyssen and Mark Anderson in 1990. The conceptual framework and the first chapters of the book were developed during a residential fellowship at the Getty Center for the History of Art and the Humanities in 1993; the suggestions of Kurt Forster, Keith Moxey, Michael Holly, and my research assistant, Lori Weintrob, were invaluable. T. J. Clark, Tony Kaes, and Anne Wagner have commented instructively on papers presented at Berkeley. Mary Kelly hosted a presentation of the work in progress at the Whitney Critical Studies Program and, together with her students, offered important insights. The late Ernest Pascucci organized a conference on "Public Fear," under the auspices of the Guggenheim Museum and *ANY* magazine, the themes of which were generated from this book, and which, through discussion and a series of highly original presentations, helped enormously to expand and clarify my thinking at a crucial stage in the writing. Mark Cousins, as a generous host at the Architectural Association in London, has heard almost all the chapters over the last five years and has been a continuous source of encouragement and judicious criticism. Susan Buck-Morss, Dietrich Neumann, Edward Dimendberg, and Thomas Y. Levin have helped on questions of critical theory, Benjamin, Kracauer, and the movies. I thank those artists and architects whose work provided the main impetus to writing: Wolf Prix of Coop Himmelblau, Daniel Libeskind, Eric Owen Moss, Thom Mayne, Mike Kelley, Toba Khedoori, Martha Rosler, and Greg Lynn were always ready to share ideas and explain their projects. Sylvia Lavin, as Chair of the Department of Architecture, UCLA, has provided a stimulating context for debate and discussion.

My students at UCLA between 1993 and the present have helped me work through numerous problems. Spyros Papapetros, whose knowledge of the history and theory of animism, the uncanny, and phobia is exhaustive, was as resourceful as Holmes himself in scouring the library, and was equally generous in his critical readings of early drafts.

Roger Conover gently but insistently guided the book into press. Emily Apter asked questions and offered suggestions that gave me a sense of direction and an intellectual excitement that sustained every stage of the writing. Nicolas Apter-Vidler was generous enough to share his knowledge of dinosaurs, ants, and game software for my digital education.

Warped Space

Introduction

In this book I explore the anxious visions of the modern subject caught in spatial systems beyond its control and attempting to make representational and architectural sense of its predicament. Fear, anxiety, estrangement, and their psychological counterparts, anxiety neuroses and phobias, have been intimately linked to the aesthetics of space throughout the modern period. Romanticism, with its delight in the terrifying sublime, saw fear and horror lurking in landscapes, domestic scenes, and city streets. Modernism, while displacing many such spatial fears to the domain of psychoanalysis, was nevertheless equally subject to fears newly identified as endemic to the metropolis, forming its notions of abstraction under the sign of neurasthenia and agoraphobia and calculating its modes of representation according to the psychological disturbances of an alienated subject. Space, in these various iterations, has been increasingly defined as a product of subjective projection and introjection, as opposed to a stable container of objects and bodies. From the beginning of the century, the apparently fixed laws of perspective have been transformed, transgressed, and ignored in the search to represent the space of modern identity. Thus the body in pieces, physiognomy distorted by inner pain, architectural space as claustrophobic, urban space as agoraphobic, all warpings of the normal to express the pathological became the leitmotivs of avant-garde art. The vocabularies of displacement and fracture, torquing and twisting, pressure and release, void and block, *informe* and hyperform that they developed are still active today, deployed in work that seeks to reveal, if not critique, the conditions of a less than settled everyday life.

Thus the virtual fears of late modernity, whether expressed in the eloquent silence of Daniel Libeskind's bunkerlike interiors in the Jewish Museum, Berlin, or the even more mute casts of traditional domestic space fabricated by Rachel Whiteread in her *House* project, bear at least a family resemblance to the old phobias of modernity as imaged in the shattered perspectives of expressionism, the rigorous abstraction of purism, the unsettling dreams of surrealism, the *Merzbau* of Dada. In both, a sense of loss and mourning, informed by psychological and psychoanalytical theory, has led to an effort to construe an aesthetic equivalent; in both, the generation of this equivalent has forced the aesthetic into new and sometimes excessive modes of expression. What I have called warped space would be, in an initial formulation, a metaphor that includes all the varieties of such forcing, the attempt, however vain, to permeate the formal with the psychological.

In this sense the themes of this book continue and develop the questions raised in my earlier study *The Architectural Uncanny.* Toward the end of that book, I introduced the ideas of "dark space" and "transparency" in the context of psychological theories of doubling and identity, most particularly in the implications of Roger Caillois's notion of "legendary psychasthenia" or spatial absorption for current critiques of architectural monumentality. Noting that Jacques Lacan's theory of the mirror stage might offer an entry point for the interpretation of modernist transparency and its contemporary opaque or translucent variations, I concluded with a reference to Lacan's seminar of 1963, on the general subject of *angoisse* or anxiety. Concerned with the uncanny effects of mirroring, shadowing, and loss of face, I proposed that the soft surfaces of the new, antitransparent architecture of Rem Koolhaas and many of his contemporaries, rather than diminishing the anxiety of the modern subject in the evident absence of transparency and its substitution by reflectivity, tended to reformulate the conditions of interiority and exteriority with reference to the body. In this formulation, the paranoiac space of modernism would be mutated into a realm of panic, where all limits and boundaries would, I hazarded, "become blurred in a thick, almost palpable substance that has substituted itself, almost imperceptibly, for traditional [i.e., modern, body-centered] architecture."[1]

In the present work I have extended the question of anxiety and the paranoid subject of modernity beyond the question of the domestic uncanny (literally "the unhomely"), to consider the idea of phobic space and its design corollary warped space, understood as a more general phenomenon touching the entirety of public territories—the landscapes of fear and the topographies of despair created as a result of modern technological and capitalist development, from Metropolis to Megalopolis, so to speak. These questions are considered in the context of an earlier, apparently triumphant urbanism and monumental architectural modernity that, precisely at the moment of its greatest self-confidence and activity in the newly emerging metropolises, underwent a crisis of identity, expressed not only in the social criticism of the 1900s but also in the unsettling of representation itself, the abandonment of the historical certainties of realism in favor of an always ambiguous abstraction. Such abstraction, analyzed in the context of the new psychologies of perception, seemed to many to be itself born out of spatial fear, the "spiritual dread of space" that the art historian Wilhelm Worringer saw as the motive for the use of the "defensive" forms of geometry, as opposed to the more natural, empathetic forms of a society at one with its surroundings.

The Enlightenment dream of rational and transparent space, as inherited by modernist utopianism, was troubled from the outset by the realization that space as such was posited on the basis of an aesthetics of uncertainty and movement and a psychology of anxiety, whether nostalgically melancholic or progressively anticipatory.[2] This was on one level inevitable. With its roots in the empirical psychology and neo-Kantian formalism of the late nineteenth century—Robert Vischer's theories of optical perception, Theodor Lipps's concepts of empathy and *Raumästhetik,* and Conrad Fiedler's mentalism—the psychology of space was devoted to calibrating the endlessly shifting sensations and moods of a perceiving subject whose perceptions had less to do with what was objectively "there" than with what was projected as seen.[3] The modern preoccupation with space was thus founded on the understanding that the relationship between a viewer and a work of art was based on a shifting "point of view" determined by a moving body, a theory worked out in popular art criticism by Adolf Hildebrand and in art history by Alois Riegl. The spatial dimension rapidly became a central preoccupation for those interested in understanding the special conditions of architecture, an art that, while perceived visually, was experienced in space.[4] As summarized by Mitchell W. Schwarzer, the "emergence of architectural space" was an outgrowth of the developing sciences of optical perception and psychology, leading to what he calls a kind of "perceptual empiricism" and thence to the notion of a space that, rather than being understood as a passive container of objects and bodies, was suddenly charged with all the dimensions of a relative, moving, dynamic entity.[5] Thus the psychological theories of Hermann Lotz and Wilhelm Wundt, followed by Lipps and Vischer, which studied space as a function of the impressions of bodily movement on the mind, were joined to the implicit spatiality of Gottfried Semper's anthropology of enclosure and Richard Lucae's history of spatial aesthetics.

Perhaps the foremost exponent of spatial architecture was August Schmarsow, who countered Heinrizh Wölfflin's static psychology of the monument as reflection of the body (as outlined in his early work *Prolegomena to a Psychology of Architecture*)[6] and equally resisted Semper's theory of "dressing" or the enclosure as a result of hanging the "wall" on a structural frame. By contrast, Schmarsow posited that space, and architectural space in particular, was an active bodily creation and perception. In a series of writings between 1893 and 1895, he developed a psychological characterization of space, based on a concept of "intuited form," built up out of the sense of sight joined to "the residues of sensory experience to which the muscular sensations of our body, the sensitivity of our skin, and the structure of our body all contribute. . . . Our sense of space [*Raumgefühl*] and spatial imagination [*Raumphantasie*] press toward spatial creation [*Raumgestaltung*]; they seek their satisfaction in art. We call this art architecture; in plain words, it is the *creatress of space* [*Raumgestalterin*]."[7] Out of the child's first attempts to establish boundaries and walls in nature, followed by the building of walls, hedges, or fences and attended by the gradual development of geometry, architectural organization emerges as the abstraction of natural intuitions, the setting up of axes for vision and movement; vertical lines carried, so to speak, by bodies in forward motion set up depth, both virtually and literally, and thence a space for free movement. Schmarsow emphasizes the need of the body to exist with enough "elbow room" or *Spielraum,* a concept that will be adopted by Wölfflin and Benjamin to characterize the "spatial fullness" of Renaissance architecture. Thus, for Schmarsow, "the history of architecture is the history of the sense of space," and its continued life in the present depends on the renewal of this sense in contemporary terms—in "the age of railway stations and market halls"—and not on the repetition of older forms of spatial expression.[8] Inevitably, as the notion of architectural space as having a historical specificity was seized on to give new life to the historicist paradigm, the history of styles was gradually dissolved into, or replaced by, the history of spaces.[9] By 1914 this understanding of the space of humanist play had become widely accepted. Geoffrey Scott, who had, as Reyner Banham notes, served as Bernard Berenson's secretary and thus come into contact with the circle of aestheticians and historians following Lipps, wrote: "To enclose a space is the object of building; when we build we do but detach a convenient quantity of space, seclude it and protect it, and all architecture springs from that necessity. But aesthetically space is even more supreme. The architect models in space as a sculptor in clay. He designs his space as a work of art."[10]

Schmarsow's "body" paradigm for space was countered by the less haptic and more optical theories of Riegl. For Riegl, indeed, space was not always present as a foundational quality of architecture, only appearing comparatively late in the history of vision in the late Roman period. Riegl's notion of a spatial progression from the "close-up" and haptic forms of Egypt, through the "normal" distance of vision practiced by the Greeks, to the deep and ambiguous spatial form of late Rome was important in the theoretical development of perspective theory, and especially so, as we shall see, to Walter Benjamin and Erwin Panofsky.[11] Similarly, and again without the specifically corporeal ingredients of Schmarsow, Paul Frankl, in his thesis of 1913–1914, *Die Entwicklungsphasen der neueren Baukunst,* translated as *Principles of Architectural History,* grafted a spatial history of architecture since the Renaissance on the time-honored perdiodization of historicism. His four categories, spatial form, corporeal form, visible form, and purposive intention, were explored in the context of four periods or phases, with the intent of reformulating the question of style according to spatio-formal criteria that acted together to form a total building: "The visual impression, the *image* produced by differences of light and color, is primary in our perception of a building. We empirically reinterpret this image into a conception of *corporeality,* and this defines the form of the *space within,* whether we read it from outside or stand in the interior. But optical appearances, corporeality, and space, do not alone make a building. . . . Once we have interpreted the optical image into a conception of space, enclosed by mass, we read its *purpose* from the spatial form."[12]

The developmental history of space was to be canonized, so to speak, within the modernist tradition by the publication of Sigfried Giedion's *Space, Time and Architecture* in 1941.[13] For Giedion, as for most modernist architects, the invention of a new space conception was the leitmotiv of modernity itself, supported by the modernist avant-garde call for an escape from history, that affirmed the importance of space both for architectural planning and form and for modern life as a whole. The idea of space held the double promise of dissolving rigid stylistic characterization into fundamental three-dimensional organizations and of providing the essential material, so to speak, for the development of a truly modern architecture. For modernist architects these spatial theories offered a way of escaping the historicist trap of stylistic revivalism and incorporating time, movement, and social life into the conceptualization of abstract form in general, as well as implying a way of defining the terms of this new life, its relationship to nature and the body. The history of modernism, indeed, might be and has often been written as a history of competing ideas of space. At the turn of the century, Hendrik Berlage wrote on "Raumkunst und Architektur" in 1907.[14] August Endell, who had followed the lectures of Theodor Lipps in Munich, joined spatial theory to empathy theory in his *Die Schönheit des grossen Stadt* of 1908; both authors have been seen as influential on the spatial ideas of Mies van der Rohe.[15] The Dutch architects and painters in the De Stijl group, including Theo van Doesburg and Piet Mondrian, advanced their revolutionary concepts of "neoplastic" space in their own journal. In the United States, Frank Lloyd Wright took on the entire space of the continent in his vision of a "prairie" space, fit for democratic individualists. His Viennese assistant, Rudolph Schindler, dubbed this "space architecture" in a brief homage to what he called this "new medium" published in 1934.[16] In France, the reflections of Henri Bergson on time, movement, and space were quickly picked up by architects and artists, were incorporated into the popular writings of Elie Faure, and were taken up by the painter Amédée Ozenfant and the architect Le Corbusier, later to be elaborated into the latter's poetic evocation of a modernist *espace indicible* or "ineffable space."

The formal experimentation of the first avant-gardes was, in part at least, an attempt to represent the spatio-temporal dislocations of relativity in philosophy, mathematics, and later physics, while at the same time registering the psychic effects of modern life on the individual and mass subject. From the standpoint of the end of the century, we are able to register a continuity in all subsequent attempts, across media and in different artistic practices, that seek to mirror each successive stage of technological development, consumer spectacle, and subjective disquiet. What has been variously termed the "death" of the subject or its "disappearance" refers to the gradual transformation of the romantic ideal of individuality under these developments, and it is not surprising that spatial concepts reveal a similar, parallel history, from an ideal of "full-ness" to an increased sense of "flattening" and distortion.

To compare contemporary forms of expression to early twentieth-century avant-garde aesthetics may seem forced, however, or at least superficial; after all, the revivalisms of postmodernism and deconstructivism have tended to debase any sense of continuity with the architecture of the teens and twenties. Certainly, in a moment when space warp has become an almost daily experience as we are hurled at apparently mind-numbing speed through the computer-simulated corridors of the latest CD-ROM game release, early twentieth-century spatial forms may seem a little quaint, if not primitive. The geometrical attempts of the early modernists to emulate the collapsing of space and time seem on one level as distant from today's virtual reality environments as are the rusty engines of the first industrial revolution from contemporary computers. Where the effort of conception embodied in the "gravity-free" projections of an El Lissitzky, the montage experiments of a Sergei Eisenstein, the *promenades architecturales* of a Le Corbusier were replicated in laborious processes of visual representation and reproduction, the techniques of postdigital culture reproduce such forms as the effortless effects of keystroke manipulations. As exemplified in the exuberant forms of Frank Gehry's Guggenheim Museum at Bilbao, Spain, the architectural results of digital manipulations both explore hitherto unimaginable complexity and, with the mechanics of the design process now digitally linked to that of the fabrication process, work to revolutionize the mode of production itself.

Nevertheless, despite such obvious differences, the contemporary graphic effects of digital space are in fact deeply obligated to the representational experiments of modernism, in a way that carries serious implications for the theorization of virtuality. The expressionist dreams of Hermann Finsterlin and the curves of Bilbao are linked in more than an overt formalism. For while it is true that the gamut of representational techniques has been apparently increased, it is also the case that little has changed in the framing of space itself over the modern period. Perspective is still the rule in virtual reality environments; objects are still conceived and represented within all the three-dimensional conventions of eighteenth- and nineteenth-century practice. Ostensibly, there is as little to distinguish Alberti's window from a computer screen as there is to differentiate an eighteenth-century axonometric by Gaspard Monge from a wire-frame dinosaur generated by Industrial Light and Magic. What has changed is the technique of simulation and, even more importantly, the place, or position, of the subject or traditional "viewer" of the representation. Between contemporary virtual space and modernist space there lies an aporia formed by the autogenerative nature of the computer program, and its real blindness to the viewer's presence. In this sense, the screen is not a picture, and certainly not a surrogate window, but rather an ambiguous and unfixed location for a subject.

The complex intersection of traditional perspectival thought, and its modernist distortions, with contemporary digital culture has had an accordingly complicated effect on theory. On the one hand, art historians and students of cultural studies have been drawn to reinvestigate the sources of modern vision, the theoretical premises of the "techniques of the observer," as Jonathan Crary has succinctly put it.[17] On the other hand, digital enthusiasts have claimed, but not entirely proved, a new and uncharted era to be in the making. I tend to believe in a less distinct separation between modernism and the present: that a rigorous examination of traditional and modernist vision is essential to an understanding of the continuing use of these techniques in digitalization; which does not mean that the very nature of digitalization has not fundamentally altered the way in which we look and are looked at in space.

The conditions for thinking these fundamental problems in vision and spatiality were forged in the early modernist period itself, with the introduction of that particular form of virtuality known as psychological projection or introjection—a phenomenon often overlooked in the heavy-handed glorification and literalization of reality propounded by much contemporary virtual reality. The upsetting of the Albertian/Cartesian/Kantian paradigms of space and representational techniques by psychoanalysis and psychology, placing the onus of sight not on the technique but on the observer, was the first step in the formation of the relatively differentiated subject, immersed in the apparent chaos of a space-time atomic universe, a universe now represented by the distortions of cubism, futurism, expressionism, and the like.

The Renaissance discovery of perspective, however, and the subsequent theoretical and experiential permutations that have apparently placed the viewer/subject in what many historians have argued is a continual erosion, if not explosion, of the humanist viewpoint, has not been entirely obviated or denied by psycho-physiological warping, literal or phenomenal. Even as Erwin Panofsky understood that "perspective transforms psychophysiological space into mathematical space," so his recent interpreter Hubert Damisch insists on the controlling and systematic distinction between the space of the "desiring subject" (that posited both by Foucault in his interpretation of Velásquez's painting *Las Meninas,* and by Lacan in his concept of a "tableau" as the "relation through which the subject comes to find its bearings as such") and that of the Cartesian subject (the subject that "in the historically defined moment of the *cogito,* gives itself out to be the correlative of science").[18] Despite their differences, Panofsky and Damisch both conclude, however, that modernism did not entirely disturb the reign of perspectival culture: Panofsky by rejecting El Lissitzky's claim that a new "pan-geometrical" space had been created by constructivism, Damisch by registering the idea that beyond all scientific or psychoanalytical models, perspective remains "thinking in painting," a formal apparatus given to the artist similar to that of the sentence in language. For the purposes of the following reflections, we might say, echoing Damisch and agreeing with Panofsky, that the *warping* of perspectival space is tantamount to the marking of a process of *thinking* in architecture, a discursive meditation on the place of the subject and the other in space and the way in which architecture might mark a reflection on this place.[19] For, as Damisch has pointed out, any theory that perspective has accomplished its referentiality fails to take into account its increasing ubiquity and utility in video and digital representation. "Without any doubt," Damisch writes, "our period is much more massively 'informed' by the perspective paradigm, thanks to photography, film, and now video, than was the fifteenth century, which could boast of very few 'correct' perspective constructions."[20] And while modernism held onto the belief in a fundamental paradigm shift following the introduction of the theory of relativity, this shift was inevitably calculated with reference to, and in Damisch's terms within, the perspective cast.

The book is organized roughly according to the chronology of modernist spatial history, from the late nineteenth century to the present. Part I discusses the emergence of a psychological idea of space as it is joined to an increasing sense of anxiety, from the sacred horror of Pascal reflecting on the difficulties of reason and science to comprehend an ever-enlarging and potentially empty universe, to the effects of psychology on aesthetics and art history around the turn of the century, and thence to the psychological identification of spatial phobias after 1870, and especially those of agoraphobia and claustrophobia that seem to trace their origins directly to the nature of modern life and its spatial conditions. The generalization of an anxiety of modernity quickly became the leitmotiv of theories of alienation and estrangement in the sociological analyses of Georg Simmel and his contemporaries, and was thence adopted and expanded in the criticism of Siegfried Kracauer, Walter Benjamin, and others, who attempted to measure the effect of the new mass media and their technological underpinnings on the traditional forms of representation through an often despondent analysis of the deracinated subject of modern culture. Benjamin reflects the emerging sense on the part of critics and artists alike that space as a humanist construction, concretized in the perspective experiments of the Renaissance, is in the modern period gradually becoming flattened out, closed in, exhausted, in such a way as to reduce the "elbow room" of the human subject, as Benjamin put it; a sense that is countered by the post-Nietzschean imagination of Le Corbusier and Mies van der Rohe, among others, who believed that the "end of perspective" was an overcoming, a liberating leap into infinity for modernist "man." I draw out these questions in the context of early twentieth-century debates over the nature and role of spatial distortion in the montage techniques of film, and in the formal attempts of architects like Le Corbusier to design spaces that will both imply and sustain such movement in practice, precipitated literally by his move to aerial vision in the design of urban and territorial space.

Part II explores the way in which a number of contemporary artists and architects, preoccupied with the relations of space to bodies, psyches, and objects, have responded to the present conditions with projects that deploy psychoanalytical and psychological insights to put the assumed stabilities of the viewing subject into question. Here I am especially concerned with how the convergence and collision of architectural and artistic media have produced unique forms of spatial warping. Artists who have taken on the question of architecture, and architects who have taken on the question of art, have in the last decade significantly changed the way in which a genre- and practice-based space might be read. While in the work and theory of the first avant-gardes such interchanges were frequent—between architecture properly speaking, art, installation, and drama—they were by and large undertaken within a general theory of spatial construction as a universal flux, a medium, so to speak, that subsumed and informed all media. Today, however, with the boundary lines between the arts quite strictly drawn, and with no such overarching theory of space, the transgression of art and architecture takes on a definite critical role. Thus, as I point out in the chapter on Mike Kelley, sculpture does not simply "expand its field," but rather takes in the theoretical practices of architecture in order to transform its field. Similarly, architecture's manipulation as an art practice, as a design strategy, is undertaken with a full consciousness of what is being rejected or transformed in architectural terms—functionalism, for example, or the formal codes of modernist abstraction, or, again, specifically architectural typologies. In both cases the spatial results are not radically different in appearance, but the special distortions achieved in individual practices are radical.

Here, Vito Acconci's architectural installations, Rachel Whiteread's cast spaces, Toba Khedoori's floating fragments, Mike Kelley's investigations into his (repressed) memory of an architecturally bounded past, and Martha Rosler's freeway and airport photographs are seen as staging disruptive incursions into the normal patterns of spatial organization and experience and interrogations of more pathological kinds. In these works artists have deployed architectural modes of perception and projection in order to resituate the art object, but also to extend the vocabulary of spatial reference back into the lived world as criticism and comment. Architects, similarly, have self-consciously put the notion of the Cartesian subject at risk, with spatial morphings and warpings that, while seemingly based on avant-garde precedents from the twenties, necessarily construe space in post-psychoanalytical, postdigital ways. The most celebrated example of this wave of warpings is, of course, Gehry's Bilbao museum, with its twisting and thrusting volumes encased in titanium scales, itself housing a sculpture by Richard Serra, whose own *Torqued Ellipses* have pushed the limits of steel fatigue and destabilized the viewing subject in extreme ways. But a range of other experiments, including the utopian expressionism of Coop Himmelblau, the fractured geometries of Eric Owen Moss, the attenuated and half-submerged figurations of Morphosis, the unhomely voids of Daniel Libeskind, the inhuman yet animistic blobs, skins, and nets of Greg Lynn, all contribute to the sense of a new kind of spatial order emerging in architecture, one that, as I argue, has more than a visual similarity with earlier avant-garde experiments, but that also demands an extension of reference and interpretation with regard to its digital production and reproduction.

In this book I have not sought to provide a comprehensive account of the history of the idea of space in modern culture—a subject with an already extensive bibliography and still giving rise to lively contemporary debates.[21] The analysis of spatial questions has preoccupied a number of critics and historians since the early 1970s: the work of Henri Lefebvre, Michel Foucault, Gilles Deleuze, and Paul Virilio, among many others, and more recently the studies of Bernard Cache, Victor Burgin, and Elizabeth Grosz, have added spatial category to spatial category.[22] Lefebvre's spaces—"social," "absolute," "abstract," "Contradictory," and "Differential"—have been multiplied in theory by "oblique," "Other," "perverse," "scopophilic," "paranoiac," "postmodern," "hyper," and "cyber" spaces, not to mention the Deleuzean roster of "folded," "smooth," and "striated" space. It is not my intention in this book to add to the list. Indeed, I have deliberately left definitions vague in order to allow attributions of "warped" and "warping" their full analogical and metaphorical play in a number of different contexts, from the expressionist and filmic "explosions" of the 1920s, through the psychoanalytical projections of the 1970s, to the fully fledged warp techniques of digital imaging and virtual movement.

If there is a single consistency in my treatment of space, it is that I am less interested in the purity of single definitions from philosophy or psychoanalysis, or in the literal fashioning of space that seems to be warped, than I am in the intersection of the two: the complex exercise of projection and introjection in the process of inventing a paradigm of representation, an "imago" of architecture, so to speak, that reverberates with all the problematics of a subject's own condition. Here, Lefebvre's classification of three types of intersecting space proves useful, despite his subordination of psychoanalysis to production. For Lefebvre it was important to distinguish between "spatial practice" properly speaking (the process of the production and reproduction of space, as well as the relationship of society to space); "representations of space," or conceptualized space (the "space of planners, urbanists, technocratic subdividers and social engineers"); and "representational spaces" or spaces that are "directly *lived*," overlaid on actual physical spaces, and appropriated symbolically.[23] Victor Burgin has made good use of these distinctions in his clarification of the debate between Mike Davis, Ed Soja, and Fredric Jameson over the implications of the latter's analysis of the Hotel Bonaventure in Los Angeles, pointing out that the apparent differences among the three writers refer less to arguments in kind than to differing levels of spatial interest. In this regard, my own criticism is consciously limited to that of representational space, or the space produced by architects, artists, and critics, as it is marked by the one spatial practice left unanalyzed by Lefebvre: that of the *post-psychoanalytical imaginary,* as it seeks to trace out the sites of anxiety and disturbance in the modern city.[24]

Finally, while touching on aspects of psychology and psychoanalysis, I am not in any way attempting to develop a coherent theory of psychological space, and certainly not one that might lead to an architecture more suited to the contemporary subject and its technological extensions. Nor am I claiming that the examples in architectural, urban, and artistic practice that I cite are in any sense psychological structures, or can be seen as exemplary signs of the psyche at work in object formation. No particular formal or nonformal event can be claimed for psychoanalysis; but many such experiences and experiments can form the subjects of an interpretation informed by psychoanalysis, one that might in some way throw light on the endlessly shifting relations of spatial construction to identity.

At times, however, I have taken the decidedly poetic liberty of shifting the emphasis of psychoanalytical interpretation from subject to object. That is, as Mark Cousins has observed, I have from time to time imagined that a psychoanalysis *of* architecture might be possible—as if architecture were on the couch so to speak—that would reveal, by implication, and reflection, its relationship with its "subjects." Thus personified as the "other," architecture and its relationship to space may be, in Lacanian terms, figured as the mirror, and thence the frame of anxiety and shape of desire.[25] I have indulged in this somewhat perverse reversal of orthodox theory as a way of stressing the active role of objects and spaces in anxiety and phobia. While of course recognizing that psychoanalysis traces the roots of such neuroses to etiologies of sexuality, of desire for the other, of castration anxiety, and so forth, I have wanted to preserve the initiatory role of space and objects in anxiety production, and especially with regard to the representation of such anxiety in art. Thus, despite the "heredity thesis" of Charcot and his followers, I have preferred to retain a sense of agoraphobic and claustrophobic space as generator of fear; similarly, I have preserved the sense of the "window" as transparent cut between inside and out, even as I recognize Freud's wish to see it as displacement for another scene. Along these lines, I am as intrigued by the phantom vision of the wolves through the window as I am by the primal scene they mask; by the warehouses and horse-infested streets of Little Hans's Vienna, as much as by the disclosure of the "real" origins of his phobic disorder. My strategy is perhaps best illustrated with reference to Lacan's explanation of the Pascalian "void" or "vacuum" as reflecting the philosopher's interest in desire. Interpreting Pascal's scientific experiments on the vacuum as an attack on contemporaries who were horrified by desire, and constructing, so to speak, a Lacanian Pascal functioning according to the rules of "desire for the other," Lacan noted:

> This void does not at all interest us theoretically. For us it has almost no more sense. We know that in the vacuum can still be produced knots, solids, packets of waves, and everything you want. And for Pascal, precisely because, save for nature, the whole of thought until then had held in horror whatever could have a void somewhere, it is that which is drawn to our attention, and to know if we too do not surrender from time to time to this horror.[26]

While admitting the psychoanalytic relevance of Lacan's emphasis, I would emphasize, in contradiction to Lacan, that it is what the void can hold, and its continuous propensity to inspire horror, that interests me most. Indeed, it is the nature of these strange "knots, solids, packets of waves," this "everything you want" that may be produced in a vacuum, or by a vacuum, that is the underlying question of this book.[27] All representations of anxiety or horror in the face of the void, these phantom shapes are, as occasion demands, sometimes named architecture, sometimes urban spaces; and their proliferation and mutation has been the object of representation in the arts for more than a century. Their recent entry into virtual space has simply multiplied their potential for morphing, and obscured still further their place and role in relation to their subjects, we who "from time to time surrender to their horror."

One final note. I want to emphasize that in discussing cultural responses to the psychological identification of various phobias, and in analyzing the textual accounts of psychoanalysis for their spatial implications, I am in no way intending to comment on or diminish the importance and severity of mental disturbance, its various etiologies and possible cures.

Part I

Horror Vacui

Constructing the Void from Pascal to Freud

Le silence éternel de ces espaces infinis m'effraie.
Blaise Pascal, *Pensées*

In 1895, in the midst of his studies on anxiety neuroses, obsessions, and phobias, Freud addressed himself to a French audience with the aim of "correct-
ing" Jean-Martin Charcot on the nature of such phenomena.[1] He began by
putting to one side a specific kind of obsession, an example of which was exhibited by the philosopher Pascal and was apparently well enough known to
stand with little explanation:

> I propose in the first place to exclude a group of intense obsessions which
> are nothing but memories, unaltered images of important events. As an
> example I may cite Pascal's obsession: he always thought he saw an abyss
> on his left hand "after he had nearly been thrown into the Seine in his
> coach." Such obsessions and phobias, which might be called *traumatic,*
> are allied to the symptoms of hysteria.[2]

Freud uses this example to point to the difference between what he calls "intense obsessions," which are little more than simple memories or "unaltered
images of important events," and "true obsessions," which combine a forceful
idea and an associated emotional state; he further distinguishes these true obsessions from phobias, where the emotional state is one of anxiety (*angoisse* in
the original French version). Here I am not so concerned with Freud's dismissal
of this abyssal anxiety, nor why he felt so confident in excluding Pascal from
the realm of true obsession or of phobia, but rather with the place held by the
seventeenth-century philosopher in the history of such neurosis, a place that

was secure enough in the medical tradition to warrant its initial and immediate exclusion by Freud.

In a footnote to this article, Freud acknowledged his debt to the latest French work on phobias, J. B. E. Gélineau's *Des peurs maladives ou phobies,* published in 1894. If we follow this trail backward, we find that Gélineau's contemporaries are themselves somewhat obsessed with Pascal's obsession, often termed "Pascal's disease" in reference to the newly psychologized phobia of "la peur des espaces," or, as the German psychologist Westphal had termed it in his study of 1871, "agoraphobia." For many French psychologists, indeed, Pascal had become a founding case for this phobia, the more important as a celebrated French example of a mental disease all too closely connected with German psychology, especially following the siege of Paris in 1871.[3]

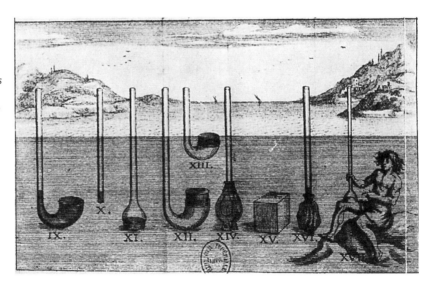

1. Blaise Pascal, "Experiments with the Equilibrium of Liquids and the Weight of Air," *Traitez de l'équilibre des liqueurs et de la pesanteur de la masse de l'air* (Paris, 1663).

It would seem, in any event, that Pascal was bound to be a perfect exemplar of the disease as the preeminent and school-textbook theorist of the void, of "l'horreur du vide," of "l'infini" and "le néant."[4] His well-known philosophical and scientific interests in the variety of vacuums, psychological and empirical, were no doubt endowed with additional veracity for late nineteenth-century enthusiasts of the case study by the reported incident on the banks of the Seine. Thus hardly a study on the newly "discovered" spatial phobias failed to mention his case, one that resonated with all the literary and philosophical traditions and commonplaces of French secondary education. Charles Binet-Sanglé, writing in 1899 and convinced that Pascal suffered from the equally popular malady of "neurasthenia," traced his entire religious philosophy to his celebrated obsession.[5]

Interest in Pascal's affliction was not, however, an invention of the psychologizing climate of the 1870s. Indeed, the anecdote seems to have been well enough established in popular lore over the two centuries after his death to have served seventeenth-century biographers, eighteenth-century theologians and *philosophes,* and nineteenth-century romantics as a dramatic example of the relations between spatial experience and psychological-philosophical enquiry. The general sense of the legend was described by the nineteenth-century critic George Saintsbury, who tells the story in great detail in his article "Pascal" for the eleventh edition of the *Encyclopedia Britannica,* with some skepticism but nevertheless according it great importance. For him, as for numerous earlier commentators, the anecdote is held to explain Pascal's second great "conversion" of 1654 when he joined his sister Jacqueline in seclusion at Port-Royal. Saintsbury writes:

> It seems that Pascal in driving to Neuilly was run away with by the horses, and would have been plunged in the river but that the traces fortunately broke. To this, which seems authentic, is usually added the tradition (due to the abbé Boileau) that afterwards he used at times to see an imaginary precipice by his bedside, or at the foot of the chair on which he was sitting.[6]

The apparent concurrence of the accident and his second and final "conversion" to religion was too dramatic to be ignored. As Saintsbury suggests, the traditional story originated in 1737, some seventy-five years after Pascal's death, in a letter written by the abbé Boileau reassuring one of his penitents who suffered from imaginary terrors:

> Where they see only a single way, you see frightening precipices. That reminds me of M. Pascal—the comparison will not displease you. . . . This

great genius always thought that he saw an abyss at his left side, and he would have a chair placed there to reassure himself. I have this on good authority. His friends, his confessor, and his director tried in vain to tell him that there was nothing to fear, and that his anxiety was only the alarm of an imagination exhausted by abstract and metaphysical studies. He would agree, . . . and then, within a quarter of an hour, he would have dug for himself the terrifying precipice all over again.[7]

This anecdote was given more force in 1740 by the discovery of the *Recueil d'Utrecht,* with its report of the report of the accident on the bridge at Neuilly in a "Mémoire" on the life of Pascal which cited a M. Arnoul de Saint-Victor, the curé of Chambourcy, who "said that he had learned from the Prior of Barrillon, a friend of Mme Périer [Pascal's sister], that M. Pascal a few years before his death, going, according to his custom, on a feast day, for an outing across the Neuilly Bridge, with some of his friends in a four or six horse carriage, the two lead horses took the bit in their teeth at the place on the bridge where there was no parapet, and falling into the water, the reins that attached them to the rear broke in such a way that the carriage remained on the brink of the precipice, which made M. Pascal resolve to cease his outings and live in complete solitude."[8]

These anecdotes took their place in the Pascal hagiography, to be readily exploited by critics and supporters. Thus, as Jean Mesnard notes, Voltaire accused Pascal of madness on the basis of the "relation of cause and effect" he established "between the accident at the Neuilly Bridge and this curious illness from which Pascal suffered,"[9] while Condorcet in his eulogy of 1767 joined both incidents together and linked them to Pascal's conversion of 1654.[10] And it was perhaps yet another tradition, one that held that Pascal had in his earlier life conceived of a public transport system for Paris, with carriages running along fixed routes at specified times, that helped to sustain this synthetic myth of a philosopher of the void, scientist of the vacuum, practical inventor, and celebrated recluse falling prey to the conjunction of his own fantasies and carriage accidents.[11] In this way three very separate pathologies—a void to the side of the body, a fear of falling into the Seine, an interest in spatial circulation—were by the end of the eighteenth century combined in a Pascalian myth.

Despite Voltaire's scorn, Pascal remained a powerful source for reflecting on the void and especially for late eighteenth-century architects like Etienne-Louis Boullée and Claude-Nicolas Ledoux, who were increasingly led to reformulate the progressive ideal of Enlightenment space under the influence of Boileau, Burke, and Rousseau. Pascal's resistance to the open transparency of rationalism was seen as a way of symbolically and affectively exploiting the ambiguities of shadow and limit, remaining a sign of potential disturbance beyond and within the apparently serene and stable structures of modern urbanism.[12] But it was not until the mid-nineteenth century that Pascal's composite myth was summoned up to authorize a new medical pathology. The doctor Louis-François Lélut, in a communication to the Académie des Sciences Morales in 1846,[13] advanced the idea that Pascal's second conversion stemmed from a mental pathology precipitated by his accident. His diagnosis was only the first of many to be repeated in different versions to the end of the century.[14]

By the 1860s, and despite the skepticism of Victor Cousin and Sainte-Beuve, Pascal's malady had become a commonplace of dinner conversation. Jules and Edmond de Goncourt, on 2 September 1866, directly draw the comparison between Pascal's vertigo and the new theories of neurosis: "Pascal, the sublime depth of Pascal? And the saying of the doctor Moreau de Tours, 'The genius is a neurotic!' There's another showman of the abyss!"[15] Edmond twenty-three years later recalls that the old Alphonse Daudet was planning a book on "suffering" ("la douleur") with "a eulogy of morphine, a chapter on the neurosis of Pascal, a chapter on the illness of Jean-Jacques Rousseau." Daudet, Goncourt notes, had suggested the *névrose* of Pascal as a thesis subject to his son Léon Daudet.[16] This seemingly innocent proposal apparently haunted the young Daudet (though he did not in fact pursue the research), who recounted a nightmare on the subject to Goncourt ten days later. He had dreamed, he said, that "Charcot brought him Pascal's *Pensées*, and at the same time showed him inside the brain of the great man, that he had with him the cells in which these thoughts had lived, cells absolutely empty and closely resembling the honeycombs of a dried-up hive."[17] Perhaps it was Alphonse Daudet himself who was haunted by Pascal, for in December of the next year, discussing the fear of mirrors in Georges Rodenbach's *Le règne du silence* (1891), where the author recalls the popular tradition in which the devil sometimes makes his face known, Goncourt relates: "One of us asked dreamily if the dead did not leave their image behind, returning at certain hours of the day. And Daudet compared the living life of this silent thing to the living silence of Pascal's stars."[18]

It was Maurice Barrès, in his 1909 lecture on behalf of his Ligues des Patriotes, who drew together all the Pascalian myths into a narrative of an internally developed illness out of which developed a thinker who, with singular heroism in Barrès's terms, broke with the prevailing spirituality of the church and philosophy. Struck by the fact that, coming from a solid and even stolid bourgeois and religious upbringing, surrounded by the comforts of dwellings and family, Pascal nevertheless "lived in anguish," he undertook an enquiry into the roots of his suffering, his *angoisse* and his *douleur*. Rejecting out of hand theories of poverty, worldly excess, or the misfortunes of his age, Barrès concluded that "the suffering of Pascal did not come from outside" but from "a great interior tragedy." Pascal had, he pointed out, been "tortured by physical pain from infancy until his death"; it was an illness that changed its nature all the time—a malady "subject to change" as Pascal himself noted. "At the age of a year he fell into a decline and exhibited phobias. He could not look at water without flying into a great rage. He could not see his father and his mother one after the other without crying and struggling violently."[19] From the age of eighteen, his sister recounted, he suffered every day: only able to drink hot water, drop by drop; paralyzed from the waist down, walking with the help of crutches; his lower limbs always cold; and, "it is said, but this is not certain, that beginning in 1654 he always thought there was an abyss on his left side." In his later years he could neither talk, read, nor work and suffered convulsions and headaches, dying at the age of thirty-nine. Descartes, Barrès recounted, recommended bed rest and soup: "this is today," Barrès concluded, "the classic treatment of neurasthenics."[20] Such infirmities, added to the "rigor and intensity of his thought," led, Barrès thought, to the "sublime unhappiness," the "anguish" of the philosopher. Not the "vertigo" of a philosopher who despairingly finds a "Christian" solution to his problems, but rather a scientific spirit, beset by phobias, who searches for the truth of phenomena with a sense of the powerlessness of science to discover the essential secret of the universe, a philosopher who, so to speak, makes a virtue out of his suffering: hence, for Barrès, the fear of "the eternal silence of these infinite spaces."[21]

Here, for Barrès, is the one outside influence that he admits as formative for Pascal's thought: that of space and its earthly precipitate, architecture. In nostalgic pilgrimages, recounted in articles published in the *Echo de Paris* in 1900 and reprinted in *L'angoisse de Pascal,* the conservative ideologue of *la patrimoine* visits the birthplace, family houses, and haunts of Pascal, as if to recapture the essence of his character through a metonymy, the rooted stones juxtaposed to the metaphysical philosophy. But in searching for roots, Barrès not unexpectedly finds ruins: at Clermont-Ferrand, the birthplace of Pascal is about to be demolished: "Already a wing of the building has no roof; the poor rooms where the Pascals lived in so noble an atmosphere of order, discipline gape open, naked and soiled with that abjection characteristic of disemboweled apartments."[22] The theoretical void has been repeated by the architectural: the inhabitants of Clermont are, Barrès proposes, no less culpable in this than those of Paris "who ferociously destroy every historical vestige, to the point that Paris . . . is perhaps of all towns in France the most empty of memories." For Barrès, "we form an attachment to the places where genius has lived insofar as they form it and help us understand it."[23] The recuperation of memory, the encounter with the traces of history, is sought again in Barrès's pilgrimage to the Château de Bien-Assis, the seat of the Périer family in the countryside outside of Clermont. Among the half-ruined walls, in the light of the setting sun, Barrès succeeds in capturing what for him is the spirit of the Port-Royal philosopher, not in the town but on the soil of a long-established manor.

Such nostalgia for a "deep France" is to be expected from Barrès; more surprising is his revelation of the true *place* of Pascalian understanding, situated precisely on the right bank of the Seine, the scene of his purported accident, and the "material setting" of his thought. This was a "sacred site," stated Barrès, one that should be accorded its real importance in the explanation of Pascal's 1654 conversion, that "magnificent hallucination" that was apparently so "fertile." "We are authorized to understand," he concluded, "how, under the influence of a shock, parts of ourselves enter into activity, elaborate images and feelings that we do not know we harbor in our innermost recesses."[24] Pascal's near-fall into the Seine, then, loosens the *replis* or folds of the psyche; spatial phobia, here, would be the release of images of the void, providing the means for its spiritual comprehension.

Whether or not Pascal's second conversion in 1654 was precipitated or reinforced by the celebrated accident, it is significant that some four years later he was to write the fragment "De l'esprit géométrique," among other questions an examination of the geometrical understanding of the void.[25] In this brief essay Pascal pressed the theory of perspective to the limits, in an introduction intended for a textbook for the Port-Royal "petites écoles." As Hubert Damisch notes, it was Pascal who drew the conclusion that because "a space can be infinitely extended, . . . it can be infinitely reduced."[26] To illustrate the "paradox" of these two infinities, Pascal gave the example of a ship endlessly drawing near to the vanishing point but never reaching it, thus anticipating the theorem of Desargues whereby infinity would be inscribed within the finite, contained "within a point," a basic postulate of projective geometry. But whether or not the meeting of parallel lines at infinity would be geometrically verifiable, the "obscurity," as Descartes called it, remained: the ship endlessly disappearing toward the horizon, the horizon point endlessly rising, the ship infinitely close to, and infinitely far from, infinity.[27] Here geometrical theory coincides almost too neatly with the interlocking relations of agoraphobic and claustrophobic space, diagnosed by the doctors who, in the 1870s, found in Pascal their most celebrated patient.

Agoraphobia

Psychopathologies of Urban Space

The rapid growth of big European cities toward the end of the nineteenth century, the transformation of the traditional city into what became known as *die Grosstadt* or metropolis, engendered not only a vital culture of modernism and avant-garde experiment, but also a culture of interpretation dedicated to the study and explanation of these new urban phenomena and their social effects, supported by the emerging new disciplines of sociology, psychology, political geography, and psychoanalysis. The pathology of the city, already fully present in the organicist metaphors of romantic, realist, and naturalist novelists from Balzac through Hugo to Zola, gained new and apparently scientific validation in the last quarter of the nineteenth century. By the late 1880s the diagnoses of the American George Miller Beard, who had in 1880 identified neurasthenia as the principal mental disease of modern life, were commonplaces of urban criticism. The Great City was seen to shelter a nervous and feverish population, overexcited and enervated, whose mental life, as Georg Simmel noted in 1903, was relentlessly antisocial, driven by money.[1] Max Nordau's "degeneration" was joined with Charcot's interpretation of neurasthenia to construct a climate of interpretation in which the metropolis figured as the principal agent of the "surmenage mental" of modern civilization, as Charles Richet termed it.[2]

Of special interest was the *space* of the new city, which was now subjected to scrutiny as a possible cause of an increasingly identified psychological alienation—the Vienna Circle was to call it "derealization"—of the metropolitan individual, and, further, as an instrument favoring the potentially dangerous behavior of the crowd.[3] Metropolis rapidly became the privileged territory of a host of diseases attributed directly to its spatial conditions, diseases that took their place within the general epistemology of Beard's neurasthenia and Charcot's hysteria, but with a special relationship to their supposed physical causes. Among these, and the earliest, were Carl Otto Westphal's and Henri Legrand du Saulle's agoraphobia and Benjamin Ball's claustrophobia, to be followed by a host of other assumedly phobic conditions.

Agoraphobia

The extension of individual psychological disorders to the social conditions of an entire metropolis was on one level perhaps no more than metaphorical hyperbole. On another level, however, the "discovery" of these new phobias seems to have been a part of a wider process of remapping the space of the city according to its changing social and political characteristics. Whether identifying illnesses like agoraphobia or claustrophobia as predominantly bourgeois phenomena, or investigating the more threatening illnesses of the working classes, from vagabondage to ambulatory automatisms, doctors were at once reflecting and countering an emerging and generalized fear of metropolis. By the First World War, "metropolis" had come to imply both a physical site and a pathological state which, for better or for worse, epitomized modern life; Carl Schorske, echoing Nietzsche, has characterized the sentiment as "beyond good and evil."[4]

It was in these psychopathological terms that the Viennese architect Camillo Sitte attacked what he saw as the spatial emptiness of the new Ringstrasse, contrasting its apparently limitless and infinite expanses to the compositional qualities and smaller scale of traditional squares and streets.[5] Supporting his nostalgic evocation of the past by the new psychology, he wrote: "Recently a unique nervous disorder has been diagnosed—'agoraphobia' [*Platzscheu*]. Numerous people are said to suffer from it, always experiencing a certain anxiety or discomfort, whenever they have to walk across a vast empty place."[6] Underlining his point by couching it in the form of an aesthetic principle of monumental scale, Sitte proposed wittily that even statues might suffer from this disease:

We might supplement this observation on psychology with an artistic one: that also people formed out of stone and metal, on their monumental pedestals, are attacked by this malady and thus always prefer (as already mentioned) to choose a little old plaza rather than a large empty

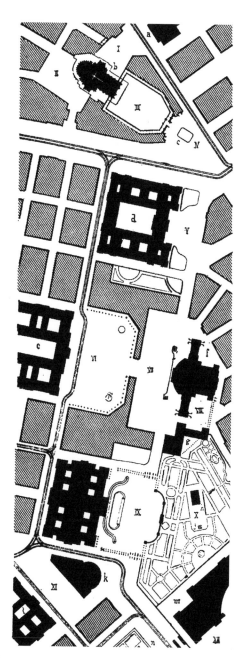

2. Camillo Sitte, "Vienna. Transformation of the Western Portion of the Ring-strasse," *Der Städte-Bau nach seinen künstlerischen Grundsätzen. Ein Beitrag zur Lösung modernister Fragen des Architektur und monumentalen Plastik unter besonderer Beziehung auf Wien* (Vienna: Carl Graeser, 1889).

one for their permanent location. What dimensions should statues on such colossal plazas have? They should be at least double or triple life size, or even more. Certain artistic refinements are, in such a case, utterly impossible.[7]

Sitte extended his argument by associating the causes of this new sickness of agoraphobia with the new space of urbanism. In traditional cities, with their small, intimate and human-scaled spaces, the illness was unknown.

Agoraphobia is a very new and modern ailment. One naturally feels very cozy in small, old plazas and only in our memory do they loom gigantic, because in our imagination the magnitude of the artistic effect takes the place of actual size. On our modern gigantic plazas, with their yawning emptiness and oppressive ennui, the inhabitants of snug old towns suffer attacks of this fashionable agoraphobia.[8]

The "universal trend of the time," concluded Sitte, was the fear of open spaces.[9]

Sitte was, of course, ironically using the new psychology to "prove" an observation that had become a commonplace of the aesthetic criticism of urbanism since the brothers Goncourt had complained of the "American deserts" created by the cutting of the modern boulevards. But such a merging of aesthetic and psychological criteria was quickly adopted by countermodernists and latter-day Ruskinians searching for psychological grounds on which to combat modernist planning, as well as by modernists who argued that such primitive psychological regressions should be overcome.[10]

Sitte's "fashionable disease" was in fact only some thirty years old in 1899: initially diagnosed by a number of doctors in Berlin and Vienna during the late 1860s, who were struck by the common responses of a number of their patients to public spaces, with the first comprehensive memoir published by the Berlin psychologist Carl Otto Westphal in 1871. The symptoms of what he called "agoraphobia" included palpitations, sensations of heat, blushing, trembling, fear of dying and petrifying shyness, symptoms that occurred, Westphal noted, when his patients were walking across open spaces or through empty streets or anticipated such an experience with a dread of the ensuing anxiety.[11]

Their fears were to a certain extent alleviated by companionship but were seriously exacerbated by the dimensions of the space, especially when there seemed to be no boundary to the visual field. A variety of terms were used to name this disease. Sitte had used the term *Platzscheu;* the year before the publication of Westphal's article, another doctor, Benedikt, had dubbed it "Platzschwindel" or dizziness in public places, and it had been variously called "Platzangst," "Platzfurcht," "angoisse des places," "crainte des places," "peur d'espace," "horreur de vide," "topophobia," and "street fear." The term "agoraphobia" had been already defined in Littré and Robin's *Dictionnaire de médecine* of 1865 as a "form of madness consisting in an acute anxiety, with palpitation and fears of all kinds," and with the support of Westphal it would emerge, despite the objections of a few French psychologists, as the generally accepted term.[12]

Westphal recounted three major cases that would be repeated in the literature for decades: a commercial traveler who experienced rapid heartbeats on entering a public square, or when passing by long walls, or through a street with closed shops, at the theater, or in church; a shopkeeper who found it impossible to cross squares or streets when the shops were closed and could not travel on the omnibus or attend the theater, concert, or any gathering of people without feeling a strange anxiety, accompanied by rapid heart palpitation; and an engineer who felt anxiety the moment he had to cross a square, especially if deserted, and felt as if the pavement were rushing as if in a torrent beneath his feet. These patients found a certain relief in physical aids: a walking stick or the presence of a friend for example. Westphal cited the case, reported by a Dr. Brück from Driburg, of a priest who was terrified if he was not covered by the vaulted ceiling of his church, and was forced when in the open to walk beneath an umbrella.[13]

If agoraphobia was by definition an essentially spatial disease, many psychologists insisted that it was equally an urban disease, the effect of life in the modern city. Westphal's engineer, indeed, stated that he felt less anxiety in a large space not surrounded by houses than in a space of the same size in a city: open nature was refreshing, the city was terrifying. Indeed, writing in 1880, Gélineau had argued for the term "kénophobie" as better characterizing this fear of the void that "strikes only the inhabitant of cities . . . developing under the influence of that debilitating atmosphere of the big towns that has been called *malaria urbana.*"[14] Legrand du Saulle two years earlier had refused the word "agoraphobia" precisely because, in his terms, it limited the disturbance to one specific kind of public space; he preferred the vaguer term "peur des espaces" as comprising all spatial fears: "the patients suffer from fear of space, of the void, not only in the street but also in the theater, in church, on an upper floor, at a window giving onto a large courtyard or looking over the countryside, in an omnibus, a ferry or on a bridge."[15] Legrand's synthetic description of the disease was as dramatic as it was unambiguous in characterizing its setting:

> The fear of spaces, ordinarily compatible with the most robust health, is frequently produced at the very moment when the neurotic leaves a street and arrives at a square, and it is marked by a sudden anxiety, an instantaneous beating of the heart. The patient, then prey to an indefinable emotion, finds himself isolated from the entire world at the sight of the void that is presented to him and frightens him immeasurably . . . he feels as if he is destroyed, does not dare to descend from the sidewalk to the roadway, makes no step either forward or backward, neither advances nor retreats, trembles in all his limbs, grows pale, shivers, blushes, is covered with sweat, grows more and more alarmed, can hardly stand up on his tottering legs, and remains unhappily convinced that he could never face this void, this deserted place, or cross the space that is before him. If one's gaze were suddenly to be plunged into a deep gulf, if one were to imagine being suspended above a fiery crater, to be crossing the Niagara on a rigid cord or feel that one was rolling into a precipice, the resulting impression could be no more painful, more terrifying, than that provoked by the fear of spaces.[16]

He concluded: "no fear without the void, no calm without the appearance of a semblance of protection."[17]

The symptoms were similar for all patients:

> This anxious state . . . is ordinarily accompanied by a sudden feebleness of the legs, an overactivity of the circulation, by waves of tingling, by a sensation of numbness starting with chills, by hot flushes, cold sweats, trembling, a desire to burst into tears, ridiculous apprehensions, hypo-

chondriac preoccupations, half-spoken lamentations, and by a general disturbance that is truly painful, with different alternations of facial coloration and physiognomical expression.[18]

Legrand's own observations confirmed Westphal's in every detail. A "Madame B," the vivacious and sociable mother of three children, experienced the symptoms on returning from vacation and finding herself unable to cross the Champs-Elysées, the boulevards, or large squares unaccompanied.[19] Fearful of empty churches without benches or chairs, of eating alone in spacious hotel dining rooms, and of being in carriages when there were no passersby in the street, she even needed help in mounting the wide stair to her apartment. Once indoors, she was never able to look out of the window onto the courtyard, and filled her rooms with furniture, pictures, statuettes, and old tapestries to reduce their spaciousness. She lived, noted Legrand, "in a veritable bazaar": "the void alone frightened her."[20] Legrand's second case was a "M. Albert G," an infantry officer, interested in literature, poetry, music, and archaeology, who was unable to cross deserted public squares out of uniform. Again his fear was evoked by the void, whether on terraces or in a large Gothic church.[21] Legrand concluded, agreeing with most other students of agoraphobia, that "it was the space that caused him anxiety."[22]

To the fear of empty and open space was added that of crowded and populated places. Legrand noted: "It has been remarked that the fear of spaces is produced among certain patients in a very frequented place, or among crowds," a form of anxiety that was quickly assimilated to the more general study of crowd behavior as sketched by Gustave Le Bon.[23] The supplement to Littré's dictionary, published in 1883, had already defined agoraphobia in this way, as a "sort of madness in which the patient fears the presence of crowds and, for example, cannot decide to cross a busy street."[24]

In these ways, the notion of agoraphobia was quickly extended in popular parlance to embrace all urban fears that were seemingly connected to spatial conditions. Entire urban populations, it was thought, might become susceptible to the disease as a result of specific events. Thus Legrand remarked on the change in the behavior of Parisians following the siege of Paris by the Germans in 1871. Describing a patient whose agoraphobia seemed to be precipitated or at least aggravated by overindulgence in strong stimulants such as coffee,[25] he found an increase in the abuse of coffee among women workers to be directly linked to the famine of the population during the Commune, leading to the dangerous abuse of all kinds of stimulants, a habit that had been continued after the withdrawal of German troops. In Legrand's terms, the successive closing and sudden opening of the city, its passage so to speak from claustrophobia to agoraphobia, had the effect of fostering the veritable cause of spatial fear.[26]

By 1879 agoraphobia had been joined by its apparent opposite, "claustrophobia," popularized in France by Benjamin Ball in a communication to the Société Médico-psychologique.[27] He cited the case of a young soldier with a fear of contact, a "délire de propreté," accompanied by a panic fear of being alone in a closed space, a sensation of being in a passage getting narrower and narrower to the point of being able to go neither forward or back, an intolerable terror that was generally followed by a flight into the fields. A second patient panicked while climbing the stairs of the Tour Saint-Jacques. Neither could remain in their apartments when the doors were closed.[28] Ball, disagreeing with Beard, who had proposed to categorize all morbid fears of space under the general heading "topophobia," asserted the special characteristics of claustrophobia and agoraphobia, which were to be treated as linked but distinct psychoses.

But whether the etiology of these spatial disorders was traced to visual causes, as in Moriz Benedikt's hypothesis that agoraphobia was a form of vertigo produced by the lateral vision of the eyes, or ascribed to heredity, as generally agreed by doctors from Legrand and Charcot to Georges Gilles de la Tourette, both agora-and claustrophobia were inevitably ranked among the most characteristic of anxieties produced by life in the modern city— exaggerated but typical forms of the all-pervasive neurasthenia. Gilles de la Tourette, concerned to modify the overencompassing category of Beard, identified agoraphobia with a special state of "neurasthenic vertigo [*une vertige neurasthénique*]," accompanied by "a sensation of cerebral emptiness accompanied by a weakness of the lower limbs. . . . A veil spreads before the eyes, everything is grey and leaden; the visual field is full of black spots, flying patches, close or distant objects are confused on the same plane." Such vertigo was increased, he observed, by the daily commute to and from the job; sufferers were "pushed to creep along walls, follow houses, and flee the crossing of wide squares."[29]

For Gilles de la Tourette, neurasthenia proper had to be distinguished from agoraphobia on the grounds that the latter was an inherited disease, and largely incurable; he described a case falsely diagnosed as *neurasthénie constitutionelle* or hereditary neurasthenia, but which Gilles claimed was rather a vertigo, or agoraphobia, that was inherited directly from the patient's mother whose "life had been tormented by the fear of spaces, by an agoraphobia that had poisoned her entire existence."[30] Such hereditary disorders were most evident, according to Gilles, in large cities, among clerks, laborers, and accident victims who "once touched by hysterical neurasthenia ... become part of those marginalized by the large towns, vagabonds" suffering from incurable mental stigmata.[31]

Gilles de la Tourette was here following his teacher Charcot, whose celebrated *Tuesday Lectures* featured many cases of vagabondage associated, according to the doctor, with agoraphobia. For Charcot, as he explained in his fourteenth lesson, 27 March 1888, these "hysterical-epileptic attacks, these vertigos, this anxiety erupting at the moment when a public square has to be crossed, all this is very interesting as an example of the combination of different neuropathic states that, in reality, constitute distinct and autonomous morbid species," and that were, of course, hereditary.[32] He presented the case of a young man who suffered from such attacks of epilepsy, agoraphobia, and vertigo, who described his inability to cross the Place du Carrousel or the Place de la Concorde without fear of their emptiness and a corresponding sensation of paralysis. Charcot easily identified the malady as "what one would call agoraphobia, a special nervous state the knowledge of which we owe to Professor Westphall [sic] of Berlin (in German: *Platzangst, Platzfurcht*)." But the patient went on to describe other symptoms that occurred at night in an enclosed railway carriage: "I was frightened, because I had the sense of being closed in. I don't like to stay in a narrow space, I feel ill." For Charcot this added another dimension: "It is not only agoraphobia, you see, it is as well claustrophobia, as Dr. Ball says." To conclude this synthetic case, Charcot diagnosed a profound vertigo that resulted in a sense of falling, whether in trains or when climbing towers.[33]

William James, while not a little scornful of "the strange symptom which has been described of late years by the rather absurd name of *agoraphobia*," like Charcot subscribed to the notion of heredity, but linked it to a primitive survival handed down from animals to man:

The patient is seized with palpitation and terror at the sight of any open place or broad street which he has to cross alone. He trembles, his knees bend, he may even faint at the idea. Where he has sufficient self-command he sometimes accomplishes the object by keeping safe under the lee of a vehicle going across, or joining himself to a knot of other people. But usually he slinks around the sides of the square, hugging the houses as closely as he can. This emotion has no utility in a civilized man, but when we notice the chronic agoraphobia of our domestic cats and see the tenacious way in which many wild animals, especially rodents, cling to cover, and only venture on a dash across the open as a desperate measure—even making for every stone or bunch of weeds which may give a momentary shelter—when we see this we are strongly tempted to ask whether such an odd kind of fear in us be not due to the accidental resurrection, through disease, of a sort of instinct which may in some of our ancestors have had a permanent and on the whole a useful part to play?[34]

Neither Charcot's nor James's belief in heredity nor Freud's opposing view that, as he noted in his German translation of the *Leçons du mardi,* "the more frequent cause of agoraphobia as well as of most other phobias lies not in heredity but in abnormalities of sexual life,"[35] would remove the urban and spatial associations from the illness. It was as if, no matter what the particular circumstances of individual patients or the arguments of doctors, the cultural significance of agoraphobia was greater than its medical etiology. The resonance of a sickness associated with open or closed spaces, of symptoms that whatever their cause seemed to be triggered by the new configurations of urban space introduced by modernization, was irresistible to critics and sociologists alike. Summarizing and extending the geographical range of Beard's "American" neurasthenia, Charcot's former student Fernand Levillain claimed all cities as the privileged sites of "surmenage intellectuel et des sens" and neurasthenia: "It is in effect in the great centers of agglomeration that all the types of *surmenage* we have reviewed are collected and developed to their maximum."[36] Despite his belief in Charcot's theory of heredity, and his criticism of Beard for having included the phobias within simple neurasthenia, Levillain nevertheless admitted that the neurasthenic inhabitant of the big city might well experience otherwise hereditary maladies in a less acute form—agoraphobia, claustrophobia, monophobia (fear of solitude and isolation), fear of touching (*délire de toucher*), and all other instances of spatial fear.

Classified as "morbid fears" and summarized in Charles Féré's *The Pathology of the Emotions,* the enumeration of phobias of all kinds became an almost obsessive part of clinical practice around the turn of the century.[37] Agoraphobia (the fear of places) was supplemented by atremia or stasophobia (fear of elevated or vertical stations), amaxophobia (exaggerated fear of carriages), cremnophobia (the fear of precipices), acrophobia or hypsophobia (fear of elevated places), oicophobia (aversion to returning home), lyssophobia (fear of liquids), hydrophobia (fear of water—also connected to agoraphobia by the fear of the sea as expanse, and of crossing a bridge), pyrophobia (fear of fire, which was often linked to claustrophobia), monophobia (fear of solitude), anthropophobia (fear of social contact), and a multitude of others, culminating in photophobia (the fear of fear itself), an illness generally subsumed under neurasthenia.[38] Not surprisingly, agoraphobia and its cognates emerged as commonplaces of conversation and lay diagnosis, especially in the context of metropolitan fears.

It is with especial interest, then, that we encounter a description of a case of agoraphobia in a nineteenth-century architect in an obituary also written by an architect, and with all the marks of a psychological case study of the epoch. Appearing in *L'Architecture* in September 1890, this was composed by the celebrated Beaux-Arts architect Julien Guadet on the death of his colleague Louis-Jules André, and details a malady that bears every relationship to the spatial phobias we have been discussing, connecting them directly to the professional experiences of architectural practice.[39] It was, Guadet writes, a long-drawn-out illness which, while diminishing in degree, never disappeared. Not wishing to accuse his former teacher of mental illness, Guadet claims to be ignorant of its medical name; he nevertheless displays familiarity with medical descriptions as he compares it to a certain kind of vertigo, one, he notes, that is felt by every architect:

What is its name for the doctors? I do not know. But I am not deceived in giving it the name of apprehension: a very physical apprehension, anxiety of the body and the senses, and not of the mind. Who among us, on a roof, on scaffolding, has not felt at least once the painful sensation of vertigo? One is used to heights, and yet suddenly, without cause, an un-expected feebleness paralyzes one, makes one inert, the will itself is pow-erless to react; nevertheless if the frailest stick is in one's hand, if a bar, a rope, a thread that the least effort would break seems to guide and lead one, then confidence is reborn, and the vertigo is dissipated.[40]

Vertigo, then, was an occupational hazard for architects; but agoraphobia was, in Guadet's terms, a special case of this sensation. For André suffered not from vertigo itself, but from a version of it "felt on the ground, in the street": "To fol-low his path was a labor for him, to rub shoulders with a passerby was a dis-comfort, to be accosted without warning by a friend was a shock." Indeed, he exhibited all the classic symptoms of agoraphobia, depicted by Guadet in al-most pathological terms: "By instinct he kept close to houses and walls in or-der to have a void on one side only; he walked with the concentration of one who crosses a ditch on a plank."[41]

Anxiety + . . . Window . . .

In the light of the common belief in what Nietzsche termed the "femininiza-tion" of fin-de-siècle culture (and thereby what he and others, including psy-chologists like Otto Weininger and Max Nordau, saw as its decadence), it is not difficult to see why, from the outset, urban phobias were assigned a definite place in the gendering of metropolitan psychopathology. Despite the predom-inance of male patients in the samples of agoraphobics and claustrophobics analyzed by Westphal and his French colleagues, these disorders were thought of as fundamentally "female" in character; it is no accident that today "agora-phobia" is commonly called "housewife's disease" by doctors. If agoraphobia and its cognates were species of neurasthenia, then it followed that all those considered prone to neurasthenic disease—the "weak," the "enervated," the "overstimulated," the "degenerated," and the "bored"—were bound to suc-cumb to mental collapse, and first in line, for the psychologists and psychoan-alysts, were women and homosexuals.

Thus, as Proust sketched out the reception of the Baron de Charlus into Madame Verdurin's salon, he was to "enter with the movements of bent head, his hands having the air of twisting a small handbag, characteristic of well-

brought-up bourgeois women, and of those that the Germans call homosexuals, with a certain agoraphobia, the agora here being the space of the salon
that separates the door from the armchair where the mistress of the salon is
seated."[42] In the published version, Proust suppressed the reference to homo-
sexuality but emphasized the agoraphobic space of entry, a "space, furrowed
with abysses, which leads from the antechamber to the small salon." Charlus
now makes his entrance with what Proust describes as the mentality of "the
soul of a female relative, auxiliary like a goddess or incarnated like a double,"
which he compares to the feelings of "a young painter, raised by a saintly
Protestant cousin," "with inclined and trembling head, eyes to the ceiling,
hands plunged into an invisible muff, the evoked form and real guardian presence of which will help the intimidated artist to cross the space . . . without
agoraphobia."[43] That the "abyss" of which Proust speaks refers back to that of
Pascal, and thence forward to his own condition as a *névrosé,* is made clear in
Albertine disparue, where he refers directly to "l'abîme infranchissable" which,
at the time of his first meeting with Gilberte, seemed to exist between himself
and "a certain kind of little girl with golden hair"; in a classic negation, and reflecting much later on the remembered image of Gilberte, he was, he noted, re-
lieved to find that this abyss was "as imaginary as the abyss of Pascal."[44]

Freud's early accounts of agoraphobia, by contrast, were largely concerned with its prevalence among women patients. Rejecting heredity as a
cause, he took issue as early as 1892 with Charcot's theory, and directly con-
tradicted his former master in his notes to his translation of the *Tuesday Lectures* where he asserted the primary importance of "abnormalities of sexual
life."[45] Equally, Freud rejected the idea that the space itself, or any material
object of obsession, was a cause. Thus in the case of a thirty-eight-year-old
woman suffering from anxiety neurosis, noted in *Studies on Hysteria* (1895), the
agoraphobia consisted of attacks of dizziness, "with anxiety and feelings of
faintness, in the street in her small native town," the first attack occurring on a
shopping expedition.[46] Freud, through a combination of questioning and lay-
ing on of hands, revealed that the source of the disorder was not the street itself, nor the existence of a recently diseased friend's house on the street, but
rather the coincidence of her expected period with the ball for which she was
shopping. The same year, in the unpublished "Project for a Scientific Psychology," Freud recounted the case of a young woman who exhibited a fear of

entering stores unaccompanied. Her agoraphobia was proved for Freud by the fact that her fears were calmed by the presence of a companion—even a small child. Freud succeeded in tracing her anxiety to the repression of a scene of molestation by a "grinning shopkeeper" when eight years old.

Following up this sexual etiology of phobia, Freud wrote to Fliess in 1896 proposing that the causes of agoraphobia in women—their fear of going out into the street—were directly linked to what he called their repressed inner desire to walk the streets, that is, to be "streetwalkers." The mechanism of agoraphobia in women would thereby be connected to "the repression of the intention to take the first man one meets in the street: envy of prostitution and identification."[47] This observation followed a detailed exposition of the notion of "anxiety" as represented in the formulation "Anxiety about throwing oneself out of the window." This observation seems to have been based on a case recounted by Freud two years earlier, of a "young married woman" who is seized with an obsessional impulse "to throw herself out of the window or from the balcony." Freud hazarded that it was "at the sight of a man [that] she had erotic ideas, and that she had therefore lost confidence in herself and regarded herself as a depraved person, capable of anything," thus succeeding in translating the obsession back into sexual terms.[48] While he had been uncertain of the relationship of this case to agoraphobia in general, by the time he writes to Fliess Freud has convinced himself of its agoraphobic dimensions. He constructs this anxiety as "Anxiety + . . . window . . . ," where the "*unconscious* idea" of "going to the window to beckon a man to come up, as prostitutes do" leads to sexual release, which, repudiated by the preconscious, is turned into anxiety. The "window" in this scheme is left as the only conscious motif, associated with anxiety by the idea of "falling out of the window." Hence, Freud argues, anxiety about the window is interpreted in the sense of falling out, and the window, opening to the public realm, is avoided.

His "evidence" in this case is a short story by Guy de Maupassant, "Le signe," published in 1886, in which the Baronne de Grangerie narrates the story of her misadventure at a window to her friend the Marquise de Rennedon. When seated at her window in her second-floor apartment overlooking the Rue Saint-Lazare and enjoying the spectacle—"so gay, this station quarter, so active, so lively"—she had noticed another woman across the street, also seated at her window, and dressed strikingly in red, even as the Baronne was dressed in mauve (both understood to be the colors of prostitution). The Baronne de Grangerie, recognizing her neighbor as a prostitute, was at first shocked and then amused to observe her; she noticed her system of eye contact with passing men and, sometimes, on closing her window, how a man would turn into the doorway. Studying the sign language with a glass, she worked out the system of winks, smiles, and slight nods of the head that made her choice of men entirely clear. The Baronne, curious, tried it out herself in front of the mirror, then, emboldened, through her own window, with "a mad desire" to see whether passing men would understand her gestures. Selecting a fair, handsome passerby and making her sign, she was covered with confusion when the man immediately responded by ascending to her apartment and, further, in order to make him leave before her husband returned, submitted to him as if she were, as he thought, a willing partner cheating on her husband for two crowns. Considering the affluence of the apartment, the man had observed, "You must really be in bad straits at the moment to *faire la fenêtre*!"[49]

In invoking Maupassant's phrase *faire la fenêtre* with regard to the formula "Anxiety + . . . window . . . ," Freud is in fact reworking this story not so much to explain the desire of imitation and the overwhelming desire to accomplish a forbidden act—the motives articulated by the Maupassant's Baronne—but rather to set up the preconditions of anxiety. Exhorting Fliess to "think of Guy de Maupassant's *faire de la fenêtre,*" and after a significant digression on the periodicity of his own impotence, Freud concludes by confirming "a conjecture . . . concerning the mechanism of agoraphobia in women." It is, he slyly hints, revealed by the very notion of "public" women, and its structure that of "envy of prostitution and identification."

One year later in "Draft M" of "The Architecture of Hysteria," enclosed with a letter to Fliess in May 1897, Freud restated his claim that "agoraphobia seems to depend on a romance of prostitution . . . a woman who will not go out by herself asserts her mother's unfaithfulness."[50] Here he derived symptoms of anxiety, which he equated with phobias, from fantasies. Fantasies themselves, he posited, "arise from an unconscious combination of things experienced and heard," according to tendencies that hide the memory from which these symptoms might have emerged. Freud compared the process of fantasy formation to a chemical process of decomposition and composition, which in the case of the fantasy distorts and amalgamates memory through fragmentation and consequent breakup of chronological relations. "A fragment of the visual scene then combines with a fragment of the auditory one into the fantasy, while the fragment set free links up with something else. Thereby an original connection has become untraceable." The "architecture" of this *Fantasiebildung* and *Symptombildung,* as Freud termed the process, was then clear, illustrated by the celebrated diagram of the analytic work on "scenes" and their symptoms. For Freud, symptoms appeared when the fantasy, previously "set up in front" of the scene, became so intense as to emerge into consciousness, whence it itself was subject to a repression that generated the symptom. He concluded: "All anxiety symptoms (phobias) are derived in this way from fantasies."[51] Beyond this, the action of repression between the preconscious and the unconscious, Freud proposed another level of repression within the unconscious itself: "there is the soundest hope," he opined to Fliess, "that it will be possible to determine the number and kind of fantasies just as it is possible with scenes." Such fantasies were, at root, family romances. He cited two examples: one, the "romance of alienation" or paranoia, which served the function of "illegitimizing the relatives in question," and the other, "agoraphobia," the romance of prostitution, "which itself goes back once more to this family romance." Hence, by a labyrinthine enough route, Freud arrived at his conclusion that "a woman who will not go out by herself asserts her mother's unfaithfulness."[52]

Much has been written, and especially on the question of phobia and gender, to qualify Freud's early analyses; the work of women analysts from Helene Deutsch to Julia Kristeva has subjected the Freudian (and Lacanian) interpretation of phobia to critical revision, to deal with questions of domesticity, gender, and the symbolic structures in which they are inscribed.[53] Most analysts have basically agreed with him on the secondary, or displaced, role of the environment in agoraphobia, where, as he summarized in the *New Introductory Lectures* of 1932, an "internal danger is transformed into an external one."[54] And yet, for the purposes of architectural and urban interpretation, in a context of the cultural understanding of space, we might rather insist that these secondary roles are primary. For if analysis reveals the hidden sources of anxiety neurosis, it is nevertheless the apartment, the window, the street, the space itself that is identified as the instigator of the initial attacks; and whether or not these spaces are symbolic of something else, or the anxiety is thence transformed into an anxiety around anxiety itself, this space remains attached to the first fear. After all, the windows at which fictional and real women stood uncertain whether either to gesture for a man to ascend, or to throw themselves out, were the physical frames, as Lacan would have it, for an anxiety that was, if not caused by, then certainly figured through private and public space and its uncertain boundaries.

When Freud turned in 1909 to the analysis of his most celebrated phobic case, that of "Little Hans," it was ostensibly to demonstrate not only that street, warehouses, carts, and horses are beside the point—they represent only "the material disguises" of his fear that stemmed from deeper-rooted hostility to the father and jealous sadistic feelings toward the mother—but that even agoraphobia might be ruled out immediately: "We might classify

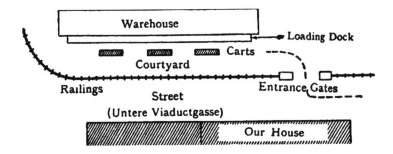

3. Sigmund Freud, position of Little Hans's house in Vienna, *Analysis of a Phobia in a Five-Year-Old Boy* (1909), fig. 2, in *Standard Edition*, 10:46.

Hans' case as an agoraphobia if it were not for the fact that it is a characteristic of that complaint that the locomotion of which the patient is otherwise incapable can always be easily performed when he is accompanied by some specially selected person—in the last resort by the physician."[55] Which was not the case in the example of Hans. Nevertheless, in Freud's account of the case, the head customs warehouse across the street from Little Hans's home, its horses and carts, and the viaduct all figured powerfully in Hans's own symbolism of fear. Freud himself goes to the trouble of mapping this spatial world in great detail, drawing a plan of the neighborhood as well as tracing the route of Hans's "desire," crossing the road in front of his house to the ramp in front of the warehouse. It is as if Freud, like his detective hero Holmes, found it necessary to draw the "scene" of the phobia, marking all the sites of every physical clue of psychic life, in order to dismiss their relevance to the investigation and reveal them as hiding something more important. And if Freud's maps of this space emphasize the importance he gave to the phobic milieu, Lacan went even further, intrigued by Little Hans's spaces, to the extent that he constructs several more maps to add to those Freud provided. Under the heading "Circuits" in the conference of 8 May 1957, during the course of the year's seminar on "The Relation of the Object," Lacan traces with forensic care the plan of Hans's Vienna.[56] First at a large scale, noting the position of Hans's house within the Ring, beside the Donau Canal, then closing in and demonstrating the position of the house vis-à-vis the Stadt Park, the Stadtbahn station, the route to the Nordbahnhof across the canal, and, picturesquely enough, Riegl's Museum für Kunst und Industrie on the Ringstrasse. This is in order to trace a first double trajectory, recounted by Hans's father, of the trip to the Schönbrunn Zoological Gardens where Hans first witnessed the giraffe, and thence to his grandmother's house. Lacan insists on these spatial details as intrinsic to the tracking down of the intersecting fantasies of Hans. He then turns to the question of the horses, tracing their appearance to the route that Hans wished to follow from his house, across the road, through the gates to the loading ramp of the Customs House. Here Lacan simply repeats Freud's own diagram. But, despite what Lacan calls "information carefully gathered," he is forced in the next session of the seminar to admit that he had been wrong—and in a most important particular: the position of the house of Hans, and its relation to the customs building. "One is blind to what one has beneath one's eyes, and that is called the signifier, the letter," he writes.[57] It had been "a hidden street," "Under the Viaduct Alley" (Untere Viaductgasse), which Freud had noted and Lacan had overlooked. Then Lacan redraws his map to take account of this, noting also that he had equally overlooked (or conflated) the existence of the Customs House with respect to the train station. Nevertheless he finds that the new facts support his first analysis—"explain all the connections at once." "Here then, the scene is set up," he concluded.[58]

In the interpretation of urban and architectural space, then, as opposed to the explanation of the anxieties of the inhabitant, phobia and fear play a fundamental role. It is as if space, with all its invasive and boundary-breaking properties, takes up anxiety for its own and carries it into the realms of aesthetic theory, representational practice, and modernist ideology indiscriminately, and

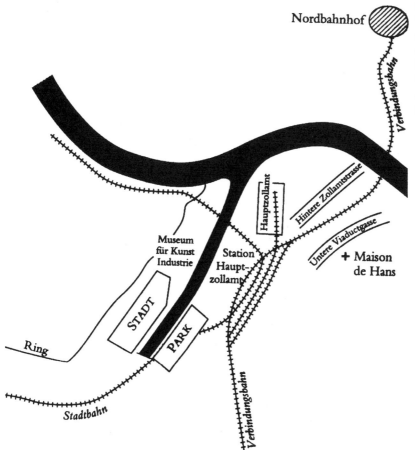

Nordbahnhof

Verbindungsbahn

Hauptzollamt

Hintere Zollamtstrasse

Untere Viaductgasse

Museum für Kunst Industrie

Station Haupt-zollamt

+ Maison de Hans

STADT

PARK

Ring

Verbindungsbahn

Stadtbahn

4. Jacques Lacan, "The Railway Network," corrected elaboration of Freud's plan of Little Hans's neighborhood in Vienna, *Le séminaire de Jacques Lacan*, book IV, p. 326.

without regard for the "scientific" ends of the psychological inquiries that initially made the connection. As Charles Melman noted, assessing the role of space in phobia from a Lacanian standpoint, "The phobic pays a tribute to space, not a symbolic tribute such as one pays to a dead father, but a tribute to the imaginary itself; and we all pay one of these. We know in effect that in space there are places that are privileged or are called sacred and are separated from the rest. The phobic is not concerned with taboo circles such as these; everything happens as if the tribute paid to space were infinite, right up to the edge of the house from which he cannot go out."[59]

Phobic Abstraction

By the end of the nineteenth century, Sitte's "fashionable" disease had become a commonplace scapegoat for all tears associated with modernity. The art historian Wilhelm Worringer even sought to expand the implications of agoraphobia, seeing it as a fundamental disease of the human condition from primitive times to the present. Writing in 1906, following what he described as a "miraculous" encounter with the sociologist Georg Simmel in the Trocadéro Museum in Paris, Worringer identified agoraphobia as the underlying cause of the ceaseless drive of art toward abstraction: "The urge to abstraction is the outcome of a great inner unrest inspired in man by the phenomena of the outside world. . . . We might describe this state as an immense spiritual dread of space."[60]

In the aftermath of what Worringer termed the "great shifting of emphasis in investigation from the objects of perception to perception itself"—the Kantian revolution—it had become clear to psychologists, aestheticians, and art historians that the conditions of perception were far from fixed and arrayed in a priori categories but rather subject to infinite variability. The "dogma of the variability of the psychical categories," in Worringer's phrase, following the psychological theories of Fechner, Volkelt, and Lipps, immediately placed perception in a field conditioned by "the checkered, fateful adjustment of man to the outer world," a field that was "ceaselessly shifting in man's relation to the impressions crowding in upon him." Abstraction, for Worringer, far from being a new and modern form, was in fact the most ancient, born precisely out of anxiety and founded on no less than a primitive fear of nature and a concomitant desire "to divest the things of the external world of their caprice and obscurity," to endow them with a regularity represented in geometric abstraction. Worringer cites "the fear of space [*Raumsheu*] which is clearly manifested in Egyptian architecture," and compares what seems to him to be a generalized *geistiger Raumscheu,* or "spiritual dread of space," to the modern malady of agoraphobia, or what he terms *Platzangst.* In the same way as "this physical dread of open places may be explained as a residue from a normal phase of man's development, at which he was not yet able to trust entirely to visual impression as a means of becoming familiar with a space extended before him, but was still dependent upon the asurances of his sense of touch," so the spiritual dread of open space was a throwback to a moment of "instinctive fear conditioned by man's feeling of being lost in the universe."[61] He characterizes this feeling as "a kind of spiritual agoraphobia in the face of the motley disorder and caprice of the phenomenal world."[62] The "sensation of fear [*Angst*]," Worringer concludes, was "the root of artistic creation."[63]

In the later *Form in Gothic,* Worringer repeated the thesis of "primitive fear" and elaborated it with respect to modern fantasies of a Rousseauesque "golden age." "Man has conceived the history of his development as a slow process of estrangement between himself and the outer world, as a process of estrangement during which the original sense of unity and confidence gradually disappears"; the reverse, he argued, was in fact true. Rather than the "poetical conception" of primitive man, the historian should reconstruct the "true primeval" man by the elimination of sentiment, leaving a "monster" in the place of "the man of paradise." This monster, helpless, incoherent, a mere "dumbfounded animal," receives unreliable perceptual images of the world that are only gradually remodeled into conceptual images. The real development, then, was not from wholeness to estrangement, but rather from the feeling of strangeness to familiarity. The original "gloomy spirit of fear," based on instinct, survives in the "deepest and most anguished insight." It is such fear, finally, that drives the search for absolutes, the rigid line, and abstraction. The capturing of shifting images on a plane surface frees objects "from their disquieting environment, from their forlorn condition in space"; such a surface resisted depth, the third dimension, which once more tended to plunge objects into the "boundless relativity" of space, and provided a security against the infinite.[64] Whenever abstraction reemerges in art, it will be, Worringer held, a symptom of individual subjugation to "the crowd": "crowd sensibility and abstract sensibility are . . . two words for the same thing." Impersonal, the "expression of the undifferentiated crowd," abstraction still marks the presence of agoraphobia and a relationship of fear to the outer world.[65]

Now while Worringer's observations were made, as Dora Vallier has recently pointed out, in strict isolation from cubist or expressionist experiments in abstract art, and while they seem, as Worringer himself claimed, to have been advanced without detailed knowledge of Georg Simmel's own investigations into the "mental life" of modernity, his juxtaposition of agoraphobia and abstraction was nevertheless a calculated reversal of the turn-of-the-century wisdom that saw the spaces created by modern abstract geometry as a direct *cause* of agoraphobia, if not of the entire psychopathology of modern urban space.[66]

Phobic Modernism

Worringer's sense of universal dread attached to space was quickly to be taken up by art historians searching for psychological explanations for visual expression, supported by Freud's own investigation of symbols and by psychoanalytical phenomenologists extending his insights to a general theory of experience. Thus, in February 1933, Ludwig Binswanger, Freud's correspondent and friendly critic and director of the Sanatorium Bellevue at Kreuzlingen, published a long article on "The Space Problem in Psychopathology."[67] A phenomenological psychoanalyst, deeply indebted to Freud, but attempting to construct a theory of the self that relied less on biology and more on existential phenomenology, Binswanger was interested in the role of spatial identification and orientation in mental illness; he analyzed his patients through a combination of belief in the self-realization embodied in a cure, and their bodily and spatial situation in the world. In the case of Lola Voss, he traced the course of a growing anxiety in a world "sunk into insignificance," where in the face of the "nothingness of the world" the self is forced more and more vainly to comprehend the source of anxiety, which is coupled with a fear of objects and people. Binswanger finds that his patient tried always to "let some *light* (which always means some space) enter into the uncanniness of her existence," recounting the struggle to make space for the self: "This shows the struggle of the existence to create space even in the nothingness of anxiety, a space in which it can move freely, breathe freely, act freely—free of the unbearable burden of the Dreadful."[68] Space is salvaged in Binswanger's account by superstition, a "foothold" that at least holds the things of the world as things; beyond this lies, for Voss as for many of his other patients, a state of being lost, of living in danger without hope of control, a state of self-abdication, dream, and delusion. Existence thus becomes a realm of a larger hostile space and a disproportionately smaller friendly space—with a loss, that is, of distance and thus of freedom in the world. Hence Lola Voss's "taboo" against spatiotemporal proximity, touch, and closeness in general. "'Walls' of taboo-like fears and prohibitions ... slid between her and the physician."[69] Binswanger concluded:

> Since existence, in this case, has totally surrendered to the Uncanny and the Dreadful, it can no longer be aware of the fact that the Dreadful emerges from itself, out of its very own ground. Hence there is no escape from such fear; man stares fear-stricken at the inescapable and all his happiness and pain now depend upon the possibility of conjuring the Dreadful. His one and only desire is to become as familiar as possible with the Dreadful, the Horrible, the Uncanny. He sees two alternatives: the first is to "capture" the Dreadful and anticipate its "inflections" with the help of words and playing on words; the second, which interferes seriously with living and life, is to put spatial distance between himself and the persons and objects struck by the Dreadful's curse.[70]

It was precisely this question of spatial proximity and distance that entered into the case history of one of Binswanger's most celebrated patients, Aby Warburg, who between 1918 and 1924 underwent treatment at Kreuzlingen and, as Michael Steinberg has noted, seems to have worked through his illness according to the principles of Binswanger's "self-realization" through writing. Beset for his entire life by anxieties, fears, and "demons" ostensibly precipitated by a sense of diminishing distance between the procedures of rational thought and the speed of modern communication, Warburg intellectually constructed his "cure" by means of a long-meditated paper reflecting on his early visit to the American southwest and his observations of the Pueblo Indians and their festivals, which he had photographed extensively in 1895.

Warburg's changing view of modernist space was from the outset articulated through a series of studies of traditional mythology and culture. Warburg, in contrast to Worringer, was originally a convinced proponent of modernist progress, a progress he attributed directly to the effects of abstraction.[71] For Warburg, indeed, the distinction between the preindustrial and the postindustrial was precisely that "reason" had supplied a sufficient *distance* between the magical forces of nature and the phobic subject; a space, as he termed it, of reason and reflection—a *Denkraum*—that insulated the fearful subject from the unknown or at best allowed the unknown to be comprehended and thus less feared.

Accordingly, in this ascription, space was beneficent, and the more the better. Indeed, the "progress" that Warburg measured seemed to increase in direct proportion to the amount of mental and physical "space" that might be conquered by society in order to create a sufficient barrier between nature and civilization. In these terms, he saw the Renaissance as a distinct turning point in progress, not simply, as his master Jacob Burckhardt had it; because of the substitution of the secular for the religious world, but because of the increasingly spatial nature of the secular world. Warburg measured this increase by, for example, what he saw as the space-filling nature of Renaissance festivals. It was partly to confirm such a proposition, hardly novel since the 1870s and largely drawn from historians like Karl Lamprecht and August Schmarsow (for whom Warburg worked in Florence in the summer of 1889), that Warburg visited the United States in 1895. Finding little to attract him in the modernized east, Warburg traveled directly to the Pueblo Indian settlements of the southwest. For Warburg, these seemed to represent, despite the layers of modernization under which they were buried, true survivals of magical, symbolic cultures. He studied the three-day festival at Oraibi and its tribal dances and ceremonies. But his real enthusiasm was reserved for the worship of the snake, its symbols and related dances. His assumption that the snake formed a propitiation for lightning, and that its handling represented the displacement of a greater fear by a lesser, was confirmed by a schoolteacher who showed him children's drawings with lightning forks with snake heads.

In 1918, however, Warburg's belief in progress was subjected to the aftershock of the war, and what now appeared less as a confidence in infinite progress and more as an elaborate defense against phobia finally collapsed in the breakdown that led to the five-year confinement and treatment under Binswanger. It was this confinement, I would hazard, that was instrumental in the development of Warburg's special understanding of modernity and its relationship to traditional culture as represented in the preparatory notes for the lecture that, with Binswanger's assent, secured his release. This lecture, the notes for which still exist, was painstakingly constructed out of the insights of his "cure" and revised recollections of his journey to the Pueblo. Entitled "Lecture on the Snake Dance," it was finally delivered in 1923.[72] In it, Warburg worked through his cure as an elaborate rethinking of modernism's progress, a virtual acceptance of the dangerous proximity of phobia and reason, and a trenchant critique of the way in which space-conquering techniques—flight, wireless, telephones—seemed to him to be eroding any possibility for a stable distance of reflection, the treasured *Denkraum.*

Ernst Gombrich has transcribed some of the notes and drafts for this lecture, in which Warburg used, so to speak, his own mental illness to develop theories of ostensibly "primitive" but evidently autobiographical mental states:

> Primitive man is like a child in the dark. He is surrounded by a menacing chaos which constantly endangers his survival. The original state, therefore, is one of fear, of those "phobic reflexes" to which Tito Vignoli . . . attached such crucial importance for the genesis of myth and ultimately of science. Our mind is in a constant state of readiness to take up a defensive position against the real or imagined causes of the threatening impressions which assail us.
>
> The phobic reflex which substitutes a known image, however menacing, for the dread of the unknown cause has an important biological function: even the most fearful imaginary cause is less fearful than the dreadful unknown. . . . In this respect the phobic reaction prepares the ground for the mastery of the world through the act of naming and thence to the dominance of logical thought.[73]

In these terms, spirituality might be interpreted as the result of universal terror, and phobia proven beneficial.

> So the Indian establishes the rational element in his cosmology by depicting the world like his own house, which he enters by means of a ladder. But we must not think of this world-house as the simple reflection of a tranquil cosmology. For the mistress of the house is the most fearsome of all beasts—the serpent.
>
> The snake ritual a dual function—act of primitive magic and a quest for enlightenment—counterpart to modern control of electricity. But the latter not without dangers—not a simple belief in universal progress. For progress had also destroyed distance. Anxieties and phobias

demand distance and reflection, detachment; causes can only be grasped through detachment and reasoning. Thus electricity annihilated *Denkraum,* the zone or space of reasoning.[74]

The pessimistic conclusion to the final publication of the snake ritual lecture no doubt stems from this fear: Warburg's photographed image of an "Uncle Sam" with a top hat proudly striding along the road in front of an imitation classical rotunda, with an electric wire stretching above his top hat, seems a symbol of the way in which what Warburg called "Edison's copper serpent" had finally wrested the thunderbolt from nature.

Telegram and telephone destroy the cosmos. Mythopeic and symbolic thought in their struggle to spiritualize man's relation with his environment have created space as a zone of contemplation or of reasoning [*Raum als Andachtsraum oder Denkraum*], that space which the instantaneous connection of electricity destroys unless a disciplined humanity restores the inhibitions of conscience.[75]

It was in September 1929 that Warburg heard the news of the successful docking of Eckener's Zeppelin in New York after evading a thunderstorm by using its instruments; for the art historian it seemed to be a triumph of science and foresight symbolizing man's conquest of the elements. In his journal he wrote: "The mercury column as a weapon against Satan Phobos."[76]

We should of course be wary of drawing too portentous conclusions from these jottings of Warburg; he himself noted, "They are the confessions of an (incurable) schizoid, deposited in the archives of mental healers," a remark that served Gombrich's own cautious approach well. But at the same time, Warburg himself noted the force of the phobic in the historian's own narratives, those "uncanny vaults where we found the transformers which transmute the innermost stirrings of the human soul into lasting forms."[77] But we might, with hindsight, see in Warburg's personal narrative of breakdown and partial recovery from modernism a sense of the inevitability of the collapse of spatial reason, as he, with such psychological pain, finally accepted the impossibility of stabilizing modern space or sheltering the subject in a world of rootless psyches.

Framing Infinity

Le Corbusier, Ayn Rand, and the Idea of "Ineffable Space"

> Our period demands a type of man who can restore the lost equilibrium between inner and outer reality. This equilibrium, never static but, like reality itself, involved in continuous change, is like that of a tightrope dancer who, by small adjustments, keeps a continuous balance between his being and empty space.
>
> Sigfried Giedion[1]

Men in Space

The pathologies of agoraphobia and claustrophobia, joined if not caused by their common site in metropolis, provided ready arguments for modernist architects who were eager to reconstruct the very foundations of urban space. Arguing that urban phobias were precisely the product of urban environments, and that their cure was dependent on the erasure of the old city in its entirety, modernist architects from the early 1920s projected images of a city restored to a natural state, within which the dispersed institutions of the new society would be scattered like pavilions in a landscape garden. Reviving the late eighteenth-century myth of "transparency," both social and spatial, modernists evoked the picture of a glass city, its buildings invisible and society open. The resulting "space" would be open, infinitely extended, and thereby cleansed of all mental disturbance: the site of healthy and presumably aerobically perfect bodies. As Sigfried Giedion figured it, this would be the space of a "tightrope dancer," balanced between individual "b:ing" and "empty space."[2]

The direct model for Giedion's acrobat was, of course, his favorite space architect, Le Corbusier, whose work represented for the Swiss historian the epitome of modernism; but, evoked in 1948, the acrobat might equally have referred to a more fictional character, the celebrated architect designed as a kind of "composite" modernist by Ayn Rand in her celebrated novel *The Fountain-head*, published in 1943.[3] Thus, on the surface at least, nothing could have seemed more serene and confident than the mental and physical being of Howard Roark in the opening scene of the novel. Here he is depicted for all intents and purposes as if in a cut from Leni Riefenstahl's *Triumph of the Will*, viewed from below as he stands poised on the edge of a cliff. On the edge of a high granite outcrop, his naked body, like some latter-day Prometheus (with whom he later identifies himself at his final trial) or futurist-cum-vorticist demigod, seems as if cut out of the material of the cliff itself—"a body of long straight lines and angles, each curve broken into planes." His face, "like a law of nature" was "gaunt," with high cheekbones betraying pure Aryan ancestry; cold gray eyes steadily betraying iron willpower; contemptuous mouth betraying a position well above the prosaic world—"the mouth of an executioner or a saint," remarks Rand, paraphrasing Hugo on Robespierre.[4]

Roark's very gaze was in the process of building, transforming his surroundings into suitable construction materials and his position into a desirable building site: "He looked at the granite. To be cut, he thought, and made into walls. He looked at a tree. To be split and made into rafters. He looked at a streak of rust on the stone and thought of iron ore under the ground. To be melted and to emerge as girders against the sky." If nature had not rendered the place perfect, surely the architect might be permitted to cut and fill a little: "These rocks, he thought, are here for me; waiting for the drill, the dynamite and my voice; waiting to be split, ripped, pounded, reborn; waiting for the shape my hands will give them."[5] While this passionate and violent account of the rape of nature by the architect deserves full analysis in the context of modernism's, and subsequently postmodernism's, pretensions to reshape the world, in this context I am more interested in Howard Roark's body, and more precisely in its position in space. For this superyouth was, almost literally, standing in midair, an Icarus before the fall:

> He stood naked at the edge of a cliff. The lake lay far below him. A frozen explosion of granite burst in flight to the sky over motionless water. The water seemed immovable, the stone—flowing. The stone had the stillness of one brief moment in battle when thrust meets thrust and the cur-

rents are held in a pause more dynamic than motion. . . . The rocks went on into the depth unchanged. They ended in the sky. So that the world seemed suspended in space, an island floating on nothing, anchored to the feet of the man on the cliff.[6]

Here, in a typical reversal, nature is yoked to man's feet, avoiding the Promethean fate.

Roark's space is recognizable enough. Lifted by Rand from the platitudes of the romantic sublime, its philosophical tone heightened, so to speak, by Nietzsche, its characteristics of absolute height, depth, and breadth had emerged in the mid-twenties as the leitmotiv of idealistic modernism. Bruno Taut had celebrated it in his attempts to fabricate crystalline cities out of the Alps to form "marble cliffs" as magical as those described by Ernst Jünger; Mies van der Rohe had envisaged it as gridded and endless—a universal system of three-dimensional graph paper, to be punctuated (materialized) in the hard steel sections of a new classicism; and Le Corbusier, who had first experienced it much like Roark standing on the edge of a cliff during his first visit to the Athenian Acropolis, and elevated it into a principle, termed it "l'espace indicible."[7]

This last concept was first articulated in 1933, on the occasion of Le Corbusier's return to Athens for the first time since his initial visit in 1911. Now on the occasion of the fourth CIAM, in his discourse to the assembled international modern architectural community, he confessed his debt to the Acropolis in almost Nietzschean terms, remembering his first experience of the hill and its ruins as overwhelming, how he left "crushed by the superhuman aspect of things on the Acropolis," by the sight of the Parthenon, "a cry hurled into a landscape made of grace and terror."[8] It is perhaps significant that this confession was first republished in 1948 in a review of his life and work, *New World of Space,* the first chapter of which is a translation of his essay "L'espace indicible," the introduction to a special number of *L'Architecture d'Aujourd'hui* of two years earlier. With the concept of "l'espace indicible" Le Corbusier completes his acropolitan trajectory, finally assimilating the unassimilable to his architecture.

As outlined in the 1946 essay, "ineffable space," as the rather inelegant translation would have it—perhaps "inexpressible," "indefinable," or "indescribable" would be a better term—is a fundamental and indeed literally terrifying concept. The violence of the Parthenon is balanced by a spatial milieu that gives it room to "cry." What in *Vers une architecture* had been a vast "cubic volume" is now transformed into an instrument of the modernist sublime:

> The essential thing that will be said here is that the release of aesthetic emotion is a special function of space.
>
> ACTION OF THE WORK on its surroundings: vibrations, cries or shouts (such as the Parthenon on the Acropolis in Athens), arrows darting away like rays, as if springing from an explosion; the near or distant site is shaken by them, touched, wounded dominated or caressed. REACTION OF THE SETTING: the walls of the room, its dimensions, the public square . . . , the expanses or the slopes of the landscape even to the bare horizons of the plain or the sharp outlines of the mountains—the whole environment brings its weight to bear on the place where there is a work of art. . . . Then a boundless depth opens up, effaces the walls, drives away contingent presences, *accomplishes the miracle of ineffable space.*[9]

In this sense, ineffable space was, for Le Corbusier, transcendent space. Its qualities were those of container and contained; he compared it to a sounding board, resonating and reverberating with the "plastic acoustics" set up by the natural and man-made objects that inhabited it. Objects, if possible freestanding, generated force fields, took possession of space, orchestrated it and made it sing or cry out with harmony or pain. Such space, Le Corbusier claimed in 1946, was a discovery of modernity—"the fourth dimension" that a number of artists had used to "magnify space" around 1910. "The fourth dimension is the moment of limitless escape evoked by exceptionally just consonance of the plastic means employed." And when correctly employed, this space had a strangely powerful effect on the very buildings that defined it and set it in motion: "In a complete and successful work there are hidden masses of implications, a veritable world which reveals itself to those it may concern," wrote Le Corbusier, adding, with a contempt worthy of Roark, "which means: to those who deserve it." This feeling—like that described a few years earlier by Freud, who in a letter to Romain Rolland called it "oceanic"—was virtually religious in nature: "I am not conscious of the miracle of faith, but I often live that of ineffable space, the consummation of plastic emotions."[10]

In a virtual replay of the explosion that demolished the Parthenon, ineffable space dissolves walls and opens the inside to the outside, an outside now simply framed in order to testify to its visual existence, but open more or less panoramically around the entire building. Ineffable space would then be that dreamt and idealized, worked and realized experience that matched the heights of Periclean Greece.

This developed theory of space, articulated in the presence of the Acropolis in 1933, was sensed and intuited on his first visit to it in 1911. His travel journal of that early journey also evoked a certain fear, an awe, sometimes a confessed terror in his appreciation of spatial experience. Thus, beyond the appreciation of the Parthenon as a type form, a "product of selection" to be compared to the modern automobile, uneasy words surround his attempt to understand it and its site, words like "violence," "terror," "sacrifice." The Parthenon is a "terrible machine," it holds something "du brutal" "de l'intense."[11] In traditional aesthetic terms, that is, Le Corbusier is removing the object from the category of the beautiful and reestablishing it, along Nietzschean lines, in its proper order of the terrifying sublime. This is explicit in the account of his first visit to the Acropolis: "Voici que se confirme la rectitude des temples, la sauvagerie du site . . . L'entablement d'une cruelle rigidité écrase et terrorise. Le sentiment d'une fatalité extra-humaine vous saisit. Le Parthenon, terrible machine . . . "[12] Such rhetoric, of course, was itself traditional—Ernest Renan's *Prière sur l'Acropole,* which Le Corbusier had bought and read, contains much of the same. But what was new, and what went beyond the Wölfflinian formalism already a part of Le Corbusier's intellectual baggage, was the expression of the Parthenon and its attendant structures as objects fully activated in space and by space; no longer the "infinite space" which, Corbusier noted, "sweetened the images of Athos," but a space closed, "contracted;" "L'Acropole,— ce roc—surgit seule au coeur d'un cadre fermé."[13] A frame formed by the surrounding mountains, that operated, in Le Corbusier's simile, like a shell holding a pearl. Nature came first, but meaning was formed by architecture: "Les temples sont la raison de ce paysage." The exterior is an interior.

Heightening the experience of this space for the young Le Corbusier was, inevitably, the sense that here was to be found the very essence of architecture,

5. Le Corbusier, sketches of the Acropolis, *Vers une architecture*, p. 155.

Fig. 11. — Propylées et Temple de là Victoire Aptère.

(fig. 11). La mer qui compose avec les architraves (fig. 12), etc. Composer avec les infinies ressources d'un art plein de richesses périlleuses qui ne font de la beauté que lorsqu'elles sont en ordre :

Fig. 12. — Les Propylées.

"the essence of artistic thought," its root and apogee. Here the awe provoked by the experience of the Acropolis itself was intensified by an anxiety that preceded the visit and infused the entire stay in Athens. Le Corbusier, as he records in his journal, arrived in Athens at 11:00 in the morning; but inventing "a thousand pretexts not to ascend" the Acropolis, he waited till sunset before climbing toward the Propylaea.

We are reminded of another visitor, Sigmund Freud, for whom the Acropolis was an equally forbidding cultural monument, who had also seized on numerous pretexts not to encounter Athens, was unaccountably depressed at the very thought of the trip, and who, on finally being confronted with the Acropolis in the summer of 1903, delayed his visit until the following afternoon, putting on a clean shirt for the occasion. Interestingly enough, both Le Corbusier and Freud experienced a similar feeling of disbelief, of unreality, at the first sight of the mountain. As Le Corbusier expressed it, "To see the Acropolis is a dream that one caresses without even dreaming of realizing it."[14] For Freud, as he wrote to Romain Rolland in 1926, the feeling was one of astonishment, on the one hand that "all this really *does* exist, just as we learnt at school," and on the other that "the existence of Athens, the Acropolis, and the landscape around it had ever been objects of doubt" in the first place. This "sense of some feeling of the unbelievable and the unreal" Freud called "derealization" [*Entfremdungsgefühl*], the opposite number, so to speak, of *déjà-vu,* and he connected it, as we know, to a feeling of guilt on behalf of his father, who had not, metaphorically at least, "come as far" as the son.[15]

For Le Corbusier, on the other hand, this sense of dreamlike half-reality signaled his arrival at the supreme architectural achievement, at the same time as defending against the terrifying thought that it might never be surpassed. Suffusing the powerful emotion of Athenian space was the equally strong anxiety that it might not be replicable, could not be captured or reproduced: "Ceux qui, pratiquant l'*art* de l'architecture, se trouvent à une heure de leur carrière, le cerveau vide, le coeur brisé de doute, devant cette tache de donner une forme vivante à une matière morte, concevront la mélancolie des soliloques au milieu des débris—de mes entretiens glacés avec les muettes pierres."[16]

A task that was made all the more difficult, firstly because the silent stones were themselves hardly "there"—a derealization of architecture itself subjected to the ruination of centuries of ransacking, explosions, and archaeological clearing; and secondly because it was not just a question, as in the academic practices of the nineteenth century, of working out the exact recombination of the stones to "restore" the Acropolis, but rather of capturing the space itself, of restaging the dynamic intensity of forms in light in space.

Now all this could be put down to the common youthful enthusiasm shared by Rand and Le Corbusier for Nietzsche and Herbert Spencer, for a fin-de-siècle diet of antidecadence and symbolist aesthetics, motivated by a quasi-religious Wagnerianism fomented by Edouard Schuré, author of *Les grands initiés,* nourished by a good dose of Hugo's *Notre-Dame,* which for Le Corbusier, Rand, and notably for Frank Lloyd Wright had challenged the modern architect to rediscover the authentic roots of cultural and social expression, to fight the increasing hegemony of the printed word, if not the movies, and to return, cutting through the academic undergrowth, to natural forms and forces.

But in the same way as "oceanic space" was, in Freud, established through what he termed a "disturbance of memory," itself caused by a deeper anxiety (that of success and the overcoming of the father), so, for Roark and Le Corbusier, infinite space became the instrument of suppression for everything they hated about the city, if not the agent of repression of their own highly developed phobias: claustrophobia in the face of the old city, of course, but also, and linked to this, that fear identified by Simmel—the fear of touching.

Out of Touch

> The pathological symptom of *Berührungsangst,* the fear of getting into too close a contact with objects, is spread endemically in a mild degree nowadays. It grows out of a kind of hyperaesthetics, for which every live and immediate contact produces pain.
>
> Georg Simmel, "Sociological Aesthetics"[17]

It does not take an especially attentive reader to notice that Rand's characters all suffer from an intolerable fear of touching, if not from more precise phobias. Henry Cameron asks Roark: "Do you ever look at the people in the street? Aren't you afraid of them? I am. They move past you and they wear hats and they carry bundles. But that's not the substance of them. The substance of them is hatred for any man that loves his work. That's the only kind they fear."[18]

Dominique Francon's phobia was more developed: "She had always hated the streets of a city. She saw the faces streaming past her, the faces made alike by fear—fear as a common denominator, fear of themselves, fear of all and of one another, fear making them ready to pounce upon whatever was held sacred by any single one they met. She could not define the nature or the reason of that fear. But she had always felt its presence. She had kept herself clean and free in a single passion—to touch nothing."[19] Later she develops an unmistakable case of agoraphobia, confined to Gail Wynand's penthouse following her marriage. Even the reliable and sensible Katie, the luckless niece of Ellsworth Toohey and ever-patient fiancee of Peter Keating, is forced to confess a phobic interlude:

> I was working on my research notes all day, and nothing happened at all. No calls or visitors. And then suddenly tonight, I had that feeling, it was like a nightmare, you know, the kind of horror that you can't describe, that's not like anything normal at all. Just the feeling that I was in mortal danger, that something was closing in on me, that I'd never escape it, because it wouldn't let me and it was too late. . . . Haven't you ever had a feeling like that, just fear that you couldn't explain?

She thought that "maybe the room was stuffy, or maybe it was the silence," when she saw her uncle Ellsworth Toohey's shadow looming huge on the wall—a kind of uncanny apparition of his future influence. "That's when it got me. It wouldn't move, that shadow, but I thought all that paper was moving. I thought it was rising very slowly off the floor, and it was going to come to my throat and I was going to drown. That's when I screamed. And, Peter, he didn't hear."[20]

We are reminded of another modernist heroine, Virginia Woolf's Mrs. Dalloway, in the novel of the same name, and of what Clarissa Dalloway herself described as a "panic fear" that accompanied her throughout life and was precisely exacerbated in that most male and modernist of domains, the metropolis. Woolf stages this fear in the London of 1923, five years after the cessation of hostilities in World War I, and her characterization of a London in shock, of a social as well as an urban trauma, is pointed by the parallel histories of two protagonists: the socialite and party-giver Mrs. Dalloway, whose only care in life seemed to be the organization of her invitations and the hostessing of her "perfect" party; and the returned shell-shock victim Septimus Warren Smith, who gradually retreats from an intolerable world into silence. At first randomly joined by juxtaposition, these two oddly matched figures are inexorably paired and intertwined, coming together at the end of the novel when the infamous nerve doctor Sir William Bradshaw brings the news of Warren Smith's suicide to Mrs. Dalloway's party. Then what have seemed all along to be two disparate worlds, upper and middle class, external pleasure and internal pain, are seen as one. As Mrs. Dalloway pieced it together:

> What business had the Bradshaws to talk of death at her party? A young man had killed himself. And they talked of it at her party—the Bradshaws, talked of death. He had killed himself—but how? Always her body went through it first, when she was told, suddenly, of an accident; her dress flamed, her body burnt. . . .
>
> Suppose [she thought of Septimus] he had . . . gone to Sir William Bradshaw, a great doctor yet to her obscurely evil, without sex or lust, extremely polite to women, but capable of some indescribable outrage. . . . Might he not then have said. . . . Life is made intolerable. Then (she had felt it only this morning) there was the terror; the overwhelming incapacity . . . there was in the depths of her heart an awful fear.[21]

The spatial characteristics of this fear paralleled those of Rand's Katie: a necessary interiority, either mental or physical or both; hence the ascription agora- or claustrophobia. Its forms are those of stream of consciousness, of entrapment, of intolerable closure, of space without exit, finally of breakdown and often suicide; Septimus Warren Smith, as we know, anticipated Woolf's own suicide at the outbreak of the Second World War.

And if Woolf's or Rand's characters hated the city that made them sick, Le Corbusier's responses were equally pathological. Writing in 1929 on "The Street" for the journal *L'Intransigeant,* he castigated the traditional canyon, "plunged in eternal twilight."

> The street . . . rising straight up from it are walls of houses, which when seen against the sky-line present a grotesquely jagged silhouette of gables, attics, and zinc chimneys. At the very bottom of this scenic railway lies

the street, plunged in eternal twilight. The sky is a remote hope far, far above it. The street is no more than a trench, a deep cleft, a narrow passage. And although we have been accustomed to it for more than a thousand years, our hearts are always oppressed by the constriction of its enclosing walls.

The street is full of people: one must take care where one goes. For several years now it has been full of rapidly moving vehicles as well; death threatens us at every step between the twin curb-stones. But we have been trained to face the peril of being crushed between them. On Sundays, when they are empty, the streets reveal their full horror. . . . Every aspect of human life pullulates throughout their length . . . a sea of lusts and faces. It is better than the theater, better than what we read in novels. . . . The street wears us out. And when all is said and done we have to admit it disgusts us.

Heaven preserve us from the Balzacian mentality of [those] who would be content to leave our streets as they are because these murky canyons offer them the fascinating spectacle of human physiognomy![22]

The solution, for both Roark and Le Corbusier, was to profess a sublime indifference and disdain for streets and people alike, summed up in Roark's reply to Cameron's question: "But I never notice the people in the streets." And once "not noticed," of course, these people might easily be wished away in dreams of peace and quiet, emptiness, and spatial luxury:

Reason, and reason alone, would justify the most brilliant solutions and endorse their urgency. But suppose reason were reinforced by a well-timed lyricism. . . .

You are under the shade of trees, vast lawns spread all round you. The air is clean and pure; there is hardly any noise. What, you cannot see where the buildings are? Look through the charmingly diapered arabesques of branches out into the sky towards those widely-spaced crystal towers which soar higher than any pinnacle on earth. These translucent prisms that seem to float in the air without anchorage to the ground—flashing in summer sunshine, softly gleaming under grey winter skies, magically glittering at nightfall—are huge blocks of offices. . . .

Those gigantic and majestic prisms of purest transparency rear their heads one upon the other in a dazzling spectacle of grandeur, serenity and gladness.[23]

Here Le Corbusier touches on the principle that will dominate all others throughout the history of modernism, whether expressionist, functionalist, metaphysical, or idealist: transparency. A transparency that, extending the universal panopticism of Benthamite ideology, will finally render buildings subjects: subject to space, absorbed and dissolved in it, penetrated from all sides by light and air, undercut by greenery, roofs planted as gardens in the sky. Again we have returned to one of the commonplaces of modernism (perhaps the ease with which modernism fabricated its commonplaces accounts for the ease with which postmodernism fabricated its own), but it was a commonplace that rendered it absurdly easy to construct the notion of a city to end all cities, from Le Corbusier's project for Une Ville Contemporaine of 1923, to his Voisin Plan of 1925, culminating in the Ville Verte and Ville Radieuse of 1933–1935. With the proposal for the "Cartesian" skyscraper to replace the "gothic" and "too small" towers of New York, Le Corbusier joins Roark. In an elegant reversal of influence, his profile, photographed against Rockefeller Center in 1947 and published on the jacket of the English edition, seems to mirror that of Gary Cooper as he stands by his own model of rational transparency in the film of *The Fountainhead*.

But would transparency on its own serve to eradicate all those phobias, psychoses, and neuroses so dear to the metropolitan doctors? For Le Corbusier and his supporters, ineffable space had resolved the question. In a 1928 issue of *Les Cahiers de la République des Lettres* in which Le Corbusier expounded his vision of a new Paris, the old doctor Maurice de Fleury, whose work on neurasthenia had consistently championed Charcot's heredity thesis, contributed an article on "urban neuroses" flatly denying any relation between urban life and pathological disorders, claiming that all the so-called neurasthenic diseases were in fact hereditary. "These psychoneuroses, these half-madnesses, have no other cause than heredity. They are essentially constitutional maladies. The milieu, incidents, overexcitement are in no way their profound cause. What in the time of Morel and Magnan one called mental degeneration appears less and less to find its raison d'être in ardent activity." Indeed, the external stimuli em-

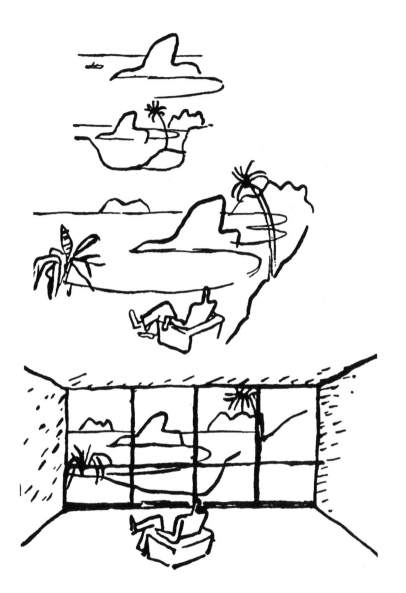

6. Le Corbusier. "This rock of Rio de Janeiro is celebrated. Around it are set the disheveled mountains; the sea bathes them. Palm trees, banana trees; tropical splendor animates the site. There one stops and installs one's armchair. A frame all around! The four oblique lines of a perspective! The room is set up in front of the site. The entire landscape in the room." *Oeuvre complète 1938–1946*, pp. 80–81.

anating from the city are veritably beneficial: "These external stimuli, which from all sides assail us, are like a bath of vital energy. They play for us, at our behest, the beneficent role of military music which relieves the step of the tired soldier, or of the orchestra whose rhythmic accents unleash the muscular strength of dancers. Let us not fear urban life too much."[24] In this way the way was cleared for the muscular energy of Le Corbusier's typical "man" working out freely like an athlete in open space. As Le Corbusier scornfully snorted in the face of late nineteenth-century decorative art: "Disorder! Neurasthenia! This art whose ebbing foam displays its broken fringe along our picture moldings is not the art of the new phenomenon which captures our imagination."[25]

Spaces of Passage

The Architecture of Estrangement: Simmel, Kracauer, Benjamin

A common and often explicit theme underlying the different responses of writers and social critics to the big cities of the nineteenth century might be found in the general concept of "estrangement": the estrangement of the inhabitant of a city too rapidly changing and enlarging to comprehend in traditional terms; the estrangement of classes from each other, of individual from individual, of individual from self, of workers from work. These refrains are constant from Rousseau to Marx, Baudelaire to Benjamin. The theme, a commonplace of romantic irony and self-enquiry and the leitmotiv of the Marxist critique of capital, was understood in both psychological and spatial terms. From Baudelaire's laments over the disappearance of old Paris ("the form of a city changes, alas, more rapidly than a man's heart") to Engels's wholesale critique of what he called "Haussmannization," the physical fabric of the city was identified as the instrument of a systematized and enforced alienation. The political critique of urban redevelopment forced by the growth of cities came together with the nostalgia of cultural conservatives lamenting the loss of their familiar quarters, creating a generalized sense of distantiation, of individual isolation, from the mechanical, mass-oriented, rapidly moving and crowded metropolis. Massimo Cacciari has written the history of this intellectual and "negative" critique of Metropolis as it emerged in the sociology of Max Weber, Georg Simmel, and their more conservative contemporaries Ferdinand Tönnies and Werner Sombart.[1]

Here I am concerned with only one aspect of this discourse of estrangement, the spatial and architectural in the writings of Simmel, Siegfried Kracauer, and Walter Benjamin as they searched for physical clues to the understanding of the social conditions of modernity. It will be my argument that, starting with the spatial sociology of Simmel, developing in the paradigmatic spaces identified and described by his student Kracauer, thence to be applied as a criterion of historical-critical analysis by Benjamin, a unique sensibility of urban space was worked out, one that was neither used as a simple illustration of social history nor seen as a mechanical cause of social change, but rather a conception of space as reciprocally interdependent with society. This sensibility was, by its very nature, attached to certain kinds of urban spaces that were, for social critics, constitutionally related to the social estrangement that seemed to permeate the metropolitan realm. In this sense, the critical strength of spatial paradigms was derived from their intimate association, if not complicity, with the material and psychological conditions of what Georg Lukács dubbed the "transcendental homelessness" of the modern world. For these writers, indeed, they existed as the tangible and residual forms of such alienation.

On one level, of course, it is already a commonplace of intellectual history to note the fundamental role of spatial form in the cultural analyses of social critics like Adorno, Kracauer, and Benjamin. The *intérieur* of Adorno, the site of his critique of Kierkegaard; the *Hotelhalle* of Kracauer, key to his reading of the detective novel as itself a "reading" of modern society; Benjamin's Parisian *passage*, the central figure of his interpretation of the nineteenth century as the prehistory of the twentieth: these emblematic spaces haunt their texts, symbolizing every aspect of the nomadism, the consumer fetishism, and the displaced individualism of modern life in the great cities. Kracauer's often-cited observation, "Spatial images [*Raumbilder*] are the dreams of society. Wherever the hieroglyphics of these images can be deciphered, one finds the basis of social reality,"[2] accurately captures the special nature of these spatial evocations: like hieroglyphs, and their modern counterparts, dreams, these spaces stand ready to be deciphered. Neither simple illustrations nor fully analyzed examples, they seem to hover in a deliberately maintained state of half-reality, now glimpsed clearly, now lost in a cloud of metaphor.

And yet it is true that the central position of these spatial paradigms in the development of critical theory has more often than not been obscured by the equal and sometimes opposite role of temporality, of their concern with historical dialectics. Thus, Adorno's own critique of Benjamin's tendencies toward spatial reification, together with a tendency on the part of critics to follow Benjamin's preoccupation with memory and post-Bergsonian philosophy, has itself worked against the nuanced interpretation of any dominant spatial images. Perhaps, also, these images are themselves almost too self-evident, too overdetermined, to be noticed as particular "constructions" in their own right. When Benjamin refers to arcades, or Kracauer to a hotel lobby, we tend to associate these forms immediately to their historical and physical referents, ignoring the degree of artifice and careful articulation that distinguishes Benjamin's "passage" or Kracauer's "lobby" from any that we might ourselves have known. For in a real sense these are purely textual spaces, designed, so to speak, by their authors; they possess an architectonics of their own, all the more special for its ambiguous status between textual and social domains; they are, so to speak, buildings that themselves serve as analytical instruments. Here the professional formation of Kracauer as an architect takes on a significant role that far surpasses, while at the same time being informed by, his actual career as a designer.

Estrangement: Georg Simmel

> Objects remain spellbound in the unmerciful separation of space, no material part can commonly share its space with another, a real unity of diverse elements does not exist in space.
>
> Georg Simmel, "Bridge and Door"

As we have seen, agoraphobia had emerged by the end of the century as a specific instance of that generalized estrangement identified by social critics as the principal effect of life in metropolis. It was, indeed, a central metaphor for the more generalized psychological interpretation of modern space undertaken by sociologists who, starting with Georg Simmel, sought to establish a science of social form and structure that treated space as a central category for modeling social relations, a point of reference for the study of individuals and groups. In the face of the crowded disorder of the modern metropolis, argued Simmel, the "sensitive and nervous modern person" required a degree of spatial isolation as a kind of prophylactic against psychological intrusion.[3] If such a personal boundary were to be transgressed, a "pathological deformation" might be observed in the individual, who would present all the symptoms of what Simmel called "fear of touching," or *Berührungsangst*. This fear of coming into too close a contact with objects was, he argued, "a consequence of hyperaesthesia, for which every direct and energetic contact causes pain."[4] Simmel's diagnosis was at once spatial and mental: the real cause of the neurosis was not, as Westphal and Sitte had implied, solely spatial. Rather, he argued, it was a product of the rapid oscillation between two characteristic moods of urban life: the overclose identification with things and too great distance from them. In both cases, as with the symptoms of agoraphobia, the question was spatial at root, the result of the open spaces of the city, those very large expanses in which the crowds of metropolis found their "impulsiveness and enthusiasm."[5]

Out of this understanding of the spatial dimensions of social order, Simmel went on to construct a theory of estrangement that was once and for all tied to the space of metropolis.[6] Defining the place and role of individuals in society by their spatial relations of proximity and distance, he added the psychological dimension to the spatial, asserting, "It is not the form of spatial proximity or distance that creates the special phenomena of neighbourliness or foreignness, no matter how irrefutable this might seem. Rather, these two are facts caused purely by psychological contents." Space as the *expression* of social conditions would then be open to the sociological gaze: "Spatial relations are only the condition, on the one hand, and the symbol, on the other, of human relations."[7] As effects of human activities, spaces were important indications of social processes, of the interaction between human beings conceived of and experienced as *space-filling*. The "empty space" between individuals, filled and animated by their reciprocal relations, was, in these terms, both a spatial and a functional concept.[8] Viewed in this way, space might allow for the study of the social boundaries that defined the limits of territorial groupings; spatial unities might be identified, within borders coincident with the locations of particular social groups. Such borders, the spatial expression of sociological and functional unity alike, intersected social space like a network of imaginary lines, articulating the activity of society as a frame isolates a picture from its background.

The metropolis presented the most exacerbated condition of these psychological boundaries. In his essay "Metropolis and Mental Life," of 1903, Simmel characterized the "psychological foundation, upon which the metropolitan individuality is erected, . . . the intensification of emotional life due to the swift and continuous shift of external and internal stimuli," as spatial by definition: "To the extent that the metropolis creates these psychological conditions—with every crossing of the street, with the tempo and multiplicity of economic, occupational and social life—it creates in the sensory foundations of mental life, and in the degree of awareness necessitated by our organization as creatures dependent on differences, a deep contrast with the slower, more habitual, more smoothly flowing rhythm of the sensory-mental phase of small town and rural existence."[9]

The social relations of the metropolitan inhabitant would then be intellectual rather than oral and emotional; the conscious would dominate the unconscious; habits would be adaptable and shifting, rather than rooted and apparently eternal; the impersonal would overcome the personal; objective distance would replace subjective empathy. The fundamental cause of these differences was the nature of metropolitan temporality, the speeded-up tempo of life itself and its regulation according to the standards of "punctuality, calculability, and exactness." For Simmel,

> the metropolis is the proper arena for this type of culture which has outgrown every personal element. Here in buildings and educational institutions, in the wonders and comforts of space-conquering technique, in the formations of social life and in the concrete institutions of the State is to be found such a tremendous richness of crystallizing, depersonalized cultural accomplishments that the personality can, so to speak, scarcely maintain itself in the face of it.[10]

It was the very nature of social relations in the big city that forced distance and thus alienation, for self-defense and for functional reasons. And distance was first and foremost a product of the omnipotence of sight; as opposed to the knowledge of individuals based on intimacy and oral communication in a small community, metropolitan connections were rapid, glancing, and ocular:

> Social life in the large city as compared with the towns shows a great preponderance of occasions to *see* rather than to *hear* people. . . . Before the appearance of omnibuses, railroads, and streetcars in the nineteenth century, men were not in a situation where for periods of minutes or hours they could or must look at each other without talking to one another.

The greater perplexity which characterizes the person who only sees, as contrasted with the one who only hears, brings us to problems of the emotions of modern life; the lack of orientation in the collective life, the sense of utter lonesomeness, and the feeling that the individual is surrounded on all sides by closed doors.[11]

This distance was necessarily reinforced by the very character of daily life itself. In *The Philosophy of Money,* Simmel wrote,

> For the jostling crowdedness and the motley disorder of metropolitan communication would simply be unbearable without such psychological distance. Since contemporary urban culture, with its commercial, professional and social intercourse, forces us to be physically close to an enormous number of people, sensitive and nervous modern people would sink completely into despair if the objectification of social relationships did not bring with it an inner boundary and reserve. The peculiar character of relationships, either openly or concealed in a thousand forms, places an invisible functional distance between people that is an interior protection and neutralization against the overcrowded proximity and friction of our cultural life.[12]

In his series of excursuses to his essay on social space, Simmel treated a number of characteristic types—the poor, the adventurer, the stranger—as indicative of the power of space to determine role. The last of these, the stranger, was most exemplary. If, Simmel stated, wandering was equivalent to the *liberation* from every given point in space and was the conceptual opposite to *fixation* at such a point, then the sociological form of the stranger combined these two characteristics in one. That is, the stranger was not the "wanderer who comes today and goes tomorrow but the person who comes today and stays tomorrow." Fixed within a particular spatial group, the stranger was one who has not belonged from the beginning. "In the stranger," Simmel concluded, "are organized the unity of nearness and remoteness of every human relation," in such a way that in relationship to the stranger "distance means that he who is close by is far, and strangeness means that he who also is far is actually near."[13] Here Simmel anticipated Freud's reflections on that form of estrangement known as the uncanny, where relations of the familiar and the unfamiliar—*das Heimliche* and *das Unheimliche*—become ambiguous and merge with one another. Simmel, himself the epitome of the stranger, cultivated, urban, Jewish, and excluded from the normal academic career of his contemporaries Weber and Dilthey, thus defined the role of a being at once strange and estranged in the money economy of capitalism.

Hotelhalle: Siegfried Kracauer

Of all Simmel's students and followers, it was Siegfried Kracauer who, trained as an architect, most profoundly absorbed these lessons of spatial sociology, and especially of the analysis of spatial formations applied to the understanding of estrangement.[14] From his student experience in Berlin in 1907, when he had taken detailed notes at Simmel's lecture on "The Problem of Style in Art," to the completion of his still unpublished monograph on Simmel in 1917, Kracauer found in Simmel a methodological guide to the present. And while his early architectural designs between 1916 and 1918 were by no means infused with a direct sociological "distance," when redescribed in his later autobiographical novel *Ginster,* they took on the character of moments in a slow development toward what Ernst Bloch would recognize as the personality of "the detached hero concerned about nothing and entirely without pathos."[15]

Thus, his project for the Military Memorial Cemetery, designed in Frankfurt in 1916, was, in Kracauer's recollection, a moment of transition between a reliance on traditional models—the cemetery of Genoa and the cathedral of Milan—with their implications of mystery and the labyrinthine picturesque, toward an ironic and distanced vision of the character appropriate to modernity, and a modernity deeply implicated in the forms of war: "To hide the tombs like Easter eggs, this project seemed too soft for these times of general war. Such times called for a cemetery where their horror would be reflected. In place of using the sketches he had developed until then, Ginster . . . elaborated a system of a cemetery that was similar to a project of military organization." Thence the "scientifically lined up," rectilinear tombs set at right angles along allées lined by geometrically cut foliage, surrounding a funerary monument that took the form of an elevated cube with a stepped-back quasi-pyramidal top that served to display the names of the dead: "During these years of war, the key word for the ruling classes," Kracauer observed, "was simplicity."[16]

Even the "prettiness" of his design for a *Siedlung* at Osnabrück, drawn up in November 1918, with its "little detached houses and gardens with pitched roofs," seemed to "Ginster-Kracauer" to be premature at the very least: in the present conditions of war, "they would," he observed, "inevitably be destroyed," and if not, these pretty houses would become the objects of destruction in a new war, attaching the workers to their defense. "Certainly," concluded Kracauer, "one could not house workers in holes, but it would be perhaps more suitable to place tombstones in the gardens."[17] Similar transformations from symbolism to rationalism were to be traced in the projects of the Swiss architect Hannes Meyer for *Siedlungen* and cemeteries between 1919 and 1923: the Freidorf housing estate near Basel, 1919–1921, with its "Palladian," almost neoclassical layout, but with pitched roofs, and the project for the central cemetery in Basel, 1923, which seems to echo the contemporary interest in the revolutionary architecture of the late eighteenth century, seem to mirror the projects of Kracauer, even though Meyer's later move toward the new objectivity would doubtless have been condemned by Kracauer.

Kracauer's account of his self-distancing from architectural practice seems to have been accompanied by a growing awareness of the distancing powers of architectural space itself, or, rather, the potential of space to act as a powerful emblem of social estrangement. Kracauer characterized his 1917 essay on Simmel as an "existential topography," comparing it to those developed by Simmel himself. In his subsequent writings, the concept of an inhabited topography was extended literally with the aid of Simmel's sociology to the spaces of modern life: the hotel lobby, which became the focus of an unpublished essay on the detective novel in 1922–1925; the "pleasure barracks" of the cafés and music halls, together with their despondent counterparts, the unemployment exchanges, described in his study of white collar workers in 1930; the boulevards or "homes for the homeless" that form the setting of his life of Offenbach published in 1936.

Of these, the hotel lobby (*Hotelhalle*), seen by Kracauer as the paradigmatic space of the modern detective novel, and thus as epitomizing the conditions of modern life in their anonymity and fragmentation, was perhaps the most Simmelian in its formulation.[18] Kracauer compared the modern hotel lobby to the traditional church; the one a shelter for the transient and disconnected, the other for the community of the faithful. Using Simmel's categories of spatial description, Kracauer elaborated the distinction between what he termed *erfüllter Raum*, or the "inhabited space" of *Verknüpfung*, or "communion," and the void or empty space of physics and the abstract sciences—what he characterized as the *ratio* of modern life. Shut out of the religiously bonded community, the modern urban dweller could rely only on spaces, like that of the hotel lobby, "that bear witness to his nonexistence." Detached from everyday life, individual atoms with no connection save their absolute anonymity, the hotel guests were scattered like atoms in a void, confronted with "nothing" (*vis-à-vis de rien*); stranded in their armchairs, the guests could do little more than find a "disinterested pleasure in contemplating the world."[19] In this way, "the civilization that tends toward rationalization loses itself in the elegant club chair," in the ultimate space of indifference. Even the conventional silence of the setting parodied that of the church. Kracauer quoted Thomas Mann in *Death in Venice:* "In this room there reigned a religious silence which is one of the distinctive marks of grand hotels. The waiters serve with muffled steps. One hardly hears the noise of a cup or tea-pot, or a whispered word."[20] In Kracauer's vision of spatial alienation,

> Rudiments of individuals slide in the nirvana of relaxation, faces are lost behind the newspaper, and the uninterrupted artificial light illumines only manikins. It is a coming and going of unknowns who are changed into empty forms by forgetting their passwords, and who parade, imperceptible, like Chinese shadows. If they had an interiority, it would have no windows.[21]

The mystery of the lobby, proper site of the detective novel, was no longer religious but base, a mystery among the masks; Kracauer cited the detective novel by Sven Elvestad, *Death Enters the Hotel:* "One sees thus once again that a grand hotel is a world apart, and this world resembles the rest of the big world. The clients wander here in their light and carefree summer life, without suspecting what strange mysteries evolve among them."[22] Here, the "pseudo-individuals," or guests, spread themselves like molecules in "a spatial desert without limits," never destined to come together, even when compressed within the *Grossstadt.*

Their only link, Kracauer concluded, was indifferent enough: what he called, suggestively, the strategic grand routes of convention.[23]

Vagabondage

> Would it be the case that vagabondage leads to hysterical neurasthenia, or rather the reverse, that neurasthenia leads to vagabondage?
>
> Jean-Martin Charcot, *Leçons du mardi*

It was the analysis of these "strategic routes" that formed the basis of Walter Benjamin's study of the big city, research that under the title of *Passagen-Werk*—work on the "passages" or covered shopping arcades of Paris—took up the last ten years of his life. Evoking the urban flâneur, Benjamin extolled the art of "slow walking" as the instrument of modern urban mapping. Franz Hessel, whose *Promenades in Berlin* he reviewed with special interest, seemed, for Benjamin, to take this art to its highest form. At once recording the streets and spaces of modern Berlin, with an irony that exposed the shallow propositions of architect-planners, and searching to record the rapidly vanishing old city with minute observations, Hessel bore witness to a moment of transition that would, for Benjamin, never be repeated: "The flâneur is the priest of the *genius loci*. This discreet passerby with his priesthood and his detective's flair, there surrounds his erudition something like that around Chesterton's Father Brown, that master of criminalistics."[24] But the dandified figure of the stroller was complemented in Benjamin by another, more subversive image: that of the vagabond who alone, criminal and exiled, possessed the marginal vision that transgressed boundaries and turned them into thresholds, a way of looking that engendered what Benjamin called the "peddling [*colportage*] of space."[25] Writing of the Place du Maroc in Belleville, Benjamin noted this strange power of names, spaces, and allegorical signification to construct, as if under the influence of hashish, a complex and shifting image beyond that of their material existence. Entering the deserted square on a Sunday afternoon, Benjamin found himself not only in the Moroccan desert but also in a colonial monument: "the topographic vision intersected in it with an allegorical signification, and it did not for all that lose its place at the heart of Belleville. But it is ordinarily reserved for drugs to be able to arouse such a vision. In fact, the names of streets, in these cases, are inebriating substances that render our perception richer in strata and in spheres. One could call the force with which they plunge us into this state an 'evocative virtue.'"[26] Referring to the many cases of "ambulatory automatism" examined by Charcot and his followers, Benjamin compared this perception to that of the vagabond amnesiac: "It is not the association of images that is here decisive, but their interpenetration. This fact should also be remembered in order to understand certain pathological phenomena: the sick man who wanders the city during the hours of night and forgets the way back has perhaps felt the ascendency of this power."[27]

In using the metaphor of the amnesiac, Benjamin was evoking a tradition of medical cases in which from the 1880s doctors had attempted to link the incidence of certain neurasthenias to social class and even race. For if agoraphobia and claustrophobia were, at least in the majority of cases studied, spatial afflictions of the middle class, another variety of urban disorder, named by Charcot "ambulatory automatism," seemed more prevalent among the working class and especially the out-of-work. For Charcot and his followers ambulatory diseases were inevitably associated with the criminal activity of vagabondage, seemingly differentiated only in terms of degree. They were most evident, Charcot wrote, among those "without avowed profession, without fixed domicile, in a word vagabonds, those who often sleep under bridges, in quarries or lime kilns and who are exposed at any instant to the blows of the police."[28]

Charcot presented two kinds of cases to the audience of his Tuesday lessons. The first were those of vagabonds properly speaking, the second those of workers who were evidently suffering attacks of hysterical of epileptic amnesia. In the first category, the case of a Hungarian Jew who suffered from a "manie des voyages" was of especial interest, as perhaps indicating to Charcot the hereditary nature of what he called this "Israelite" disease: "He is Israelite, you see it well, and the sole fact of his bizarre peregrinations presents itself to us as mentally submitted to the regime of instincts."[29] In the second classification, Charcot concentrated on the case of a young delivery man whose periodic loss of memory led to his wandering through and outside Paris for days on end.

Here is a man walking the streets of Paris for 14 hours. It goes without saying that he must have looked appropriate; if not, he would have been stopped by the police. He must have had his eyes open, or else he would have brought attention to himself. . . . So he must have acted as you or I would on the street, but he was unconscious.[30]

In the light of the repeated nature of these excursions, Charcot diagnosed ambulatory automatism caused by epilepsy. In a nice literary touch, the doctor noted that he was fascinated by the apparent coincidence between his patient's amnesia or somnambulism and that depicted by Shakespeare in *Macbeth:* "If I wanted to define this patient's mental state, I would, like both the poet and physician, say that here is a patient who appears asleep but who behaves like you and me, and we, of course, are awake."[31]

In transposing what for Charcot was an attempt to demonstrate the heredity or racial aspects of vagabondage (the case of his "wandering Jew" was celebrated) into a metaphor for pathological vision, Benjamin was privileging a particular point of view: not that of the doctor-observer, but that of the patient. Such a pathological reading of the city now took on a critical aspect, to be emulated by the writer/flâneur as he sought to recapture the primal resonances of natural paths in the urban labyrinth. Only a dreamlike state of suspension might enable the wanderer to cross between physical surroundings and their mental contents.

Viewed through these lenses, the urban street regained something of the original terror of the nomadic route. Where, Benjamin noted, the original track or road had always carried with it associations of the "terrors of wandering," embedded in the mythical consciousness of the tribes, the street engendered a new form of terror, that of the boredom inspired by its "monotonous ribbon of asphalt." Drawing these two terrors together, and still to be found buried in the subterranean ways of the modern city, was the figure of the labyrinth, site of endless wandering—the Métro.[32]

This underground, which was for Benjamin in some way an equivalent to the unconscious of the city, was to be explored with all the techniques of the geographer. Reading the city "topographically," Benjamin tried to recapture its strange, landscape character. He cited Hofmannsthal's vision of Paris as a "landscape composed of pure life," and added that if this was so, it would be a veritable "volcanic landscape": "Paris is, in the social order, the pendant to Vesuvius in the geographical order." In his imagination, Paris was transformed into the semblance of an antique excavation, with its ruins, its sacred places, and even its entrances to the underworld. In this sense, it was also like a dream; hence his fascination with those "passages, architectures where we live once again oneirically the life of our parents and our grandparents, as the embryo in the womb of its mother repeats phylogenesis. Existence flows in these places without particular accentuation, as in the episodes of dreams. Flânerie gives its rhythm to this somnolence."[33] Like the troglodyte inhabitants of Gabriel Tarde's vision of a future underground society, Benjamin's flâneurs were tracing the final paths through the traditional city. The development of the boulevards represented only the first stage in the process of the eventual dissolution of the urban fabric.

Implicitly, through the accumulated citations of the *Passagen-Werk,* Benjamin traces a history of modern vision in which the rise of deeper and more public perspectives in the public realm was accomplished at the expense of individual interiority. In the Biedermeier interiors of the 1830s, with their windows shaded by layers of drapery out of urban sight, the point of view was entirely from the inside: "It is thus something like a perspective which opens from the interior toward the window." In the panoramas and arcades, perspective is partially exteriorized but still shut in, a "suffocating perspective." In the broad open vistas of Haussmann, the development was sustained with all the inexorable logic of modern spatialization: from claustrophobia to agoraphobia. It remained only for the project of modernist transparency to complete the process. Describing the peregrinations of Hessel, the modern wanderer, Benjamin saw him as the witness to the very "last monuments of an ancient art of dwelling":

> The last: because in the imprint of the turning point of the epoch, it is written that the knell has sounded for the dwelling in its old sense, dwelling in which security prevailed. Giedion, Mendelsohn, Le Corbusier have transformed the place of abode of men into the transitory space of all the imaginable forces and waves of air and light. What is being prepared is found under the sign of transparency.[34]

The ideology of transparency, the battle cry of modernism, was, as Benjamin recognized, the agent of a spatial dissolution to which only the flâneur was privy: "the sensation of the entirely new, of the absolutely modern, is a form of becoming as oneiric as the eternal return itself. The perception of space that corresponds to this conception of time is the transparency of the world of the flâneur."[35]

What for Le Corbusier represented a liberation from the closed and infected Balzacian quarters of the nineteenth-century city was, in the historically nuanced terms of Benjamin, the substitution of the void for the home. Without comment Benjamin copied a passage from Sigfried Giedion's *Bauen in Frankreich* of 1928: "The houses of Le Corbusier define themselves neither by space nor by forms: the air passes right through them! The air becomes a constitutive factor! For this, one should count neither on space nor forms, but uniquely on relation and interpenetration! There is only a single, indivisible space. The separations between interior and exterior fall."[36] These "new spatial conditions of modernity," as Benjamin elsewhere observes, were as present in the city as in the house: "The 'ville contemporaine' of Le Corbusier is an old village on a major road. Except for the fact that it is now taken over by cars and airplanes that land in the middle of this village, nothing has changed."[37] The ironic assertion of timeless space here gave force to Benjamin's belief that, finally, space had been destroyed by time. That this process had begun in the late eighteenth century only made the nineteenth the more hallucinatory in retrospect, suspended as it were between a past of walls and doors and a future of voids.

Benjamin wrote his review of Hessel's book in 1929. Some ten years later, the art of flânerie had been banished from Berlin and Paris, Benjamin himself had been forced into exile, thence to suicide, and Kracauer was in New York, writing his analysis of the filmic history that, in technique and substance, had in his eyes given rise to the birth of the Nazi propaganda film. One of these films, depicting the visit of Hitler and his architect Speer to the conquered city of Paris, seemed uncannily to fulfill Sitte's original prophecy that agoraphobia would become the modern disease par excellence. Describing the vision of a vast, empty Paris, the image of the "void" behind the propaganda, Kracauer wrote:

> The Führer is visiting the conquered European capital—but is he really its guest? Paris is as quiet as a grave. . . . While he inspects Paris, Paris it-

self shuts its eyes and withdraws. The touching sight of this deserted ghost city that once pulsed with feverish life mirrors the vacuum at the core of the Nazi system. Nazi propaganda built up a pseudo-reality iridescent with many colors, but at the same time it emptied Paris, the sanctuary of civilization. These colors scarcely veiled its own emptiness.[38]

What Benjamin and Hessel, Kracauer and Simmel were able to comprehend with their meticulous readings of the modern city, that "mnemotechnical auxiliary of the solitary walker," was that in the face of modern planning and its supporting politics, what the nineteenth-century was pleased to call "city" was rapidly in the process of disappearing. Nothing we have seen during a century of urban redevelopment seems to contradict these observations from the first quarter of our era, which lead us to the conclusion that a certain strain of modernist architecture, at least, was intent on transforming the world into Kracauer's nightmare of rationalism triumphant, a gigantic hotel atrium.

Dead End Street

Walter Benjamin and the Space of Distraction

> Vision seems to adapt itself to its object like the images that one has of a town when one contemplates it from the height of a tower; hearing is analogous to a view taken from outside and on the same level as the town; touch, finally, relates to (the understanding) of whoever comes in contact with a town from close up by wandering through its streets.
>
> G. W. Leibniz[1]

We seldom look at our surroundings. Streets and buildings, even those considered major monuments, are in everyday life little more than backgrounds for introverted thought, passages through which our bodies pass "on the way to work." In this sense cities are "invisible" to us, felt rather than seen, moved through rather than visually taken in. A city might be hidden by landscape, distance, darkness, or atmosphere, or then again there may be some hidden influence at work in the observing subject to render it unseen or unseeable. This influence, which we might call, following Walter Benjamin, an optical unconscious, has been much discussed in recent theory, a discussion generally revolving around the nature of modern opticality, its technical, institutional, and psychological construction in the context of mass, metropolitan, postindustrial society and subjecthood. In this chapter I want briefly to look at one particular aspect of this debate, one that returns to Benjamin's own formulation of why cities are not seen, his celebrated remark, in the essay "The Work of Art in the Age of Mechanical Reproduction," that "architecture has always represented the prototype of a work of art the reception of which is consummated by a collectivity in a state of distraction,"[2] a comment that has been much taken up by critics interrogating the idea of "distraction," but little studied in terms of its spatial implications.[3]

Here, rather than survey its place in the study of technology and visual technique, I want to look more closely at the "space" implied by, and projected from, such a formulation: the space of distraction, so to speak. I will try to show that what Benjamin meant by this tantalizing aphorism is set in a more complex argument about the character of modern space and modern subjects, one that stems from his study of the German baroque mourning play, or *Trauerspiel*, and that in turn situates distraction and its spatial character firmly in the domain of the "modern baroque" as delineated by art and architectural historians from Wölfflin and Riegl to Giedion. I will argue that the tropes of interpretation initially developed to understand the exaggerated and indeterminate spatial forms of the baroque—a space that was seen to represent if not hasten the collapse of Renaissance humanism—were a consistent influence on Benjamin's interpretation of the city, and ones that allowed him to frame the question in terms that went beyond the "visuality" of Riegl to imply the complete collapse of perspectival space in modernity.

Blind Alleys

Benjamin's remark about distraction, usually joined to a discussion of his concept of the "loss of aura," is generally understood to refer to the distracted state of mind of the urban dweller, jaded, bored, or swamped by the flood of visual and social stimuli of the modern city, along the lines of Georg Simmel's reworking of nineteenth-century neurasthenic pathology applied to metropolis. Benjamin himself employs the concept more precisely, however, linking it to the opposition he is drawing between a traditional spectator of a work of art in a state of concentration, and a mass audience lacking concentration and thus "absorbing" the work of art. In the case of buildings, only a tourist will evince that "attentive concentration" characteristic of the art lover. In this Benjamin would seem to be echoing his friend Siegfried Kracauer, whose influential essay of 1926 on Berlin's "picture palaces" was titled "Cult of Distraction." But here, in the apparent genealogy of distraction Simmel-Kracauer-Benjamin, we have to pause in the face of what seem to be serious differences in the use of this word. The German *Zerstreuung* might mean, at one and the same time, distraction, diversion, amusement, diffusion, preoccupation, absentmindedness,

scattering, dispersion, and so on. To take just one example of such differentia-
tion: Kracauer clearly uses the word to delineate the "need for entertainment,"
the "addiction to distraction" of the Berlin masses, seeking relief from the conditions of their workday lives; he is concerned to describe the movie houses of
Berlin as palaces of distraction, optical fairylands, "shrines to the cultivation of
pleasure." "The Gloria Palast," he remarks, with implications Benjamin would
have appreciated, "presents itself as a baroque theater."[4] Benjamin, however,
while his reference to the movies, stars in the context of his statement "the
masses seek distraction [*die Massen Zerstreuung suchen*]" implies a general ad-
herence to Kracauer's arguments, immediately moves beyond Kracauer's interest in "surface" to investigate the phenomenological conditions comprised by
"distraction," within which buildings and the city are experienced.[5] Building
on Riegl's historical analysis of visual cultures as developing from the tactile to
the optical, Benjamin emphasizes the twofold nature of architectural appropriation in the city: "by use and by perception—or rather by touch and sight
[*taktil und optisch*]." Tactile as opposed to optical perception is, Benjamin
claims, following Simmel, accomplished by habit, custom, or usage (*Gewohn-
heit*). But for Benjamin this is not, as Simmel implied, a kind of appropriation
lost to modern cities, rendered subservient to the visual; rather habit and use
determine the optical reception of buildings: "As regards architecture, habit determines to a large extent even optical reception." Through habit and use, the
rapt attention of an individual observer of a work of art is dispersed, so to
speak, in the custom of "noticing the object in an incidental [*beiläufig,* casual]
fashion." Distraction here, rather than an active search for over-the-top pleasures, represents an absentmindedness common to a subject in a state of habitual activity: in front of the film, even, "the public is an examiner but an
absent-minded one [*ein zerstreuter*]."

That his discussion of the tensions between the tactile and the optical
does not necessarily imply a negative judgment of the former is made clear in
earlier writings that imply a more positive role for "distraction" in the face of
architecture and the city, one that will activate a deeper understanding of urban topography than simple visual inspection. Thus, writing to Gershom
Scholem from Assisi in November 1924, Benjamin describes a visit, which took
place appropriately enough in a "dense autumn fog," in which he says he

looked at too many paintings yet did not have enough time to be able to concentrate on architecture. For my inductive way of getting to know the topography of different places and seeking out every great structure in its own labyrinthine environment of banal, beautiful, or wretched houses, takes up too much time and thus prevents me from studying the relevant books. Since I must dispense with that, I am left only with impressions of the architecture. The first and most important thing you have to do, is to feel your way through a city.[6]

Here tactile knowledge of the urban labyrinth is seen as an important precondition to true urban knowledge, a view to be repeated in different ways throughout his exploration of the Parisian underground during his years working on the arcades project. A first metaphor for describing the space of distraction might then be the labyrinth, a Nietzschean metaphor for modernity that would certainly embrace the "art of losing one's way" beloved of Benjamin's city walks. The invisible city would here be the underground, the realm of the dead, the dreamscape across the threshold, all domains treasured by Benjamin in his Berlin and Parisian explorations.

But what of visual as opposed to tactile space? In what respects might we begin to qualify the notion of the visual apperception and appropriation of the city in the context of our expanding understanding of distraction? If we are to believe Hubert Damisch, the question of the visibility of the city (its "readability" if not its "figurability") was posed initially in the context of the modern metropolis, its confused "image" and the breakup of communal bonds with the rise of the masses.[7] Damisch posits that the models of such visibility were engendered, framed so to speak, by the conventional perspective device of the "view through a window," a view that had the theoretical nicety of combining Alberti's transparent surface and the outside (urban) context. Damisch contrasts two scenes through a window: the one sketched by Descartes, as he interrogated the conditions for visual judgment,[8] and the other described by Edgar Allan Poe in "The Man of the Crowd" in which the narrator, sitting in the corner of a London café, deciphered the "labyrinth" of the crowd. This last scene, of course, is a direct reference to Benjamin's own citation of Poe's corner in his Baudelaire study. The implications of Damisch's contrast are clear: Descartes's rational city provided a space for judgment, Poe's labyrinthine metropolis presented nothing but apparent confusion.

Benjamin himself implies something of the same contrast. In his essay on the collector Eduard Fuchs, he alludes to the nature of Renaissance space as constructed through perspective: "The painters of the early Renaissance," he says in a footnote, "were the first to depict interior space in which the figures represented have *room to move* [Innenräume ins Bild gesetzt, in denen dargestellten Figuren *Spielraum* haben]." Here *Spielraum* has all the connotations of its literal meaning—"space for drama" or "play space," with the additional senses of "room to play," "play room," "figures in play," "elbow room."[9] Such a space, emblem of a historico-visual relationship between perspective painting and the new architecture of the Renaissance, was for Benjamin, as for Wölfflin (who is the principal source for this reference), the very space of existence "architecturally framed and founded."

Elsewhere Benjamin will qualify this space as characterized principally by its depth, where "perspectives" also meant infinite prospects, virtual rooms to move. Writing, again to Scholem, of the title of his newly completed book *One-Way Street,* he notes, "It has turned out to be a remarkable arrangement or construction of some of my 'aphorisms,' a street that is meant to reveal a prospect of such precipitous depth—the word is not meant to be understood metaphorically!—like, perhaps, Palladio's famous stage design in Vicenza, *The Street.*"[10]

But if the book itself was conceived as an essay in the clarity of Renaissance perspective, a study in depth, or at least staged depth, the themes of *One-Way Street*'s aphorisms resonate with post-Renaissance anxiety. For it is precisely this depth which has, in Benjamin's view, been put into question by habit. Under the heading "Articles Lost" in the section "Lost Property Office," he reflects on the difference between "the first glimpse of a village, a town, in the landscape" and the subsequent effacement of this first picture by routine and habit. For Benjamin, as for Riegl, the crucial visual connection is that "between foreground and distance," that shifting relationship between foreground and background (figure and ground) which makes the bas-reliefs and monuments of the late Roman period so ambiguous to interpret. In the case of a landscape, the first shock of the new is erased by habit, which collapses the distance between foreground and background—or, in scenographic terms, front stage and backstage—so that in some way the prospect vanishes. Benjamin's analogy is telling: "As soon as we begin to find our bearings, the landscape vanishes at a stroke like the facade of a house as we enter it. It has not yet gained preponderance through a constant exploration that has become habit. Once we begin to find our way about, that earliest picture can never be restored." The only resistance to such a disappearing trick would be, as Benjamin notes, that special kind of "blue distance" that "never gives way to foreground or dissolves at our approach," but rather, like a painted backdrop in the theater, simply "looms more compact and threatening" the closer it gets: "It is what gives stage sets their incomparable atmosphere."[11]

The collapse of perspective distance is perhaps the most dominant visual theme of *One-Way Street*. Even as Aby Warburg had viewed with phobic horror the implosion that had destroyed the space of judgment or reflection, the reduction of the *Denkraum* under the assault of rapid communications and technological invention, so Benjamin sees the erosion of the space for criticism: indeed, its space, he advertises, "is for rent":

> Criticism . . . was at home in a world where perspectives and prospects counted and where it was still possible to take a standpoint (point of view). Now things press too closely on human society. The advertisement . . . abolishes the space where contemplation moved and all but hits us between the eyes with things as a car, growing to gigantic proportions, careens at us out of a film screen. And just as the film does not present furniture and facades in completed forms for critical inspection, their insistent, jerky nearness alone being sensational, the genuine advertisement hurtles things at us with the tempo of a good film.[12]

Similarly, the intrusion of large-scale urban construction projects into the heart of the traditional city has removed the distance that once separated the center and the periphery, a distance confirmed by the sight of the horizon—the view of nature beyond the walls—from inside the city to outside, and that was reassuring to the dweller enclosed "in the peace of the fortress" as the elemental forces of nature were held back from contact but revealed to view. Now, a modern process of "mingling and contamination" has produced ambiguities where clarity once reigned:

7. Sasha Stone, "One-Way Street," photomontage for the cover of Walter Benjamin, *Einbahnstrasse* (Berlin, 1928).

Great cities . . . are seen to be breached at all points by the invading countryside. Not by the landscape, but by what in untrammeled nature is the
most bitter: ploughed land, highways, night sky that the veil of vibrant
redness no longer conceals. The insecurity of even the busy areas puts the
city-dweller in the opaque and truly dreadful situation in which he must
assimilate, along with isolated monstrosities from the open country, the
abortions of urban architectonics.[13]

Between the clarity of the Renaissance *Spielraum,* that space of free play for
both bodies and thoughts, and the ambiguity and mingling of modern urban
space, between deep perspectives and prospects and the opaque, flat, impacted
surfaces where the subject is rendered blind, so to speak, dependent on habit
and custom to feel its way around and through "dark space," there has occurred
a fundamental transformation, and one precisely of the same order that Benjamin was indeed describing in his characterization of the Renaissance invention of *Spielraum:* a historical change, calculated according to Riegl's theory of
the *Kunstwollen,* in the process of vision itself.

Most commentators, reading Benjamin's Baudelaire essays or taking their
cue from the message of the late "Work of Art" essay, have assumed that Benjamin construed this change as both cause and effect of the growth of industrial
metropolis. And certainly all the characteristics of modernity are to be found exacerbated in the sites of the *Passagen-Werk.* But in a recent rereading, Samuel
Weber has discovered intriguing intimations of modern visuality and the notion
of the distracted subject in Benjamin's earlier work on baroque tragedy. Developing the statement by Benjamin that *The Confused Court* (the title of a Span-
ish *Trauerspiel*) could be taken as a model for allegory, as "subject to the law of
'dispersal' and 'collectedness'" (translated by Weber "dispersion" [*Zerstreuung*]
and "collection" [*Sammlung*]), Weber extends Benjamin's statement that "things
are brought together according to their meaning; indifference to their being-
there [*Dasein*] disperses them once again." Weber posits that

the tendency toward dispersion that Benjamin discerns in the collective
structures specific to the 19th century metropolis no longer appears to
originate with the emergence of urban masses but to go back at least as
far as the 17th century in Germany. Second, the dispersed, centrifugal

structure of mass phenomena shows itself to be bound up with articula-
tory processes at work long before Baudelaire began to "fence" with "the
ghostly crowd of words."[14]

Weber further develops the notion of "distraction," or "dispersion" (picking up
on Benjamin's tell-tale use of the word *Dasein*), in terms of a comparative axis
that might see a more Heideggerian connotation in the word *Zerstreuung* than
hitherto allowed by a strict late Marxist reading of Benjamin. Weber points to
Derrida's examination of the notion of dispersion in Heidegger, and to its intimate, almost bodily, connection to the spatiality of *Dasein.* Here we might
simply note in passing that a cursory examination of Heidegger's own deployment of the term in *Being and Time* points to two major and related meanings:
the one linked to the "existential spatiality" of Dasein, and its characteristic
form of Being-in-the-World as *zerstreut,* dispersed; the other employing "distraction" as an attribute of curiosity and its propensity to "not tarrying": "curiosity is everywhere and nowhere" and therefore "never dwells anywhere."
Both these senses of dispersion and distraction would here intersect more or
less seamlessly with the Benjaminian usages of *Zerstreuung* already discussed;
or if not intersect, for Benjamin was resistant to any comparison between his
thought and that of Heidegger, then certainly alert us to the constantly shifting meaning of "distraction" in 1920s discourse.

If, however, picking up on Weber's implication, we take up the *spatial* dimension of the dispersion/distraction nexus in the context of Benjamin's
baroque study, we find that "distraction" takes on a more precise formulation,
and this precisely in relation to Benjamin's reworking of the idea of "baroque
space" as he had inherited it from Wölfflin and Riegl.

The Baroque Effect

The momentary impact of baroque is powerful, but soon leaves us with a
certain sense of desolation. It does not convey a state of present happiness,
but a feeling of anticipation, of something yet to come, of dissatisfaction
and restlessness rather than fulfillment. We have no sense of release, but
rather of having been drawn into the tension of an emotional condition.

Heinrich Wölfflin, *Renaissance und Barock,* 1888[15]

It was symptomatic of the ambiguous nature of "space" as a psychological and material concept that the initial art historical interpretation of architectural space was first worked out precisely in response to an uncertainty about the limits of architecture: that uncertainty which arose in the face of the difficulty of comprehending the nature of architectural "space" after the Renaissance—the so-called baroque space that seemed altogether to break the bounds of architectural stability and three-dimensional harmony. For Wölfflin, student of the "psychology of architecture," this was a pathological condition, reflected in the mental state of its artists: "all the most prominent baroque artists suffered from headaches," he noted, citing Milizia on Bernini and Borromini, and "there were also cases of melancholia."[16]

Thus, for Wölfflin, the baroque (which he dated from the Council of Trent) pushed the limits of (classical, Renaissance) architecture to their potential destruction. An architecture of depth and obscurity had, in his view, replaced an architecture of surface and clarity. The baroque, according to Wölfflin, introduced "an entirely new feeling of space, tending toward infinity." "Space," he wrote, "which in the Renaissance was regularly lit and which can be represented only as tectonically closed, here [in the baroque] seems to be lost in the unlimited and undefined." No longer faced with a clear, external form, "the gaze is led toward infinity."[17] Such a dissolution of space into incommensurability was explained from a psychological point of view that understood every object to be judged according to its relation to the body. Wölfflin had already espoused such a view in his thesis, *Prolegomena zu einer Psychologie der Architectur,* two years before. Noting that "a historical psychology—or rather, a psychological history of art—should be able to measure with great accuracy the acceleration of linear movement," Wölfflin spoke of what he called "the breathless haste of Arab decorative lines" and compared different arch styles to the impressions they give of slow or quick breathing. In the margins of his personal copy of the *Psychologie,* he wrote: "Baroque: irregular breathing."[18] In the baroque, that is, the capacity of the human body to empathize with the building was stretched to deformity. Such a psychological interpretation was to influence that of Jacques Lacan, whose summation of the "baroque"—"the regulation of the soul by the scopic regulation of the body"—seems to extend Wölfflin's critique.[19]

If the baroque represented a breakdown of form, it was easy to associate its characteristics with the new nervous illnesses; the baroque in architecture and painting was after all filled with rifts, breaks, and openings representing the relations between the material and metaphysical worlds. Thus Daniel Paul Schreber, writing his memoirs in the asylum of Sonnenstein, insisted that he might prove the "extraordinary experiences and observations he controlled" by reference to a baroque painting by Pradilla that he had seen in a publication on modern art. "This picture," he wrote, "is surprisingly like the picture I often see in my head: the rays (nerves) of the upper God, when they are thrust down in consequence of my nerves' power of attraction, often appear in my head *in the image of a human shape.*" Schreber, ignoring the central ascending figures of this painting of "Liebersreigen," indicated a faint image of a woman, in the far top left, in his terms "descending" with outstretched arms, although this was more than a projection on his part. In his mind, the woman was changed into a male figure of the nerves of the upper God, "almost as if these nerves were trying to overcome an obstacle to their descent," an obstacle Schreber attributed to the blocking effect of his former analyst, Flechsig, as he had attempted to counter God's omnipotence. Within the ethereal and potentially infinite space of the baroque ceiling, Schreber was able to figure his struggle for power and contact with God as rays of light representing nerves.[20]

But the critique of the baroque, however historically and formally derived, was ultimately pointed toward the larger problem of modern art, itself seen as a direct extension of, if not a pathological development from, the baroque. Wölfflin's celebrated remark of 1888, "One can hardly fail to recognize the affinity that our own age in particular bears to the Italian Baroque,"[21] underlines the extent to which these ascriptions of decline and dissolution were deliberately aimed at the modern. Wölfflin cited Carl Justi's characterization of Piranesi as having "a nature entirely modern in its passion," embodied in "the mystery of the sublime—of space and of power," and he compared this to the "same emotions which a Richard Wagner evokes to act on us."[22] The baroque was also, of course, a contemporary style; a baroque revival in German-speaking countries—the final phase of eclecticism—had already started in the 1870s, partly inspired by Semper's Opera House in Vienna. A. E. Brinckmann, writing a historical survey of architectural space in 1924 under the title *Plastik und Raum,* spoke of this "neubarock" style that emerged in the late nineteenth-century and culminated, in his terms, with the sculpture of Rodin.[23] In the late 1880s the style was supported by writers like Hans Auer who, as Mallgrave and

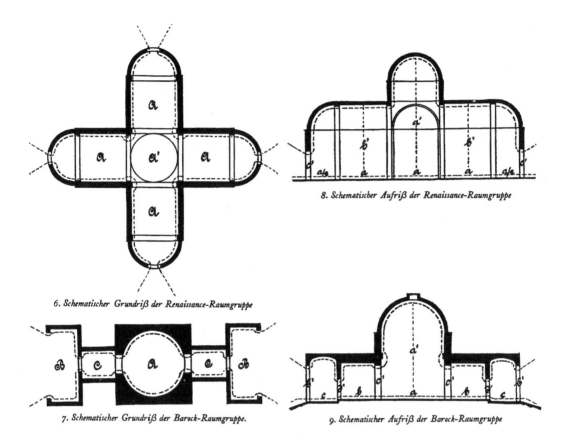

6. *Schematischer Grundriß der Renaissance-Raumgruppe*

7. *Schematischer Grundriß der Barock-Raumgruppe.*

8. *Schematischer Aufriß der Renaissance-Raumgruppe*

9. *Schematischer Aufriß der Barock-Raumgruppe*

8. A. E. Brinckmann, "Schematic Plans of Renaissance and Baroque Spatial Groups," *Plastik und Raum als Grundformen künstlerischer Gestaltung* (Munich: Piper Verlag, 1924).

Ikonomou recall, saw the baroque style "as offering spatial and formal possibilities for personal and artistic expression, but also as having some special spiritual affinity with the age of Leibniz, Voltaire, and Newton."[24]

Trying to account for the continuing force of the baroque in the present, Adolf Göller in 1887 developed a theory of increasingly rapid style change, each more jaded than the next, so that, in the context of nineteenth-century revivalism, the baroque was simply the natural follower of a Gothic and Renaissance revival.

With the progressive impoverishment of the architectural style, the charm of form also suffers and disturbing ideas intensify. In addition to the charm of form there is another achievement of the flowering of a style that dissipates only slowly: this is the feeling for high, wide *space*, which is not much subject to jading; like the feeling for masses, it is largely a product of imagination. . . . The baroque style with all of its relatives worked itself out and exhausted its potential. Like a conflagration, it consumed all imaginable combinations of its own elements of form before it was extinguished. Thus it left the sense of form utterly devastated. Since there was no longer anything capable of germinating at the scene of the fire, nothing baroque could grow again in the garden of the reawakening of architecture. . . . One architectural style arises from the ruins of another.[25]

Göller was here echoing the diagnosis of Nietzsche, who had characterized the baroque style in such terms in *Human, All Too Human* some ten years before. For Nietzsche, the baroque style was equally an art of decadence: it "appears whenever a great age of art enters its decline," when "the demands of the art of classical expression have grown too great." Its appearance, he noted, is to be "greeted with sadness—because it heralds nightfall."[26] But in his subtle analysis the baroque took on characteristics that were to influence Walter Benjamin, who, despite his sense of its melancholia, was to see in its forms and subjects a profoundly modern sensibility, one that, as Nietzsche emphasized, should not be presumptuously "dismissed out of hand." Despite its lack of "innocent, unconscious, victorious perfection," the baroque displayed, for Nietzsche, two major aesthetic strengths: those of expression and of narration. Out of the "eloquence of strong feelings and pleasures" was forged "an ugly sublime," one of "great masses, of quantity for its own sake," which reveled in "the light of twilight, of transformation, or of conflagration." Such expressions, "forbidden fruits" for preclassical and classical art, were splendidly displayed in the baroque. Equally, its narrations chose topics and themes full of "dramatic tension: those that cause the heart to quicken even in the absence of art, so close do they bring us to the heaven and hell of emotion." An art of extremes, then, and one that presses the very limits of art to excess, even disappearance.

Nietzsche's remarks haunted Benjamin's melancholic baroque of allegory, ruins, and fragments. Echoing Wölfflin's characterization of the baroque in architecture as representing the decline and decadence of the Renaissance, Benjamin wrote of the period of baroque tragic drama as one of the "Verfalls der Kunst," an epoch of decadence.[27] Against the "exact mean between excess and deficiency" achieved by Renaissance harmony, the baroque signaled "dissolution" of all forms and boundaries; the call for "unlimited space and the elusive magic of light" led to the transgression of all of architecture's "natural limits." For Benjamin, writing in the 1920s, the analogy between the baroque and the modern was more poignant still; the baroque style joined two periods of decadence by means of a symptomatic analysis of forms in tumult, disrupted forms that were emblematic of the conflicted forces of their respective epochs. Benjamin spoke of the "striking analogies with the present state of German literature" and noted the common themes between baroque tragic drama and expressionist drama, beginning with the presentation of Hans Werfels's *Trojans* in 1915.[28] As with many myths surrounding the emergence of modernism, the baroque effect was seen in terms of light and dark, rather as modernity itself was construed as poised between reason and the abyss of expressionist exaggeration. In this way, taking his cue from Nietzsche, Benjamin construed a baroque that was, as an art of expression and narration, the first modern style, allegorical and overstated, exemplified in the *Trauerspiel.*

Benjamin's subtle transformation of Wölfflin's by-then-commonplace characterization of subject and object relations relies on his critical reading of Riegl's posthumously published *The Origin of Roman Baroque Art,* and intimates that special kind of "modernity" later to be tracked down in the arcades. From Wölfflin to Riegl, as we have seen, baroque space had been essentially treated as a question of depth, of freedom from limits, but thus equally of anxiety, ambiguity and disturbance, distortion and conflict. Riegl's analysis of Michelangelo's proto-baroque Medici Chapel in San Lorenzo, published in 1907 and closely read by Benjamin, speaks of the "introduction of depth replacing the absolutely flat surface," "the tactile surface intersected/crossed by optical depth," a "resolute movement toward the optical, because space in depth, the space of the air, cannot be touched by the finger, can only be estimated in relation to that which is seen."[29] Here baroque space already holds qualities of modern space—as, in Riegl's formulation, the "optical" supersedes the "tactile."

Benjamin, following this law of optical progression, similarly identified three stages through which the concept of "play" (*Spiel*) passed before its modern manifestation: the first the baroque, the second classicism, and the third romanticism (or in his terms, modernity). The first stage Benjamin characterized as fundamentally preoccupied with the "product," the second with "production," and the third with "both."[30] These stages were characterized by different paradigmatic "settings" or "scenes," each one spatially distinct from the next, but in a kind of Hegelian development in which each carried the traces of its previous genesis.

All three periods were similar in that history was finally spatialized. In the paradigmatic and, for modernity, the primal scene of the baroque, Benjamin saw the invention of the "panorama" not so much in technical terms (this would have to wait until the end of the eighteenth century) but in its conceptual form as the spatial form of history in nature. The panorama was, in the *Trauerspiel,* exemplified in the pastoral, the diverse landscapes of which served as the settings for so much ruined monumental history. "History merges into the setting," Benjamin notes; "in the pastoral plays . . . history is scattered like seeds over the ground," and literally so, in the form of columns raised to the memory of heroes.[31] Here Benjamin draws on the study of the baroque by his conservative contemporary Herbert Cysarz, who had coined the term "panoramic" to describe history in the seventeenth century: "'In this picturesque period the whole conception of history is determined by such a collection of everything memorable.'"[32] The setting thus secularizes history, in such a way that, emulating the development of the calculus in science, "chronological movement is grasped and analyzed in a spatial image."[33]

This panoramic space of history, indeed, affected the entire form of the *Trauerspiel.* Where classical tragedy had been characterized by "spasmodic chronological progression," *Trauerspiel* "takes place in a spatial continuum, which one might describe as choreographic."[34] For Benjamin this was where the baroque revealed itself as essentially modern; as the moment when, finally, time becomes spatially measurable. He recounts an image of the moving hand of the clock in a *Trauerspiel* by Geulincx, a "celebrated clock-metaphor, in which the parallelism of the psychological and physical worlds is presented schematically in terms of two accurate and synchronized clocks; the second hand, so to speak, determines the rhythm of events in both."[35] In this double timekeeping Benjamin sees the intimation of a union between the mechanical nature of "clock time" and the aesthetic forms of modern music, as if, he imagines, the cantatas of Johann Sebastian Bach joined the philosophy of Bergson, testifying to the relations between the regular and harmonious sequence of the historical process and the "the non-qualitative, repeatable time of the mathematical sciences."[36] History would be in this metaphor both spatially and temporally measurable.

Such a mechanistic spatial-historical play that transposes "*what is vital . . . of the originally temporal data into a figurative spatial simultaneity*"[37] cannot be effected, however, without a deep distortion of space itself. From the point of view of the perceiving subject, the very effort to turn time into space turns space into a kind of reflected anamorphosis: "The creature is the mirror within whose frame alone the moral world was revealed to the baroque. A concave mirror; for this was not possible without distortion."[38]

And this distorting mirror reflected, in the *Trauerspiel,* an effectively modern subject, the worried, anxious, cunning and scheming courtier, in the spatial setting of high tragedy—the "tragic scene" prescribed by Vitruvius and illustrated by Serlio. For Benjamin, it is precisely the space of the baroque court, set within "'stately palaces and princely pavilions,'" that, in its spatialization of history on stage, allows history to be interpreted.[39] "The image of the setting, or more precisely of the court [*Hof*]," Benjamin writes, "becomes the key to historical understanding."[40]

This court setting, described in Daniel Casper von Lohenstein's preface to *Sophonisbe* as the intersection between play and scene—"Nowhere are action and setting [*Spiel und Schauplatz*] richer than in the life of those whose element is the court," Lohenstein had written[41]—becomes for Benjamin the paradigmatic space of modern action. For even when the heroes are fallen, when "the court is reduced to a scaffold," "and that which is mortal will enter the setting," the court of the *Trauerspiel* represents the timeless, natural decor of the historical process—a process that inevitably leads toward modernity.[42]

But this courtly space, however grandly represented or ostentatiously displayed, is reduced in both depth and height from that of Greek or even Renaissance tragedy. Where, as Nietzsche imagined it in *The Birth of Tragedy,* the space of the Greek theater is defined only by the skies that hover above it, where "the architecture of the scene appears like a luminous cloud formation" providing an upper stage from which the Bacchante observe the action of the play,[43] for Benjamin, the stage of the *Trauerspiel* is surmounted by lowering clouds and a disturbed sky: "For the dominant spiritual disposition, however eccentrically it might elevate individual acts of ecstasy, did not so much transfigure the world in them as cast a cloudy sky over its surface. Whereas the painters of the Renaissance know how to keep their skies high, in the paintings of the baroque the cloud moves, darkly or radiantly, down towards the earth."[44] Where the stage of Greek tragedy is a "cosmic *topos*" that reflects the communal will for "the scene" as it becomes a veritable tribunal before which the audience is assembled to witness and judge, "the *Trauerspiel,* in contrast, has to be understood from the point of view of the onlooker."[45] Communality is transformed into individuality, the space of the stage becomes an "inner world of feeling [*Innenraum des Gefühls*]" with no cosmic relationship to redeem its audience. Such concentration on inner space, on individual emotional life, is typical of the society of the court, even as the disillusioned insight of the courtier is typical of the *Trauerspiel.* Forced to play and scheme in the flattened space of an anamorphic mirror, Benjamin's baroque courtier is revealed as a dispersed subject bodily projecting itself in the ruined landscape of historical destiny, measured by the relentless ticking and turning of clocks at ever-increasing tempos, soulless in the wasteland of humanism's detritus, picking its way among the bones of fallen heroes. In this sense, in Simmelian terms, the "courtier" would be one who finds "the tempo of emotional life accelerated to such an extent that calm actions, considered decisions occur more and more infrequently."[46] For Benjamin this subject would resemble nothing more than the alienated modern metropolitan citizen.

The Explosion of Space

Architecture and the Filmic Imaginary

> I am kino-eye. I am a builder. I have placed you, whom I've created to-
> day, in an extraordinary room which did not exist until just now when I
> also created it. In this room there are twelve walls shot by me in various
> parts of the world. In bringing together shots of walls and details, I've
> managed to arrange them in an order that is pleasing and to construct
> with intervals, correctly, a film-phrase which is the room.
>
> Dziga Vertov, 1923[1]

The architecture of film has acted, from the beginning of this century, as a laboratory, so to speak, for the exploration of the built world—of architecture and
the city. The examples of such experimentation are well known, and they include the entire roster of filmic genres: science fiction, adventure, film noir, action films, documentaries. Film has even been seen to anticipate the built forms
of architecture and the city: we have only to think of the commonplace icons
of expressionist utopias to find examples, from *The Cabinet of Dr. Caligari* to
Metropolis, that apparently succeeded, where architecture failed, to build the
future in the present. Thus the recent installation of the exhibition "Expressionist Utopias" at the Los Angeles County Museum of Art, by the Viennese
architectural firm Coop Himmelblau, even suggested a kind of contemporary
completion, where at last architecture might be seen to catch up with the imaginary space of film. In recent years, other designers, searching for ways to represent movement and temporal succession in architecture, have similarly
turned to the images forged by the first, constructivist and expressionist avant-
gardes, images themselves deeply marked by the impact of the new filmic techniques. From the literal evocations of Bernard Tschumi in his *Manhattan
Transcripts* and projects for the urban park of La Villette in Paris to the more

theoretical and critical work on the relations of space to visual representation in the projects of Elizabeth Diller and Ricardo Scofidio, the complex question of film's architectural role is again on the agenda. In their new incarnation, such neoconstructivist, dadaist, and expressionist images seem to reframe many earlier questions about the proper place for images of space and time in architecture, questions that resonate for contemporary critique of the "image" and the "spectacle" in architecture and society.

And yet the simple alignment of architecture and film has always posed difficulties, both theoretically and in practice. On the one hand, it is obvious that film has been the site of envy and even imitation for those more static arts concerned to produce effects or techniques of movement and space-time interpenetration. Painting, from Duchamp's *Nude Descending a Staircase;* literature, from Virginia Woolf's *Mrs. Dalloway;* poetry, from Marinetti's *Parole in libertà;* architecture, from Sant'Elia to Le Corbusier, have all sought to reproduce movement and the collapse of time in space; and montage, or its equivalent, has been a preoccupation in all the arts since its appearance, in primitive form, with rapid-sequence photography. On the other hand, it is equally true that the Enlightenment roots of modernism ensured that film, as well as all the other arts, were bound, à la Lessing, to draw precise theoretical boundaries around the centers of their conceptually different practices—practices understood as distinct precisely because of their distinct media; each one, like Lessing's own poetry and painting, more or less appropriate to the representation of time *or* space. Thus, despite the aspirations of avant-garde groups, from dada to Esprit Nouveau, to syncretism and synesthesia, the relations of the arts still could not be conceived without their particular essences being defined: as if the arts were so many nations, romantically rooted in soil and race, each with characteristics of their own to be asserted before any treaties might be negotiated. Thus, since the late nineteenth century, film has provided a test case for the definition of modernism in theory and technique. It has also served as a point of departure for the redefinition of the other arts, a paradigm by which the different practices of theater, photography, literature, and painting might be distinguished from each other. Of all the arts, however, it is architecture that has had the most privileged and difficult relationship to film. An obvious role model for spatial experimentation, film has also been criticized for its deleterious effects on the architectural image.

Thus, when in 1933 Le Corbusier called for a film aesthetics that embodied the "spirit of truth," he was only asserting what many architects in the twenties, and more recently in the eighties, have seen to be the mutually informative but properly separate realms of architecture and film. While admitting that "everything is Architecture" in its architectonic dimensions of proportion and order, Le Corbusier nevertheless insisted on the specificity of film, which "from now on is positioning itself on its own terrain . . . becoming a form of art in and of itself, a kind of genre, just as painting, sculpture, literature, music, and theater are genres."[2] In the present context, debates as to the nature of "architecture in film," "filmic architecture," or filmic theory in architectural theory are interesting less as a guide to the writing of some new *Laocoön* that would rigidly redraw the boundaries of the technological arts, than as establishing the possibilities of interpretation for projects that increasingly seem caught in the hallucinatory realm of a filmic or screened imaginary; somewhere, that is, in the problematic realm of hyperspace.

Cineplastics

The obvious role of architecture in the construction of sets (and the eager participation of architects themselves in this enterprise), and the equally obvious ability of film to "construct" its own architecture in light and shade, scale and movement, from the outset allowed for a mutual intersection of these two "spatial arts." Certainly many modernist filmmakers had little doubt of the cinema's architectonic properties. From Georges Méliès's careful description of the proper spatial organization of the studio in 1907 to Eric Rohmer's reassertion of film as "the spatial art" some forty years later, the architectural metaphor, if not its material reality, was deemed essential to the filmic imagination.[3] Equally, architects like Hans Poelzig (who together with his wife, the sculptor Marlene Poelzig, sketched and modeled the sets for Paul Wegener's *Der Golem—Wie er in die Welt kam* of 1920) and Andrei Andreiev (who designed the sets for Robert Weine's *Raskolnikoff* of 1923) had no hesitation in collaborating with filmmakers in the same way as they had previously served theater producers.[4] As the architect Robert Mallet-Stevens observed in 1925: "It is undeniable that the cinema has a marked influence on modern architecture; in turn, modern architecture brings its artistic side to the cinema.

Modern architecture does not only serve the cinematographic set [*décor*], but imprints its stamp on the staging [*mise-en-scène*], it breaks out of its frame; architecture 'plays.'"[5] And, of course, for filmmakers (like Sergei Eisenstein) originally trained as architects, the filmic art offered the potential to develop a new architecture of time and space unfettered by the material constraints of gravity and daily life.

Out of this intersection of the two arts, a theoretical apparatus was developed that saw architecture as the fundamental site of film practice, the indispensable real and ideal matrix of the filmic imaginary, and at the same time posited film as the modernist art of space par excellence—a vision of the fusion of space and time. The potential of film to explore this new realm, seen as the basis of modernist architectural aesthetics by Sigfried Giedion, was recognized early on. Abel Gance, writing in 1912, was already hoping for a new "sixth art" that would provide "that admirable synthesis of the movement of space and time."[6] But it was the art historian Elie Faure, influenced by Fernand Léger, who first coined a term for the cinematic aesthetic that brought together the two dimensions: "cineplastics." "The cinema," he wrote in 1922, "is first of all plastic. It represents, in some way, an architecture in movement that should be in constant accord, in dynamically pursued equilibrium, with the setting and the landscapes within which it rises and falls."[7] In Faure's terms, "plastic" art was that which "expresses form at rest and in movement," a mode common to the arts of sculpture, bas-relief, drawing, painting, fresco, and especially the dance, but which perhaps achieved its highest expression in the cinema.[8] For "the cinema incorporates time to space. Better, time, through this, really becomes a dimension of space . . . unrolling under our eyes its successive volumes ceaselessly returned to us in dimensions that allow us to grasp their extent in surface and depth."[9] The "hitherto unknown plastic pleasures" thereby discovered would, finally, have the effect of creating a new kind of architectural space, akin to that imaginary space "within the walls of the brain":

> The notion of duration entering as a constitutive element into the notion of space, we will easily imagine an art of cineplastics blossoming that would be no more than an ideal architecture, and where the "cine-mimic" will . . . disappear, because only a great artist could build edifices that constitute themselves, collapse, and reconstitute themselves again

ceaselessly by imperceptible passages of tones and modeling which will themselves be architecture at every instant, without our being able to grasp the thousandth part of a second in which the transition takes place.[10]

Such an art, Faure predicts, will propel the world into a new stage of civilization, one where architecture will be the principal form of expression, based on the appearance of mobile industrial constructions, ships, trains, cars, and airplanes together with their stable ports and harbors. Cinema will then operate, he concludes, as a kind of privileged "spiritual ornament" to this machine civilization: "the most useful social play for the development of confidence, harmony, and cohesion in the masses."[11]

Spaces of Horror

Critics of the first generation of German expressionist films had already experienced such a "cineplastic" revolution in practice: the spate of immediate postwar productions in 1919 and 1920, including Paul Wegener's *Der Golem,* Karl Heinz Martin's *Von Morgens bis Mitternacht,* and, of course, Robert Weine's *Das Kabinett des Dr. Caligari,* demonstrated that, in the words of the German art critic and *New York Times* correspondent Herman G. Scheffauer, a new "stereoscopic universe" was in the making. In an analysis published at the end of 1920 that unabashedly paraphrased an earlier article by the Berlin critic Heinrich de Fries, Scheffauer hailed the end of the "crude phantasmagoria" of earlier films and the birth of a new space: "Space—hitherto considered and treated as something dead and static, a mere inert screen or frame, often of no more significance than the painted balustrade-background at the village photographer's—has been smitten into life, into movement and conscious expression. A fourth dimension has begun to evolve out of this photographic cosmos."[12] Thus the film began to extend what Scheffauer called "the sixth sense of man, his feeling for space or room—his *Raumgefühl*," in such a way as to transform reality itself. No longer an inert background, architecture now participates in the very emotions of the film—the surroundings no longer surround but enter the experience as presence: "The frown of a tower, the scowl of a sinister alley, the pride and serenity of a white peak, the hypnotic draught of a straight road vanishing to a point—these exert their influences and express their natures; their essences flow over the scene and blend with the action."[13] An advance on the two-dimensional world of the picture, the "scenic architect" of films such as *Caligari* has the ability to dominate "furniture, room, house, street, city, landscape, universe!" The "fourth dimension" of time extends space in depth, "the plastic is amalgamated with the painted, bulk and form with the simulacra of bulk and form, false perspective and violent foreshadowing are introduced, real light and shadow combat or reinforce painted shadow and light. Einstein's invasion of the law of gravity is made visible in the treatment of walls and supports."[14]

9. Walter Reimann, sketch for *The Cabinet of Dr. Caligari*, 1919.

Scheffauer provides a veritable phenomenology of the spaces of *Caligari*—a corridor in an office building, a street at night, an attic room, a prison cell, a white and spectral bridge, the marketplace; all constructed out of walls that are at once solid and transparent, fissured and veiled, camouflaged and endlessly disappearing, and presented in a forced and distorted perspective that presses space both backward and forward, finally overwhelming the spectator's own space, incorporating it into the vortex of the whole movie. In his description of the film's environments, Scheffauer anticipates all the later commonplaces of expressionist criticism from Siegfried Kracauer to Rudolf Kurtz:

A corridor in an office building: Wall veering outward from the floor, traversed by sharply-defined parallel strips, emphasizing the perspective and broken violently by pyramidal openings, streaming with light, marking the doors; the shadows between them vibrating as dark cones of contrast, the further end of the corridor murky, giving vast distance. In the foreground a section of wall violently tilted over the heads of the audience, as it were. The floor cryptically painted with errant lines of direction, the floor in front of the doors shows crosslines, indicating a going to and fro, in and out. The impression is one of formal coldness, of bureaucratic regularity, of semipublic traffic.

A street at night: Yawning blackness in the background—empty, starless, abstract space, against it a square, lopsided lantern hung between lurching walls. Doors and windows constructed or painted in wrenched perspective. Dark segments on the pavement accentuate diminishing effect. The slinking of a brutal figure pressed against the walls and evil spots and shadings on the pavement give a sinister expression to the street. Adroit diagonals lead and rivet the eye.

An attic: It speaks of sordidness, want and crime. The whole composition a vivid intersection of cones of light and dark, of roof-lines, shafts of light and slanting walls. A projection of white and black patterns on the floor, the whole geometrically felt, cubistically conceived. This attic is out of time, but in space. The roof chimneys of another world arise and scowl through the splintered window-pane.

A room; or rather a room that has precipitated itself in cavern-like lines, in inverted hollows of frozen waves. Here space becomes cloistral and encompasses the human—a man reads at a desk. A triangular window glares and permits the living day a voice in this composition. A prison-cell: A criminal, ironed to a huge chain attached to an immense trapezoidal "ball." The posture of the prisoner sitting on his folded legs is almost Buddha-like. Here space turns upon itself, encloses and focuses a human destiny. A small window high up and crazily-barred, is like an eye. The walls, sloping like a tent's to an invisible point, are blazoned with black and white wedge-shaped rays. These blend when they reach the floor and unite in a kind of huge cross, in the center of which the prisoner sits, scowling, unshaven. The tragedy of the repression of the human in space—in trinity of space, fate and man.

A white and spectral bridge yawning and rushing out of the foreground: It is an erratic, irregular causeway, such as blond ghouls might have built. It climbs and struggles upward almost out of the picture. In the middle distance it rises into a hump and reveals arches staggering over nothingness. The perspective pierces into vacuity. This bridge is the scene of a wild pursuit. . . .

Several aspects of the market place of a small town: . . . the town cries out its will through its mouth, this market place.[15]

Caligari, then, has produced an entirely new space, one that is both all-embracing and all-absorbing in depth and movement. But the filmic medium allowed the exploration of other kinds of space than the totalizing plasticity modeled by Walter Röhrig, Walter Reimann, and Hermann Warm for Weine's film. Scheffauer identifies the "flat space" of Martin's *Von Morgens bis Mitternacht* (1920), designed by Robert Neppach, where rather than being artificially constructed in the round as in *Caligari,* it was suggested in tones of black and white as "a background, vague, inchoate, nebulous."[16] Above and around this inactive space that makes the universe into a flat plane, there is only "primeval darkness"; all perspective is rendered in contrasts of white planes against blackness. There is also the "geometrical space" found in Reimann's film fantasy of Paul Scheerbart's *Algol;* in this meditation on the space of the stars, "the forms are broken up expressionistically, but space acts and speaks geometrically, in great vistas, in grandiose architectural culminations. Space or room is divided into formal diapers, patterns, squares, spots, and circles, of cube imposed upon cube, of apartment opening into apartment."[17] Finally, there is what Scheffauer terms "sculptural" or "solid" space, such as that modeled by the Poelzigs for Wegener's *Der Golem.*

Professor Poelzig conceives of space in plastic terms, in solid concretions congealing under the artist's hand to expressive and organic forms. He works, therefore, in the solid masses of the sculptor and not with the planes of the painter. Under his caressing hands a weird but spontaneous internal architecture, shell-like, cavernous, somber, has been evolved in simple, flowing lines, instinct with the bizarre spirit of the tale. . . . The gray soul of medieval Prague has been molded into these eccentric and errant crypts. . . . Poelzig seeks to give an eerie and grotesque suggestiveness to the flights of houses and streets that are to furnish the external setting of this film-play. The will of this master-architect animating facades into faces, insists that these houses are to speak in jargon—and gesticulate![18]

Pan-Geometries

In assimilating filmic space to the theoretical types of *Raum* adumbrated in German philosophy and psychology since Theodor Vischer, and in proposing the relativity of spatial forms in the face of continuous optical movement, in a way that reminds us of the historical relativity of optical forms demonstrated by Alois Riegl, Scheffauer anticipates the more scholarly account of perspectival history developed between 1923 and 1925 by Erwin Panofsky. Panofsky's essay "Perspective as Symbolic Form" set out to show that the various perspective systems from Roman times to the present were not simply "incorrect" instances of representing reality, but rather endowed with distinct and symbolic meaning of their own, as powerful and as open to reading as iconographical types and genres. Panofsky even took note of the modernist will to break with the conventions of perspective, and saw it as yet another stage of perspective vision itself. He cites expressionism's resistance to perspective as the last remnant of the will to capture "real, three-dimensional space," and El Lissitzky in his desire to overcome the bounds of finite space:

Older perspective is supposed to have "limited space, made it finite, closed it off," conceived of space "according to Euclidean geometry as rigid three-dimensionality," and it is these very bonds which the most recent art has attempted to break. Either it has in a sense exploded the entire space by "dispersing the center of vision" ("Futurism"), or it has sought no longer to represent depth intervals "extensively" by means of foreshortenings, but rather, in accord with the most modern insights of psychology, only to create an illusion "intensively" by playing color surfaces off against each other, each differently placed, differently shaded, and only in this way furnished with different spatial values (Mondrian and in particular Malevich's "Suprematism"). The author believes he can suggest a third solution: the conquest of an "imaginary space" by means of mechanically motivated bodies, which by this very movement, by their rotation or oscillation, produce precise figures (for example, a rotating stick produces an apparent circle, or in another position, an apparent cylinder, and so forth). In this way, in the opinion of El Lissitzky, art is elevated to the standpoint of a non-Euclidean pan-geometry (whereas in fact the space of those "imaginary" rotating bodies is no less "Euclidean" than any other empirical space).[19]

Despite Panofsky's skepticism, it was, of course, such a "pan-geometric" space that architecture hoped to construct through abstraction and technologically induced movement. Architects from El Lissitzky to Bruno Taut were to experiment with this new "pan-geometry" as if, in Ernst Bloch's words, it would enable them finally "to depict empirically an imaginary space." For Bloch, the underlying Euclidean nature of all space offered the potential for architecture to approach "pan-geometry" in reality; basing his argument on Panofsky's essay, he commended expressionists for having generated rotating and turning bodies that produced "stereometric figures . . . which at least have nothing in common with the perspective visual space (*Sehraum*)." Out of this procedure emerged "an architecture of the abstract, which wants to be quasi-meta-cubic." For Bloch this potential allowed modern architecture to achieve its own "symbolic allusions," even if these were founded on the "so-called Euclidian pan-geometry," criticized by Panofsky.[20] In this illusion the architects were encouraged by the cinematographers themselves, who, at least in the twenties, and led by Fritz Lang and F. W. Murnau, accepted the practical rulings of the Universum Film A.G. or Ufa, whose proscription against exterior filming supported the extraordinary experimentation in set design of the Weimar period.

Psycho-Spaces

But the attempt to construct these imaginary new worlds was, as Panofsky had noted, not simply formalistic and decorative; its premise was from the outset psychological, based on what Rudolf Kurtz defined as the "simple law of psychological aesthetics that when we feel our way into certain forms, exact psychic correspondences are set up."[21] Hugo Münsterberg, in his 1916 work *Film: A Psychological Study,* had already set out the terms of the equation film = psychological form.[22] For Münsterberg, film differed from drama by its appeal to the "inner movements of the mind":

> To be sure, the events in the photoplay happen in the real space with its depth. But the spectator feels that they are not presented in the three dimensions of the outer world, that they are flat pictures which only the mind molds into plastic things. Again the events are seen in continuous movement; and yet the pictures break up the movement into a rapid succession of instantaneous impressions. . . . The photoplay tells us the human story by overcoming the forms of the outer world, namely space, time, and causality, and by adjusting the events to the forms of the inner world, namely, attention, memory, imagination, and emotion.[23]

Only two years later, in one of his first critical essays, Louis Aragon was to note this property of the film to focus attention and reformulate the real into the imaginary, the ability to fuse the physical and the mental, later to become a surrealist obsession. Seemingly anticipating the mental states of Breton's *Nadja* or of his own *Paysan de Paris,* but as revealed in film, Aragon meditated on the way "the door of a bar that swings and on the window the capital letters of unreadable and marvelous words, or the vertiginous, thousand-eye facade of the thirty-story house . . . ". The possibility of disclosing the inner "menacing or enigmatic meanings" of everyday objects by simple close-up techniques and camera angles, light, shade, and space established, for Aragon, the poetic potential of the art: "To endow with a poetic value that which does not possess it, to willfully restrict the field of vision so as to intensify expression: these are two properties that help make cinematic decor the adequate setting of modern beauty."[24]

For this, however, film had no need of an artificially constructed "decor" that simulated the foreshortening of perspective or the phobic characteristics of space; the framings and movements of the camera itself would serve to construct reality far more freely. In his later 1934 essay on "Style and Medium in the Motion Pictures," Panofsky himself argued against any attempt to subject the world to "aesthetic prestylization, as in the expressionist settings of *The Cabinet of Dr. Caligari,*" as "no more than an exciting experiment." "To prestylize reality prior to tackling it amounts to dodging the problem," he concluded: "The problem is to manipulate and shoot unstylized reality in such a way that the result has style."[25]

Metropolitan Montage

The City as Film in Kracauer, Benjamin, and Eisenstein

> The street in the extended sense of the word is not only the arena of fleeting impressions and chance encounters but a place where the flow of life is bound to assert itself. Again one will have to think mainly of the city street with its ever-moving anonymous crowds. The kaleidoscopic sights mingle with unidentified shapes and fragmentary visual complexes and cancel each other out, thereby preventing the onlooker from following up any of the innumerable suggestions they offer. What appears to him are not so much sharp-contoured individuals engaged in this or that definable pursuit as loose throngs of sketchy, completely indeterminate figures. Each has a story, yet the story is not given. Instead, an incessant flow of possibilities and near-intangible meanings appears. This flow casts its spell over the *flâneur* or even creates him. The *flâneur* is intoxicated with life in the street—life eternally dissolving the patterns which it is about to form.
>
> Siegfried Kracauer, "Once Again the Street"[1]

The Lure of the Street: Kracauer

From the mid-twenties on, critics increasingly denounced what they saw as the purely decorative and staged characteristics of the expressionist film in favor of a more direct confrontation with the "real." If, as Panofsky asserted, "the unique and specific possibilities of film" could be "defined as *dynamization of space* and, accordingly, *spatialization of time*," then it was the lens of the camera, and not any distorted set, that inculcated a sense of motion in the static spectator, and thence a mobilization of space itself: "Not only do bodies move in space, but space itself does, approaching, receding, turning, dissolving and recrystallizing as it appears through the controlled locomotion and focusing of the camera and through the cutting and editing of the various shots."[2] And this led to the inevitable conclusion that the proper medium of the movies was not the idealization of reality, as in the other arts, but "physical reality as such."[3] Marcel Carné's frustrated question "When will the cinema go down into the street?," calling for an end to artifice and the studio set and a confrontation of the "real" as opposed to the "constructed" Paris, was only one of a number of increasingly critical attacks on the architectural set in the early thirties.[4]

Among the most rigorous of the new realists, Siegfried Kracauer, himself a former architect, was consistent in his arguments against the "decorative" and artificial, and in favor of the critical vision of the real that film allowed. From his first experience of film as a pre–World War I child to his last theoretical work on film published in 1960, Kracauer found the street to be both site and vehicle for his social criticism. Recalling the first film he saw as a boy, entitled significantly enough "Film as the Discoverer of the Marvels of Everyday Life," Kracauer remembered being thrilled by the sight of "an ordinary suburban street, filled with lights and shadows which transfigured it. Several trees stood about, and there was in the foreground a puddle reflecting invisible house facades and a piece of sky. Then a breeze moved the shadows, and the facades with the sky below began to waver. The trembling upper world in the dirty puddle—this image has never left me."[5] For Kracauer, the aesthetic of film was first and foremost material, not purely formal, and was essentially suited to the recording of the fleeting, the temporally transient, the momentary impression—that is, the modern—a quality that made the "street" in all its manifestations an especially favored subject matter. If the snapshot stressed the random and the fortuitous, then its natural development in the motion picture camera was "partial to the least permanent components of our environment," rendering "the street in the broadest sense of the word" the place for chance encounters and social observation.[6] But for this to work as a truly critical method of observation and recording, the street would first have to be offered up as an "unstaged reality"; what Kracauer considered film's "declared preference for nature in the raw" was easily defeated by artificiality and "staginess," whether the staged "drawing brought to life" of *Caligari* or the more filmic staging of montage, panning, and camera movement. Fritz Lang's *Metropolis,* of 1926, was an example of this latter kind of staging, where "a film of unsurpassable staginess" was partially redeemed by the way in which crowds were treated "and rendered through a combination of long shots and close shots which provide exactly the kind of random impressions we would receive were we to witness this spectacle in reality."[7] Yet for Kracauer, the impact of the crowd images was obviated by the architectural settings that remained entirely stylized and imaginary. A similar case was represented by Walter Ruttmann's *Berlin, Symphonie einer Grossstadt* (1927), where in a Vertov-like manipulation of shot and montage the director tried to capture "simultaneous phenomena which, owing to certain analogies and contrasts between them, form comprehensible patterns. . . . He cuts from human legs walking in the street to the legs of a cow and juxtaposes the luscious dishes in a deluxe restaurant with the appalling food of the very poor."[8] Such formalism, however, tended to concentrate attention not on things themselves and their meaning but on their formal characteristics. As Kracauer noted with respect to the capturing of the city's movement in rhythmic shots, "tempo is also a formal conception if it is not defined with reference to the qualities of the objects through which it materializes."[9]

For Kracauer, the street, properly recorded, offered a virtually inexhaustible subject for the comprehension of modernity; its special characteristics fostered not only the chance and the random, but more importantly the necessary distance, if not alienation, of the observer for whom the camera eye was a precise surrogate. If, in the photographs of Marville or Atget, one might detect a certain melancholy, this was because the photographic medium, intersecting with the street as subject, fostered a kind of self-estrangement allowing for a closer identification with the objects being observed. "The dejected individual is likely to lose himself in the incidental configurations of his environment, absorbing them with a disinterested intensity no longer determined by his previous preferences. His is a kind of receptivity which resembles that of Proust's photographer cast in the role of a stranger."[10] Hence, for Kracauer and his friend Walter Benjamin, the close identification of the photographer with the flâneur, and the potential of flânerie and its techniques to furnish models for the modernist filmmaker: "The melancholy character is seen strolling about aimlessly: as he proceeds, his changing surroundings take shape in the form of numerous juxtaposed shots of house facades, neon lights, stray passers-by, and the like. It is inevitable that the audience should trace their seemingly unmotivated emergence to his dejection and the alienation in its wake."[11] In this respect, what Kracauer saw as Eisenstein's "identification of life with the street" took on new meaning, as the flâneur-photographer moved to capture the flow of fleeting impressions that Kracauer's teacher Georg Simmel had characterized as "snapshots of reality." "When history is made in the streets, the streets tend to move onto the screen," concluded Kracauer.

The Critic as Producer: Benjamin

Other critics were more optimistic about the potential of filmic techniques to render a version of reality that might otherwise go unrecorded, or better, to reconstrue reality in such a way that it might be critically apprehended. Thus Walter Benjamin's celebrated eulogy of the film as liberty of perception, in "The Work of Art in the Age of Mechanical Reproduction," was a first step in the constitution of the filmic as *the* modern critical aesthetic:

> By close-ups of the things around us, by focusing on hidden details of familiar objects, by exploring commonplace milieus under the ingenious guidance of the camera, the film, on the one hand, extends our comprehension of the necessities which rule our lives; on the other hand, it manages to assure us of an immense and unexpected field of action. Our taverns and our metropolitan streets, our offices and furnished rooms, our railroad stations and our factories appeared to have us locked up hopelessly. Then came the film and burst this prison world asunder by the dynamite of the tenth of a second, so that now, in the midst of its far-flung ruins and debris, we calmly and adventurously go traveling. With the close-up, space expands; with slow motion, movement is extended. . . . An unconsciously penetrated space is substituted for a space consciously explored by man. . . . The camera introduces us to unconscious optics as does psychoanalysis to unconscious impulses.[12]

Unconscious optics, the filmic unconscious, was, for Benjamin, itself a kind of analysis, the closest aesthetic equivalent to Freud's own *Psychopathology of Everyday Life,* in its ability to focus and deepen perception.

In this characteristic, film obviously outdistanced architecture; Benjamin's remark that "architecture has always represented the prototype of a work of art the reception of which is consummated by the collectivity in a state of distraction" was made in this very context: the assertion of the "shock effect" of the film as that which allows the public, no longer distracted, to be put once more in the position of the critic. Thus the only way to render architecture critical again was to wrest it out of its uncritically observed context, its distracted state, and offer it to a now attentive public—that is, to make a film of the building.

Or of the city. In an evocative remark inserted apparently at random among the unwieldy collection of citations and aphorisms that make up the unfinished *Passagen-Werk,* Walter Benjamin opened the possibility of yet another way of reading his unfinished work: was it not perhaps the sketch of a screenplay for a movie of Paris?

> Could one not shoot a passionate film of the city plan of Paris? Of the development of its different forms [*Gestalten*] in temporal succession? Of the condensation of a century-long movement of streets, boulevards, passages, squares, in the space of half an hour? And what else does the flâneur do?[13]

In this context, might not the endless quotations and aphoristic observations of the *Passagen-Werk,* carefully written out on hundreds of single index cards, each one letter-, number-, and color-coded to cross-reference them to all the rest, be construed as so many shots, ready to be montaged into the epic movie "Paris, Capital of the Nineteenth Century"; a prehistory of modernity, finally realized by modernity's own special form of mechanical reproduction?

While obviously no "film" of this kind was ever made, an attempt to answer the hypothetical question "What would Benjamin's film of Paris have looked like?" would clarify what we might call Benjamin's "filmic imaginary." Such an imaginary, overt in the *Passagen-Werk* and the contemporary essay "The Work of Art in the Age of Mechanical Reproduction" and covert in many earlier writings from those on German baroque allegory to those on historical form, might, in turn, reveal important aspects of the theoretical problems inherent in the filmic representation of metropolis. For, in the light of Benjamin's theories of the political and social powers of mechanical reproduction as outlined in his "Conversations with Berthold Brecht," it is clear from the outset that any project for a film of Paris would in no way have resembled other urban films of the interwar period, whether idealist, expressionist, or realist. Rather it would have involved Benjamin in an act of theoretical elaboration that, based on previous film theory and criticism, would have constructed new kinds of optical relations between the camera and the city, film and architecture. These would no doubt have been established on the complex notion of "the optical unconscious," an intercalation of Freud and Riegl, that appears in Benjamin's writings on photography and film in the late twenties and early thirties.[14]

On one level Benjamin's fragmentary remark is easily decipherable: what he had in mind was evidently an image of the combined results of the flâneur's peripatetic vision, montaged onto the history of the nineteenth century and put in motion by the movie camera. No longer would the implied movement of Bergsonian mental processes or the turns of allegorical text have to make do as pale imitations of metropolitan movement; now the real movement of the film would, finally, merge technique and content as a proof, so to speak, of the manifest destiny of modernity. In this sense, Benjamin's metaphor of a Parisian film remains just that: a figure of modernist technique as the fullest expression of modernist thought, as well as the explanation of its origins.

Certainly it is not too difficult to imagine the figure of Benjamin's flâneur, Vertov-like, carrying his camera as a third eye, framing and shooting the rapidly moving pictures of modern life. The etchings of Jacques Callot, the thumbnail sketches of Saint-Aubin, the "tableaux" of Sébastien Mercier, the rapid renderings of Constantin Guys, the prose poems of Baudelaire, the snapshots of Atget are all readily transposed into the vocabulary of film, which then literally mimics the fleeting impressions of everyday life in metropolis in its very techniques of representation. Indeed, almost every characteristic Benjamin associates with the flâneur might be associated with the film director with little or no distortion. An eye for detail, for the neglected and the chance; a penchant for joining reality and reverie; a distanced vision, apart from that distracted and unselfconscious existence of the crowd; a fondness for the marginal and the forgotten: these are traits of flâneur and filmmaker alike. Both share affinities with the detective and the peddler, the ragpicker and the vagabond; both aestheticize the roles and materials with which they work. Equally, the typical habitats of the flâneur lend themselves to filmic representation: the banlieu, the margins, the zones, and outskirts of the city; the deserted streets and squares at night; the crowded boulevards, the phantasmagoric passages, arcades, and department stores; the spatial apparatus, that is, of the consumer metropolis.

On another level, however, if we take the image literally rather than metaphorically, a number of puzzling questions emerge. A film of Paris is certainly conceivable, but what would a film of "the *plan* of Paris" look like? And if one were to succeed in filming this plan, how then might it depict the development of the city's "forms"—its boulevards, streets, squares, and passages—at the same time as "condensing" a century of their history into half an hour? How might such a film, if realized, be "passionate"? If, as Benjamin intimates, the model of the film director was to be found in the figure of the flâneur, how might this figure translate his essentially nineteenth-century habits of walking and seeing into cinematographic terms? It seems that step by step, within the very movement of Benjamin's own metaphor, the ostensible unity of the image is systematically undermined; as if the result of making a film of the plan of Paris were to replicate the very fragmentation of modernity that the metropolis posed, the flâneur saw, and the film concretizes. Benjamin's image thus emerges as a complex rebus of method and form. Its very self-enclosed elegance, beginning with the film and ending with the flâneur as director (a perfect example of a romantic fragment turning in on itself according to Schelling's rules), seems consciously structured to provoke its own unraveling. It is as if Benjamin inserted his cinematographic conundrum into the formless accumulation of the *Passagen-Werk*'s citations and aphorisms to provoke, in its deciphering, a self-conscious ambiguity about the implied structure of his text, and, at the same time, a speculation on the theory of film that he never wrote.

For it was not simply that the flâneur and the filmmaker shared spaces and gazes; for Benjamin these characteristics were transferred, as in analysis, to the spaces themselves, which became, so to speak, vagabonds in their own right. He spoke of the phenomenon of the "*colportage* or peddling of space" as the fundamental experience of the flâneur, where a kind of Bergsonian simultaneity allowed "the simultaneous perception of everything that potentially is happening in this single space. The space directs winks at the flâneur."[15] Thus the flâneur as ragpicker and peddler participates in his surroundings, even as they cooperate with him in his unofficial archaeology of spatial settings. And, to paraphrase Benjamin, what else does the filmmaker do for a viewer now opened up "in his susceptibility to the transient real-life phenomena that crowd the screen"?[16]

Architectural Montage: Eisenstein

Here we are returned to Eisenstein's "street," reminded, in Benjamin's desire to have shot a "passionate" film, of Eisenstein's own long analyses of the notion of filmic "ecstasy," the simultaneous cause and effect of movement in the movie. The "ecstatic" for Eisenstein was, in fact, the fundamental shared characteristic of architecture and film. Even as architectural styles had, one by one, "exploded" into each other by a kind of inevitable historical process, so the filmmaker might force the shot to decompose and recompose in successive explosions. Thus, the "principles of the Gothic . . . seem to explode the balance of the Romanesque style. And, within the Gothic itself, we could trace the stirring picture of movement of its lancet world from the first almost indistinct steps toward the ardent model of the mature and postmature, 'flamboyant' late Gothic. We could, like Wölfflin, contrast the Renaissance and Baroque and interpret the excited spirit of the second, winding like a spiral, as an ecstatically bursting temperament of a new epoch, exploding preceding forms of art in the enthusiasms for a new quality, responding to a new phase of a single historical process."[17]

But Eisenstein goes further. In an essay on two Piranesi engravings for the early and late states of the *Carceri* series, he compares architectural composition itself to cinematic montage, an implicit "flux of form" that holds within itself the potential to explode into successive states.[18] Building on his experience as architect and set designer, Eisenstein developed a comprehensive theory of what he called "space constructions" that found new meaning in the romantic formulation of architecture as "frozen music": "At the basis of the composition of its ensemble, at the basis of the harmony of its conglomerating masses, in the establishment of the melody of the future overflow of its forms, and in the execution of its rhythmic parts, giving harmony to the relief of its ensemble, lies that same 'dance' that is also at the basis of the creation of music, painting, and cinematic montage."[19] For Eisenstein a kind of relentless vertigo is set up by the play of architectural forms in space, a vertigo that is easily assimilable to Thomas De Quincey's celebrated account of Coleridge's reaction to Piranesi's *Carceri,* or, better, to Gogol's reading of the Gothic as a style of endless movement and internal explosions.[20]

And if Eisenstein is able to "force," to use Manfredo Tafuri's term, these *representations* of architectural space to "explode" into the successive stages of their "montage" decomposition and recomposition, as if they were so many "shots," then it is because, for Eisenstein, architecture itself embodies the principles of montage; indeed its especial characteristics of a spatial art experienced in time render it the predecessor of the film in more than simple analogy.

In the article "Montage and Architecture," written in the late thirties as a part of the uncompleted work on montage, Eisenstein sets out this position, contrasting two "paths" of the spatial eye: the cinematic, where a spectator follows an imaginary line among a series of objects, through the sight as well as in the mind—"diverse positions passing in front of an immobile spectator"—and the architectural, where "the spectator moved through a series of carefully disposed phenomena which he observed in order with his visual sense." In this transition from real to imaginary movement, architecture is film's predecessor. Where painting "remained incapable of fixing the total representation of an object in its full multi-dimensionality," and "only the film camera has solved the problem of doing this on a flat surface," "its undoubted ancestor in this capability is . . . architecture."[21]

Here, Eisenstein, former architect and an admitted "great adherent of the architectural aesthetics of Le Corbusier," turned to an example of the architectural "path" that precisely parallels that studied by Le Corbusier himself in *Vers une architecture* to exemplify the "promenade architecturale": the successive perspective views of the movement of an imaginary spectator on the Acropolis constructed by Auguste Choisy to demonstrate the "successive tableaux" and "picturesque" composition of the site.[22] Eisenstein cites Choisy's analysis at length with little commentary, asking his reader simply "to look at it with the eye of a film-maker": "It is hard to imagine a montage sequence for an architectural ensemble more subtly composed, shot by shot, than the one which our legs create by walking among the buildings of the Acropolis." For Eisenstein the Acropolis was the veritable answer to Victor Hugo's assertion of the cathedral of a book in stone: "the perfect example of one of the most ancient films."[23] Eisenstein finds in the carefully sequenced perspectives presented

10. Auguste Choisy,
"The Acropolis, First
Sight of the Platform,"
from "Le pittoresque
dans l'art grec," *Histoire
de l'architecture,* 2 vols.
(Paris: Gauthier-Villars,
1899), 1:415.

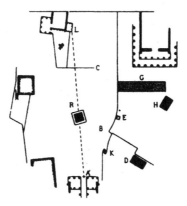

11. Sergei Eisenstein,
"Montage and Architec-
ture," diagrams of the
successive positions of
the Acropolis as de-
scribed in perspective
by Auguste Choisy.

by Choisy the combination of a "film shot effect," producing an obvious new impression from each new, emerging shot, and a "montage effect," where the effect is gained from the sequential juxtaposition of the shots. The filmmaker speculates on the desirable temporal duration of each picture, finding the possibility that there was a distinct relationship between the pace of the spectator's movement and the rhythm of the buildings themselves, a temporal solemnity being provoked by the distance between each building.

Le Corbusier, who is apparently less faithful in his reproduction of Choisy's sequence, concentrates on the second perspective, shown together with the plan of the visual axis of entry from the Propylaea to the former statue of Athena. For the architect, this demonstrates the flexibility of Greek "axial" planning, as opposed to the rigidity of the academic Beaux-Arts: "False right angles have furnished rich views and a subtle effect; the asymmetrical masses of the buildings create an intense rhythm. The spectacle is massive, elastic, nervous, overwhelming in its sharpness, dominating."[24] The plan of the mobile and changing ground levels of the Acropolis is only apparently "disordered." There is an inner equilibrium when the entire site is viewed from afar.

In this common reliance on Choisy we might be tempted to see the final conjunction of architectural and filmic modernism; the rhythmic dance of Le Corbusier's spectator (modeled no doubt on the movements of Jacques Dalcroze) anticipating the movement of Eisenstein's shots and montages. For both analysts, the apparently inert site and its strangely placed buildings is almost literally exploded into life, at once physical and mental. For both, the rereading of a canonical monument has provided the key to a "true" and natural modernist aesthetic.

And yet, as both ceaselessly reiterated, such correspondences were, when taken themselves too literally, false to the internal laws of the two media, architecture and film. If Le Corbusier agreed that "everything is Architecture," he also called for film to concentrate on its own laws; Eisenstein, similarly, abandoned a career as architect and stage designer precisely because the film offered a new and different stage of representational technique for modernity. For Le Corbusier architecture was a setting for the athletic and physical life of the new man; its objects and settings the activators of mental and spiritual activity through vision; for Eisenstein architecture remained only a *potential* film, a necessary stage in aesthetic evolution, but already surpassed.

Both would have agreed with Robert Mallet-Stevens, who was troubled by the invasion of the decorative into filmic architecture, the potential to create "imaginary" forms that illustrated rather than provided settings for human psychological emotions. Mallet-Stevens warned against the tendency to view architecture as a photogenic aid to film, thereby creating a "foreseen" dynamic that in real space would be provided by the human figure: "the ornament, the arabesque, is the mobile personage who creates them."[25] Rather than expressionist buildings imitating their cinematic counterparts, he called for a radical simplification of architecture that would, in this way, offer itself up naturally to the filmic action, always preserving the distance between the real and the imaginary. "Real life is entirely different, the house is made to live, it should first respond to our needs."[26] Properly handled, however, architecture and film might be entirely complementary. He cited a screenplay by Ricciotto Canudo that would perhaps realize this ideal:

> It concerned the representation of a solitary woman, frighteningly alone in life, surrounded by the void and nothingness. The décor: composed of inarticulate lines, immovable, repeated, without ornament: no window, no door, no furniture in the "field," and at the center of these rigid parallels a woman who advanced slowly. Subtitles become useless, architecture situates the person and defines her better than any text.[27]

In this vision of a cinematic architecture that would return through its own laws of perspective to the essential characteristics of building, Mallet-Stevens echoed Le Corbusier and anticipated Eisenstein. In his depiction of a decor framed as the very image of isolation, agoraphobic or claustrophobic, he also answered those in Germany who were attempting to "express" in spatial distortion what a simple manipulation of the camera in space might accomplish.

Such arguments between these two possibilities of filmic architecture have hardly ceased with the gradual demise of cinema and the rise of its own "natural" successors video and, more recently, digital hyperspatial imaging. That their influence on architecture might be as disturbing as those observed by Le Corbusier and Mallet-Stevens is at least possible to hazard, as buildings and their spatial sequences are designed as illustrations of implied movement or, worse, as literal fabrications of the computer's-eye view.

X Marks the Spot

The Exhaustion of Space at the Scene of the Crime

The exact position of the X that in common lore marked the most significant spot at the scene of the crime has more than often been in doubt. Precise in terminology, and of course in geometrical accuracy, the spot has been, so to speak, on the move throughout the last century and a half of modern criminological practice. The place of the body might be marked by tape and chalk on the ground to which it had fallen; the alleged site of the crime might be gridded with painstaking care in order to provide a coordinate system by which to situate the evidence, carefully collected in labeled bags for presentation in court; the tracks of the criminal, the traces of blood, the dispersed weapons, and their hastily jettisoned ammunition might all be gathered together and plotted on the special kind of map that criminologists have defined as appropriate to fix the "scene" of the crime in legally tenable terms. But all this precision, as fictional and real defenders have demonstrated since Edgar Allan Poe, falls apart at the slightest questioning of a spatial kind. The question of *what* has generally been easily answered, at least until the most sophisticated technologies (such as those of DNA analysis) have proved too much "beyond a doubt" to be believable. The question of *where,* however, has always been readily thrown into obscurity, by the simple trick of denouncing the various projections, suppositions, and assumptions that are gathered around any exercise in mapping. Objects can be presented in the courtroom, but spaces have always to be imagined, and represented; and representation has, from the early nineteenth century at least, been an art, controlled by psychological projection and careful artifice, more than a science.

This was no doubt the message of Georges Bataille when, in his brief review of the photographic album *X Marks the Spot* (issued appropriately enough by the Spot Publishing Company of Chicago in 1930),[1] he remarked on the custom of publishing photos of criminal cadavers, a practice "that seemed equally popular in Europe, certainly representing a considerable moral transformation in the attitude of the public to violent death."[2] To illustrate the point, Bataille selected an image from this "first photographic history of Chicago gangland slayings" depicting the corpse of an assassinated gangster found in the ice of Lake Michigan, the figure face up, as if frozen while floating, a literal monument to its own death. In one sense, of course, this image has no relation to the "X marks the spot" announced in the title of the album, to the custom of marking the position of the victim after the removal of the body; there was in this case no mark to be left on the ice following the excavation of the frozen corpse, and its place of discovery was destined to be effaced forever with the subsequent thaw. For an instant, then, the corpse acted as its own mark, one to be rendered permanent only in the police photo. And this photograph, as Georges Didi-Huberman has pointed out, was itself an enigmatic record: "First one doesn't see very much, insofar as the image evokes a pure and simple yet chaotic site—a black and white magma. Then one recognizes the man frozen (and presumably assassinated) *trapped in the ice* of Lake Michigan."[3] Transformed into an anamorphic vision by virtue of the flattening surface of the ice and the angle of the photo, the dead gangster has been doubly recomposed, first as a marker of the site of his own death, secondly as a visually encoded hieroglyphic image of that mark. Further, whatever place was marked by the position of the body, it was not the site of the assassination itself, but rather the place where the gangster had ended up, propelled by the currents of the lake and frozen by chance on rising to the surface. A mark therefore of the ever-exilic, ever-transitory place of death in modern urban life, but at the same time of the consistent popular and judicial fascination with the nature and signs of that place.

This signal of Bataille's interest in the position and role of X in marking the spot of death in the city anticipated by eight years his more developed reflection on Nietzsche's proclamation of the "death of God,"[4] an essay in which the role of the mark is now played by a monument—the Obelisk of Luxor erected in the Place de la Concorde in 1836—and the "spot" is that of the guillotine erected for the execution of Louis XVI. In this process of transformation, in which a police inquiry into a murdered gangster is enlarged to encompass the death of God, the mystery—who was the victim and who the murderer?—is similarly deepened, both by the historical age and mysterious origins of this X in Egypt and by its subsequent deracination and transposition to modern Paris. The circumstances of its reutilization, and the subsequent history of its interpretation and reception in the *place* or Place de la Concorde, when joined to the monumental history of this Place itself, establish for Bataille the appropriate *mise-en-scène* in which to stage Nietzsche's fool, running into the public square with lantern lit in broad daylight, crying: "I'm looking for God!"

The obelisk held a special place in Bataille's symbolic topography. For by virtue of its origin in history and its monumental role in space, it potentially reconciled time *in* space, effacing the one in favor of the latter, at the same time as it opened the way, through a process of desymbolization, and by its insistent presence, to a negation of all historical meaning. X, then, marks the spot not only of the proclamation of the death of God and of the actual murder, but also of the threshold of all ensuing consequences and potentialities, or rather, the place from which it would be possible to imagine any such future. The conjuncture of the Place de la Concorde and the obelisk was thus an entirely appropriate "place" for a Nietzschean inquiry. The place itself had indeed been the object of almost as many redefinitions and imposed identities as the obelisk—as a *place,* that is, its place was singularly unstable in both political and architectural terms.

Put in terms of a criminal investigation—the forensic study of "the scene of the crime" preparatory to bringing a suspect to trial—Bataille's scenario would certainly be troubling to a police method that relied on physical evidence faithfully collected and recorded by that instrument of the "real," the camera. The distortion of the visual field produced an image that could be reassembled into the figure of a corpse only through an equal and opposite distortion, a sideways reading, so to speak, that in itself cast doubt on the original form. Further, at the same time as the site of the discovery of the body acted as the stable context for inferring the nature and perpetrator of the murder, its unstable coordinates unfixed the evidence and disseminated the clues into a spatial void. *Space,* infiltrating and dispersing *place,* had put the tangibility and thereby the veracity of courtroom exhibits into doubt. The crime takes place in space, which in turn renders its exact position unstable.

And yet this very spatial dimension of the crime, a commonplace of city novels from Poe's Paris and Conan Doyle's London to Chandler's Los Angeles, has been largely overlooked in criticism, in favor of the material evidence presented by traces and objects—a preoccupation shared by police methods and recently underlined in the heated debates over the "bloody glove" in the Simpson trial. In this trial, the "fit" of the glove, and its possible purchase by Simpson, were less important in the end than its position in space, its potential for having been "planted," its obvious immobility in the evidence photos disturbed by the defense's clever manipulation of its equally obvious potential for movement. Similarly, blood, which indelibly marked socks and vans belonging to the accused, thus creating a trail that police hoped would trace the crime back to the culprit, was demonstrated to be equally mobile, as it moved from site to station to laboratory and back to crime site again. Indeed, the entire trial was destabilized by a defense that exploited space against object, that knew how to set in motion every fixed premise and stable clue by situating it in a field of other spaces and sites that raised the possibility of doubt as to its fixed place. The fluidity of space was pitched against the stability of place; the object consistently displaced by its spatial field.

Here we are reminded of that canonical tale of the spatial displacement of evidence, Poe's "The Purloined Letter," later to be reconstituted as a psychoanalytical fable of automatism of repetition by Jacques Lacan.[5] Poe's very title, Lacan cautions, is a warning of the story's implications: he points out that the word "purloined," translated by Baudelaire as *volée*, "stolen," is derived from the Anglo-French *pur* (as in purpose, purchase, purport) and the Old French *loing, loigner, longé* ("alongside"), making a word that implies the action of "putting aside," "putting alongside," or even "putting in the wrong place." Such attributes of displacement, when joined to the action of "stealing"—for purloining also implies a theft, if not one involving outright confiscation—intimates the complex matrix of intersecting double scenes staged by Poe's narrative. The first (Lacan significantly terms it the "primal scene"), in the royal *boudoir* (perfect scene for a primal crime), finds the Queen receiving a letter, surprised by the King and in confusion "hiding" the letter by leaving it open on a table, only to witness the Minister substitute his own letter for hers and make off with it together with the power its ownership conveys. The second (a repetition of the first) is in the Minister's apartment, and stages Dupin discovering the letter in full view hanging from the mantleshelf, and himself substituting a letter with a motto for the Minister to reflect on when opening what he thinks is the Queen's. These two spaces of "putting in the wrong (therefore the right) place," of putting the evidence in full view so as to hide it from those who would think it hidden, are separated in Poe's story by the intermission—a scene of search and of the relentless thoroughness of the police investigation; an investigation that the Prefect of Police has to admit comes up empty-handed.

The premise of this search is simple enough, and has been repeated to infinity. Anticipating that a clever thief would hide his spoils cleverly, the police "search *everywhere.*" "Everywhere" for Poe, and for the Prefect, involves a scientific survey of every possible space: the entire building is searched, room by room, the furniture first. Every possible drawer is opened, on the premise that "such a thing as a *'secret'* drawer is impossible" to conceal against a method that measures accurately "the fiftieth part of a line" in order to account for the mathematically calculated bulk of every compartment. Even the space behind and between books, the space in the binding and the pages is submitted to this probing inspection. The surface of the house itself is "divided . . . into compartments," which are numbered, and "each individual square inch throughout the premises, including the two houses immediately adjoining," is scrutinized with a microscope.[6] This search would be, Lacan remarks, a veritable "exhaustion of space," whereby the entire "field in which the police presumes, not without reason, that the letter should be found" is submitted to a kind of *quadrillage* of exactitude in such a way that "had the letter been deposited within the range of their search," the police would have found it.[7]

We should not be surprised to find the Prefect's search methods systematically taught in contemporary police practice. The training manual "Basic Course Unit Guide: Crime Scene Search Technique," developed for the Commission on Peace Officer Standards and Training of the state of California (c. 1985), advocates geometrically controlled search patterns (as opposed to a "point-to-point" search that is "very often disorganized"), such as the "strip search" in lanes defined by stakes and lines; the "double strip (grid)" search; the "quadrant (or sector)" search that in indoor situations would divide the "building into rooms," the "bookshelf into sections," and the "cupboard into [gridded] sections"; the "circular (spiral or concentric)" search; the "wheel (or radiate)" search; the "area search," and finally the aerial search. Tips for teaching these methods describe how students should test out each method of search in the context of specific rooms and spaces, carefully photographing, sketching, describing in notes, collecting, marking, and preserving the result-ing "evidence."[8]

Poe's spatial field of crime scenes is, in a similar sense, three-dimensional; both the map constructed by the police search and the map of the displaced, purloined letter are construed in space and time (the one holding that we will find the letter given time, the other that the letter will never be found because it is not "looked for" in the right field), so that the eventual intersection of the two fields effectuated by Dupin results in a kind of warping—producing a Klein bottle form that returns the letter to its receiver, but by a path that twists the space of purloining to enter and exit Dupin's own desk. The poetics of crime and its revelation transform the geometrical space of rational detection into a knot of abyssal proportions.

It is worth noting, in the context of this argument, that Dupin's success was not a triumph of visual acuity. Dupin did not see the letter with any more precision that the Prefect. Rather, his feat was the result of intellectual intro-jection, precisely a feat of not seeing, conducted in a black box specifically set up for reflection, not vision: Dupin's "little back library, or book closet" sur-rounded by "curling eddies of smoke" with the two friends "sitting in the dark." "If there is any point requiring reflection," observed Dupin, as he for-bore to enkindle the wick, "we shall examine it to better purpose in the dark."[9]

Such a refusal of vision, in favor of interior reflection, is consistent with the arguments of Walter Benjamin, himself an avid student of Dupin, that space, or rather "architecture," is experienced primarily in a state of "distrac-tion," a state that ignores the visual characteristics of the building in favor of its haptic and tactile environment, a "dark space," as Eugène Minkowski would have it, where vision is unconscious and "losing one's way" is the key to knowl-edge. In the same way, Dupin notes the peculiar characteristic of "overly-large lettered signs and placards of the street" that, like the purloined letter, "escape observation by dint of being excessively obvious."[10] Indeed, we might infer that the thorough spatial search launched by the Prefect was itself less visual than me-thodical, a search conducted according to habitual and customary premises. Af-ter all, the crime itself was accomplished in full view of the victim and seen by her, and the perpetrator was content to leave the stolen letter equally in full view.

Lacan's identification of the three kinds of gaze characterizing the inter-subjectivity of the scenes of Poe's narrative supports this interpretation of the "unseeing" look. According to Lacan, "the first is a gaze that sees nothing: that of the King and of the police"; "the second, a gaze that sees that the first sees nothing and deceives itself in seeing hidden what it hides—the queen and the minister"; "the third sees that the first two gazes leave what is to be hidden exposed to whomever would seize it—the minister and Dupin."[11] When set in a spatial field, whether enclosed or open, this unconscious blindness becomes a pathological condition that late nineteenth-century analysts would identify as a return to the haptic, a tactophilia, that in its "close-up" vision approximated to the early stage of child development or (as applied to the history of vision by historians like Alois Riegl) to the optical structure of ancient Egypt. Only a haptic-driven optics, Riegl argued, could produce works like the pyramids, which revealed themselves in their three-dimensional totality to a viewer standing at their base—almost touching; a Greek temple, by contrast, demanded to be viewed from a "normal" distance and in three-quarter view. Late Roman monuments required neither a close-up nor a normal viewing point, but rather confused the viewer by (as in the case of the cylindrical Pantheon) oscillating between figure and ground, or more precisely by providing no fixed ground against which to be seen. Riegl's analysis, while obviously oversimplified in its reliance on a biological model of development to determine the historical development of vision, nevertheless contains the premise, utilized by cultural critics and artists throughout the twentieth century, that vision, which has a "history," as Victor Burgin has stressed, is always confused by its unconscious, its determining relations to touch and the other nonvisual senses, when as a bodily projection it finds itself in space. Thus, against the optical stupidity of the police, interested, as Fredric Jameson points out in his brilliant essay on Raymond Chandler, more in the control of administration than in the prevention of crime, is posed the intuitive brilliance of the detective: the optical unconscious's underdog, in the person of Dupin, Holmes, Marlowe, et al.

Los Angeles of course, was, the location of criminal spatial dissemination par excellence. As Jameson notes, it is Los Angeles, more than any other city, that since the thirties has consistently anticipated the breakdown of class and character-type division embedded in the more stratified cities of old Europe, a breakdown that is precisely the result of its spatial character—"a spreading out horizontally, a flowing apart of the elements of the social structure."[12] The unstructured nature of the city and its society drives the detective into space, so to speak: no longer confined, like Dupin and Holmes, to the space of his own mental analysis and problem solving—the intuitive rationalist, the mathematician of chance—the Los Angeles detective "is propelled outwards into the space of his world and obliged to move from one kind of social reality to another incessantly, trying to find clues."[13] Time and space become commingled in a complex narrative in which the murder, to take an example at random, is committed only at the end of the book, rendering it a "senseless accident" rather than, as classically the case, the ultimate object of the search. Similarly, the objects that once formed a growing body of evidence, of clues painstakingly collected, tabulated, and preserved, now are described and "collected" for the sake not of the search but of a generalized sense of place, a nostalgia for products, often entirely incidental to the case at hand, representing the author's knowledge of the world he evokes and authenticating a picaresque narrative for its own sake: "The author's task is to make an inventory of these objects, to demonstrate by the fullness of his catalogue, how completely he knows his way around the world of machines and machine products, and it is in this sense that Chandler's descriptions of furniture, his description of womens' clothing styles, will function: as a naming, a sign of expertise and knowhow."[14] These objects, then, have lost the fetish character of clues, and certainly no longer carry the fetish character of their status as products, but instead gain, in their generalized dissemination through the space of the novel, an overwhelming aura of criminality per se, as if every beer bottle, cigarette, ashtray, and car were invested with a potential seediness, as if even the spaces in which they are set, the run-down motels, the nondescript bars, the diners, were carriers of a low-grade criminal infection that has transformed the entire city into a scene of perpetual and undifferentiated crime. Even the space of the law was contaminated by such ubiquity of the lawless: a space that was to be identified, as Chandler himself noted, with the precinct station—"beyond the green lights of the precinct station you pass clear out of this world into a place beyond the law."[15] For Chandler and Los Angeles in general, this place has passed into the world itself.

As we have seen, Georges Bataille's interest in gangland photos takes its inspiration from this sense of the latent criminality of space. Bataille's observations on the gangster photo album were set in the context of his enquiry into architectural monumentality and the nature of public space in modern culture, an investigation begun in the articles "Architecture," "Espace," and "Musée" in *Documents* and continued, as Denis Hollier has demonstrated, throughout his writings.[16] Here Bataille began to explore that profound destabilization of the realm of the monumental operated by the force of space itself and, more precisely, the psychological power of space considered as a fluid, boundary-effacing, always displaced and displacing medium. In his brief article "Espace" published in the first issue of *Documents* in 1930, Bataille characterizes space as a "loutish" and errant child of philosophy, a breaker of protocol and an offender against propriety, a "scallywag at odds with society."[17] Its most powerful distinguishing quality was its "discontinuity."

A clue as to Bataille's meaning may be gleaned from his first qualification of the word "espace" as a "question des convenances." "Convenance," or suitability, had always been a loaded term, in architecture especially, where it referred to the classical codes of appropriateness of a genre or an order to a particular program—at its simplest, regulating the application of the orders and constraining decoration to a rigid social hierarchy. But evidently the *convenances* of which Bataille speaks are very different from those of the classical canon, or rather, even as they rely on former canons, they are conceived in order to establish entirely new mixed genres and canons, not of social hierarchy but of its dissolution; not of social propriety, but of its withering away; new genres and canons, that is, of power and eroticism represented in space, precisely through the abilities of space itself to dissolve boundaries, as, that is, transgressive by nature, breaking the boundaries of all conventions, social or physical.

Rather than the dignified astronomical and geometrical entity imagined by the philosophers, space was in fact a bad object—abject and ignoble in its ubiquity, endlessly invading the protected realms of society and civilization with the disruptive forces of nature. As the images illustrating Bataille's article demonstrate, space is for him a vehicle of masquerade ("it seems that an ape dressed as a woman is no more than a division of space," runs the caption to a photograph of a chimpanzee dressed like a traditional maid, with shopping basket, seated in a jungle setting). It is equally a ritual of sexual initiation ("space . . . takes the form of an ignoble initiation rite"), or, alternatively, of cannibalism ("space might become a fish swallowing another"). Finally, space would be the instrument that undermines the very foundations of legal society. A fourth photograph, of the collapse of a prison in Columbus, Ohio, is given a caption, drawn from the last paragraph of the article: "Obviously it will never enter anybody's head to lock the professors up in prison *to teach them what space is* (the day, for example, the walls collapse before the bars of their dungeons)."[18] Space has thus not only confounded the geometers, but it has demonstrated its disruptive power in the face of the most defended of institutions, reducing, so to speak, the Benthamite panopticon, constructed according to the laws of classical optics, to a formless heap of rubble. In this sense, Bataille argues, space is "pure violence," escaping time and geometry to affirm its presence as the expression of the *here-now,* the instantaneous, the simultaneous, and, by extension, the event. Space would be not simply an agent of the *informe,* a "formless" recently reconstrued by Rosalind Krauss and Yve-Alain Bois as a key to the rereading of what they see as a continuously present countercurrent in the avant-garde art of the twentieth century, but also the virulent and ubiquitous instrument of Bataille's campaign against objecthood, on behalf of the erosion of all conventional boundaries.[19]

Part II

Home Alone

Vito Acconci's Public Realm

> Public space is leaving home.
> Vito Acconci

If utopian reconstruction was the preferred method of twenties modernism, wholesale destruction the aim of postwar redevelopment, and nostalgic repetition the dream of postmodern aestheticism, then the present seems to be embracing a combination of strategic planning and tactical incursion as a way of intervening among the blighted remains of capitalism's last cities. And while the forms of this new procedure vary widely, from neosurrealist carnival to deconstructive collapse, the sensibility is common: total rebuilding, total demolition, or total revival are all blocked by the inertia of the "already built" and the "institutionally confirmed." Only a nomadic, fast-moving, small-scale, and intrusive organism can operate in the interstices of what William Gibson, returning for a moment from cyberspace, has called "Nighttown,"[1] in order to transform its aging structures, not by radical change but by gradual mutation. Here the biological analogy, long dormant in the realm of functionalist thought, returns with all the force of the new biochemical science to characterize the activities of transgressive designers: cyborgs are formed from the forced union of natural and mechanical elements; parasites attach themselves to existing structures; viruses invade apparently healthy cells.

The language of the new architectural form is deliberately derived from the vocabulary of pandemic and plague, as if, following the tradition of urban pathologies since the eighteenth century, the object were infected with the same illness attacking the subject, the city fallen prey to the same epidemic as its citizens. But the resulting strategy is radically different from the propaedeutic urbanism invented to insulate and empower the nineteenth- and early twentieth-century middle classes. Now the disease is turned back, so to speak, on the city, as a weapon in the hands of its carriers—those heirs of the so-called "dangerous and laboring classes" that were once the objects of fascinated attention and rigorous exclusion for planners and their civic clients. In the new sites of domestic biological warfare, design strategies envision the triumph of the homeless, of people with AIDS, of people of color, and of all those marginalized by gender or sexual preference, not through armed combat but through spatial revolution.

For this newly embattled society, space no longer holds the utopian promise of universalist modernism, nor the all-subsuming warmth of sixties communitarianism. Space, rather, is considered to be an already occupied terrain, a territory to be surveyed carefully, invaded silently, and with preparations made for partial retreat. The new avant-garde is no longer a joyful proclaimer of future technological or formal bliss; it is personified instead by the squatter, the panhandler, the vagrant, the unwanted stranger. It was Georg Simmel who, in the context of the huge population movements and urban invasions of the turn-of-the-century metropolis, characterized the unsettling force of this stranger who was not the "wanderer who comes today and goes tomorrow but the person who comes today and stays tomorrow."[2] In a fundamental updating of this characteristic, the squatter appropriates, the homeless refuses to move, the vagabond ignores fixed boundaries, with all the powers of a "nomadology" that, at last resort, hits and runs.

The results of this shift in tactics are architecturally demonstrated not simply in stylistic shifts but in deliberate changes of scale, ranging from the demonumentalized to the dismantled. All pretense of a piecemeal utopia à la Karl Popper (Colin Rowe), or a postmodern utopia of the fragment (Michael Graves), is dropped; what is left is a shrapnel-like shard, a sharp-pointed splinter, a remnant, a castoff, an irreducible piece of junk (Coop Himmelblau). These are not left to lie where they fell in some dystopian wasteland of the edge or the margin; they are honed into tools, weapons, and instruments of insertion, opening rifts and faults in the apparently seamless fabric of the city to let in its new inhabitants.

In the construction of this practice that transgresses all spatial boundaries, the traditional limits of art and architecture have been readily broken; a treaty of mutual sustenance forged by the Beaux-Arts in the nineteenth century has been arrogated in favor of mutual plunder. Thus an architect taking his cue from the surrealist and Fluxus movements (Frank Gehry) will collaborate with an artist taking his cue from the monumentalizing tradition of architecture (Claes Oldenburg). Within art practice itself, the architectural analogy—of structure, form, and landscape—common to the minimalist and earthwork art of the fifties and sixties is dissolved into a general concern with shelter (Krzysztof Wodiczko) and prosthetics (Elizabeth Diller and Ricardo Scofidio).

In this context, the recent work of Vito Acconci takes on a paradigmatic role. Over the last decades, in projects that range from the construction of "furniture" to the design of entire public spaces, Acconci has deliberately challenged the traditional commonplaces of architecture, both in the construction of domesticity and in the planning of the public realm. Starting with "constructions" that register the nomadic life of postindustrialism—"instant house," "mobile home," "trailer camp," and even "umbrella city" (1980–1982)—and moving through a range of domestically scaled objects—"storage unit," "overstuffed chair," "turned tables" (1984–1987)—Acconci has systematically taken apart the house and home of the American dream, finally arriving at the construct of the *Bad Dream House* (1984, 1988). Acconci's bad dream is indeed a nightmare, at least to those who would invest the house with all the values of home. Against the proponents of family values settled firmly in Ralph Lauren cottages, Acconci, long before Murphy Brown, decided to leave home. Or rather, to turn his experience of "home alone" to advantage. Gradually working outward from his body—the only shelter on which he could rely—Acconci developed the instruments of survival through a process of undressing and flaying, of appropriation and renaming.

Thus, projects like those for the *Adjustable Wall Bra* or the *Clam Shelter* (1990) stand as the metonymic devices of a reflection on the fundamentals of shelter. Here Acconci plays on the gamut of "original" shelters proposed as the basis for architecture since the "primitive hut" of Vitruvius. But rather than seriously inventing a new typology, Acconci prefers to create tropes—architecture as clothing, architecture as natural enclosure—that operate on the poetic edge of architectural belief. These constructions, in turn, are instantly removed from the genre of mere illustration by their insertion into that most sacred of architectural domains, use. For they are not only analogical forms; they

12. Vito Acconci,
Adjustable Wall Bra,
1990.

literally operate on two levels, that of the installation and that of the usable object. Further, both the *Adjustable Wall Bra* and the *Clam Shelter* work within an already critical tradition of counterarchitectural practice; they refer, that is, to the surrealist proposition (André Breton versus Le Corbusier) that architecture should return to an intrauterine state far removed from its rationalistic, technologically determined modern condition. The concept of uterine architecture, developed by Tzara in the thirties and illustrated by Matta, referred to the cave and the tent as potential sources of reformulation, as against the constructed models of huts and temples long treasured by the classical and modernist traditions, from the abbé Laugier to Le Corbusier. Acconci, shifting ground, transposes the notion of origins literally to the metonymic forms of bra and shell, revealing architecture as a play of partial objects standing in, so to speak, for their lost originals—breast and uterus—but at the same time reversing their original signification by making the container stand for the contained. Sitting in or covered by the bra, the subject becomes breast; sitting under or crawling into clam shell, the subject is put in the position of clam. In neither case can we be certain of the seriousness of the proposal; in neither case can we reject it as outside the bounds of the architectural discourse. In neither case, finally, because of the manifestly temporary, experimental, and open-ended nature of the installation, does it fall into the category of a caricatural play *on* architecture—a problem faced by many critical statements made by architects in architecture over the last twenty years. The "I(r)onic Columns" of Charles Moore and Robert Venturi, ubiquitously scattered from the Piazza d'Italia in New Orleans to the Oberlin Art Gallery, might be faintly amusing when first viewed, but their status as jokes is eroded by their unrepeatability. By contrast, the malleability and transmutability of the bra-clam combos ensures a range of possible contexts and significations that is, in architectural terms at least, virtually inexhaustible. Similarly, Acconci's fluorescent furniture projects of 1992 propose the double reading of furniture at once transformed through light (Dan Flavins you can sit and sleep in) and readily utilized, as already prefigured in the Multi-beds of 1991.

In the same way, Acconci's play on the spatial relations of shelter, with obvious political resonance in the context of contemporary homelessness, avoids the positivism of projects, like those of Krzysztof Wodiczko, that attempt at once to ironize and to solve the homeless problem. Acconci, taking up the theme of mass-produced mobile housing advanced in the twenties by those who would have turned aircraft and tank production to peacetime uses, invents a more ambiguous kind of shelter: one that is both a city of mobile homes and a display of mobile life. Once within his Mobile Linear City that pulls out from the rear of a flatbed truck, with all the practical affect of a technological solution, the inhabitant is framed by a series of increasingly small "housing units," each performing a different function, from living to dining to sleeping, until the end unit with its services is reached. But the project is more than a comment on the functional divisions of mass housing; it is also a carefully constructed theatrical presentation of the "house" as a kind of anthropological exposition of the everyday. The resulting spectacle, reminiscent of Guy Debord's polemical analysis of the televisual "spectacle de la maison" in the late 1950s, is produced deliberately by a witty inversion of private and public space that forces a space—closed up until used—to be opened up to the outside once in use.

At the larger scale of the public institution, Acconci likewise follows the subversive path, first sketched by Georges Bataille, that sees the architectural monument as a literal crystallization of power and cultural accretion; as an almost geological phenomenon. From the simple institutional critique represented by the State Supreme Court Lawn project, Carson City, 1989, where a half-sized replica of the court building is buried in the ground in order to offer the new roof as a kind of "people's court," to the North Carolina Revenue Building, Raleigh, 1991, which is turned into an island by cutting a moat around it and inserting a slanting mirror beneath it so that it seems to float, all the verities of institutional stability are put into question. This recurring theme of reversal and submersion, which brings roofs, so to speak, down to earth, is repeated in the housing scheme for Regensburg (1990), where the pyramidal roofs are literally "put into people's hands."

On another level, Acconci works to disturb the clarity of the forms that endowed each institutional type with legibility among the gamut of types that constituted the surveillance society. The project for Las Vegas City Hall, for example, deliberately presents a double and monstrous reading of a city hall as church by means of a giant cross placed against, but peeling away from, its end wall, reflecting the signs of the casinos. Here the doubling of the building in a critical form is supplanted by a doubling of the reading that announces the city hall as a church, and this in turn as a casino.

This questioning of the limits of the program and its representation is taken to further extremes in the school projects. In the Longview School, Phoenix (1990), Acconci constructs a "school outside the school," as if the result of an explosion whereby the pieces of the original school were scattered, tilted, turned over. Such a literal deconstruction of the school, where elements of existing buildings are dismembered and dismantled—as if the kit of architectural parts carefully assembled by the typologically sophisticated architects of the seventies was now taken by an unruly child and scattered on the floor— is more than a caricature of subversive overturning, however. Each element is given a new and public use as it comes to rest outside the institution it apparently destroys. As Acconci writes, "The function of public art is to de-design."[3]

Here the landform itself is brought into play as an active agent of the almost carnivalesque overturing of the school. In the Longview design, as well as in the Lafontaine Avenue School in the Bronx (1990), the ground rises up as if in a post-quake wave threatening to swallow up the constructions placed so confidently on its surface. Nothing is stable in Acconci's world; underneath the ground, which is no more than a quagmire, there are forces always ready to rise up, swallow up, and submerge what is above ground, to the extent that the very certainties of "above" and "below" are put into doubt.

Extending the traditional aesthetic notion of "landscape," Acconci then expands his architectural criticism to the wider public spaces themselves; Autry Park, Houston (1990), constructs a seesaw out of the land, whereby the ground, in Acconci's metaphor, pivots around its own center, the resulting forms, thrust up as if by geological pressure, establishing new public spaces, seating possibilities, and boundaries. At times, this land movement absorbs the surrounding architecture in such a way as to render architecture and landscape indistinguishable. These themes are brought together in the recent project for the Square Jules Bocquet, in Amiens, France (1992). Here, the square is treated like an outdoor room, but the enclosing walls of the square, far from forming a static and comforting boundary to the place, repeat *en abyme* from the periphery to the center. What Acconci calls "ghost facades" fill the square, sometimes tilting progressively to form seats, or scaled to form accentuated perspective: "The ground," Acconci writes, "acquires the face of the building."

Each of the projects has, then, a clear political agenda, both within architecture and in society; they propose a continuous, ebullient and witty questioning of everyday life in buildings and spaces. Their reversals and inversions, their sexual and bodily innuendoes play with the unbreakable tension between bodies and objects, ourselves and the ground on which we walk. In the process, Acconci has succeeded in transforming the rules of the architectural game, and, for those architects and urban designers who would look and listen, has proposed strategies to study in tackling the blasted quarters of Los Angeles, Chicago, or New York. Further, he has extended the very lenses with which we look at our spaces, domestic and urban, private and public, investing them and their containers with diabolical life so that we can no longer see any comforting distinctions between buildings, spaces, and the public art that decorates them. "Public art," he writes, "builds up, like a wart, on a building." It is in the interstices of such rhizogenic growths that the homeless, the conspiratorial, the until-now forgotten might shelter, meet, and even live.

Full House

Rachel Whiteread's Postdomestic Casts

As we have seen, the notion of architecture as comprised of "space," rather than of built elements like walls and columns, is a relatively modern one; it first emerged with any force at the end of the nineteenth century as a result of German psychological theories of *Raum*—one thinks of Schmarsow, Lipps, and their art historical followers Wölfflin, Riegl, Frankl, et al. Space, indeed, became one of the watchwords of modernist architecture from Adolf Loos to Le Corbusier and Frank Lloyd Wright, rapidly emerging as a primary critical term for the definition of what was "modern." Space, more even than function, became a limit term for modernity, not least for its connection with time both before and after Einstein. Space moved; it was fluid, open, filled with air and light; its very presence was a remedy for the impacted environments of the old city: the modern carrier of the Enlightenment image of hygiene and liberty. For most modernist architects, space was universal, and was intended to flood both public and private realms equally. Space in these terms, at least after Frank Lloyd Wright, was even politically charged; the Italian critic Bruno Zevi argued insistently after the Second World War that Wrightian space was synonymous with democratic space, as against a previous and undemocratic "Fascist" inattention to space.

With hindsight, the specific kinds of politics embedded in the idea of modernist space have inevitably become more ambiguous, as the trumpeted beneficence of modern architecture and its attendant "space" for contemporary living has all too clearly demonstrated its shortcomings, and as the alliances of modernist architects and unsavory patrons in the thirties have been revealed by historians. But the notion that space itself is good has hardly been erased from our mental vocabularies. This might well be a result of what one might call space's historical pedigree. As a product of theories of psychological extension—either of projection or introjection—space naturally and early on became a cure for the twin phobias of late nineteenth-century urbanism, agoraphobia and claustrophobia. To open up the city would, in Le Corbusier's terms, and in much post-CIAM rhetoric, rid it of all closed, dirty, dangerous, and unhealthy corners; and, in the absence of dramatic contrast between open and closed spaces, would rid metropolitan populations of any spatial anxiety they might have felt in the first wave of urbanization.

13. Rachel Whiteread, *House*, 1993–1994.

Perhaps the residue of this attitude partly accounted for the virulence of London County Council attacks on Rachel Whiteread's *House*. This cast of the interior space of a soon-to-be demolished terrace house was accused of standing in the way of slum clearance, of blocking the planting of healthy greenery, of making a monument to an unhealthy and claustrophobic past. On another level, that of the "house," the simple act of filling in space, of closing what was once open, would naturally counter the received wisdom of a century of planning dogma that *open* is better if not absolutely good. The "house" of Rachel Whiteread was on the surface a clear enough statement, and one carefully executed with all the material attention paid by a sculptor to the casting of a complicated figure piece. But seldom has an event of this kind—acknowledged as temporary, and supported by the artistic community—evoked so vituperative a reaction in the popular press. It was as if we had been transported back in time to the moment when Duchamp signed the *Fountain.* Since its unveiling, Whiteread's house has been portrayed in cartoons, and in the critical press, with varying degrees of allegory and irony, even its supporters resorting to punning headlines—on the order of "the house that Rachel built," "home work," "house calls," "a concrete idea," "the house that Rachel unbuilt," "home truths," "no house room to art."

But from another viewpoint Whiteread's *House,* far from undermining modernism's spatial ideology, reinforces it, and on its own terms. For, since the development of Gestalt psychology, space has been subject to all the intellectual and experiential reversals involved in the identification of figure and ground, as well as the inevitable ambiguities between the two that were characteristic, as critics from Alois Riegl to Colin Rowe have pointed out, of modernism itself. Thus many modernists have employed figure/ground reversals to demonstrate the very palpability of space. The Italian architect Luigi Moretti even constructed plaster models in the 1950s to illustrate what he saw as the history of different spatial types in architecture. These models were cast, as it were, as the solids of what in reality were spatial voids; the spaces of compositions such as Hadrian's Villa were illustrated as sequences of solids as if space had suddenly been revealed as dense and impenetrable.[1] Architectural schools from the late 1930s on have employed similar methods to teach "space"—the art of the impalpable—by means of palpable models. By this method, it was thought, all historical architecture might be reduced to the essential characteristics of space, and pernicious "styles" of historicism might be dissolved in the flux of abstraction.

In these terms, Whiteread's *House* simply takes its place in this tradition, recognizable to architects, if not to artists or the general public, as a didactic illustration of nineteenth-century domestic "space." To an architect, whether trained in modernism or its "brutalist" offshoots, her work takes on the aspect of a full-scale model, a three-dimensional exercise in spatial dynamics and statics. A not accidental side result of this exercise is the transformation of the nineteenth-century *realist* house into an abstract composition; Whiteread has effectively built a model of a house that resembles a number of paradigmatic modern houses, from Wright to Loos, from Rudolph Schindler to Paul Rudolph.

In this sense her *House* would arouse the ire of the entire postmodern and traditionalist movement in Britain and elsewhere, dedicated to the notion that "abstraction" equals "eyesore."

But it seems also true that this project touched another nerve entirely, one not dissociated from those we have mentioned but more generally shared outside the architectural and artistic community, and deeply embedded in the "domestic" character of the intervention. Whiteread touched, and according to some commentators mutilated, the house, by necessity the archetypal space of homeliness. Article after article referred to the silencing of the past life of the house, the traces of former patterns of life now rendered dead but preserved, as it were, in concrete if not in aspic. To a cultural historian, this commentary, pro and con, was strangely reminiscent of the accounts of the discovery, excavation, and subsequent exhibiting of Herculaneum and Pompeii. These disinterred cities, which had been preserved precisely because they had been filled up like molds by lava and ashes, seemed, when excavated, to have been alive only shortly before, their inhabitants caught by the disaster in grotesque postures of surprise as they went about their daily work. Much travel and fantasy literature of the nineteenth century circled around this point: the life-in-suspension represented by the mummified traces of everyday existence. A cartoon of the Whiteread *House* by Kipper Williams fed on just this fear, that of being trapped inside a space filled so violently, the space and air evacuated around a still-living body.

Nineteenth- and twentieth-century writers and literary critics, from E. T. A. Hoffmann to Henry James, subsumed this horror of domestic interment/disinterment in the popular genre and theory of the uncanny, a genre often evoked in the discussion of Whiteread's project. This characterization would have it that the very traces of life extinguished, of death stalking through the center of life, of the "unhomeliness" of filled space contrasted with the former homeliness of lived space (to use the terminology of the phenomenologist-psychologist Eugène Minkowski) raised the specter of demonic or magical forces, at the very least inspiring speculation as to the permanence of architecture, at most threatening all cherished ideals of domestic harmony—the "children who once played on the doorstep" variety of nostalgia so prevalent among Whiteread's critics. Robin Whale's cartoon of the negative impression of Whiteread's "cast" body in the wall of *House* echoes this sensibility; unwittingly it stems from a line of observations on the uncanny effects of impressions of body parts beginning with Chateaubriand's horrified vision of the cast breast of a young woman at Pompeii: "Death, like a sculptor, has molded his victim," he noted.

Added to this was what many writers saw as the disturbing qualities of the "blank" windows in the *House;* this might again be traced back to romantic tropes of blocked vision, the evil eye, and the uncanny effect of mirrors that cease to reflect the self; Hoffmann and Victor Hugo, in particular, delighted in stories of boarded-up houses whose secrets might only be imagined. The abandoned hulk of Whiteread's *House* holds much in common with that empty house on Guernsey so compelling for Hugo's fantasies of secret history in *Les travailleurs de la mer.*

Psychoanalysis, however, and especially since the publication of Freud's celebrated article on "The Uncanny" in 1919, has complicated such romantic reactions by linking the uncanny to the more complex and hidden forces of sexual drives, death wishes, and Oedipal fantasies. Taking off from the difficult formulation hazarded by Schelling in the 1830s that the uncanny was "something that ought to have remained secret and hidden but which has come to light," Freud linked this sensation to experiences of a primal type—such as the primal scene witnessed by Little Hans—that had been suppressed only to show themselves unexpectedly in other moments and guises. Joined to such primary reactions, the causes of uncanny feelings included, for Freud, the nostalgia that was tied to the impossible desire to return to the womb, the fear of dead things coming alive, the fragmentation of things that seemed all too like bodies for comfort. Here we might recognize themes that arose in some of the responses to *House,* including the literal impossibility of entering into the house itself, as well as the possibility that its closed form held unaccounted secrets and horrors. In psychoanalytical terms, Whiteread's project seems to follow the lead of Dada and surrealism in their exploration of "unhomely" houses precisely for their sexual and mental shock effect: the "intrauterine" houses imagined by Tristan Tzara, the soluble habitations delineated by Dalí, the "soft" houses of Matta offer ready examples, against which in post-avant-garde terms the *House* seems to pose itself as a decidedly *non-*uterine space, a *non-*soft environment. As critics have noted, Whiteread's notion of "art" as temporary act or event similarly takes its cue from Dada precedents.

But Freud's analysis seems lacking precisely when confronted with terms that imply a non–object based uncanny—an uncanny generated by space rather than its contents. Freud, despite a late recognition that space might be less universal than Kant had claimed, remained singularly impervious to spatial questions, and it was left to phenomenologists from Minkowski to Binswanger to recognize that space itself might be psychologically determined and thereby to be read as a symptom, if not an instrument, of trauma and neurosis. Tellingly, Minkowski writes of "black" or "dark" space, that space which, despite all loss of vision—in the dark or blindfolded—a subject might still palpably feel: the space of bodily and sensorial if not intellectual existence. It is such a space that Whiteread constructed, a blindingly suffocating space that, rather than receiving its contents with comfort, expelled them like a breath.

And it was this final reversal that seems in retrospect to have been most pointed. For what was the modern house, if not the cherished retreat from agoraphobia—that "housewife's disease" so common in suburbia, and so gendered from its first conception in the 1870s? Thrust so unceremoniously into the void, the domestic subject no longer finds a shell, clinging, as if to Géricault's raft, to the external surface of an uninhabitable and absolute claustrophobic object, forced to circulate around the edges of a once womblike space. Therein lay an origin of the uncanny feelings that arose when such desires, long repressed, suddenly reemerged in unexpected forms. In Whiteread's world, where even the illusion of return "home" is refused, the uncanny itself is banished. No longer can the fundamental terrors of exclusion and banishment, of homelessness and alienation, be ameliorated by their aestheticization in horror stories and psychoanalytic family romances; with all doors to the *unheimlich* firmly closed, the domestic subject is finally out in the cold forever.

And if *House* constitutes itself as a memory trace of former occupation and a traditional notion of dwelling, her most recent project, the winning entry for a Holocaust Memorial on the Judenplatz in Vienna (1998), takes this to a public conclusion. This project has been described by critic David Thistlewood as "a closed windowless double-cube of a building with a flat roof, and beneath a plain parapet what would appear from a distance to be vertically striated concrete walls," which on closer inspection prove to be the cast impressions of a vast library of books inside, the voids behind books "described by their gathered edges and the containing shelves," a move anticipated in *Untitled (Shelves)* of 1996. For Thistlewood, "the lost presence of the books projects outwards towards infinity, interacting with the world of real events in which the work is sited," standing for the entire archive of Jewish history.[2] In the context of the discussion of *House* the memorial does not simply, as Thistlewood notes, turn sculpture into architecture, but rather it transforms both. The interior as exterior, the "cast" of a building *as* building, with its own interior, and a cast, further, that is made of a building that never existed except in imaginary and typological form—the ark, the Temple—here intersects sculptural and architectural norms to constitute something else, a "neither-nor" of both. This crystallization of a type form, a manifestation in iconographic terms of the purely imaginary image, brings it into contact with the everyday, and with a haptic, almost felt relationship with the viewer, now become a potential toucher of books, an opener of truths, substituted for a distanced vision of monumental form.

A comparison with another submission for the same competition, the Vienna Holocaust memorial of Peter Eisenman, will clarify the point. In the Eisenman project, as in Whiteread's, the concern seems not so much to iconically represent "memory" as to emulate its processes. But where Whiteread inserts her work into the processes of everyday experience, acting on and within a subject/viewer's own memory work, Eisenman emulates those processes of remembering and forgetting in the generation of the architectural object itself, leaving traces of this generation as clues wherein the subject/viewer, attempting to reconstitute the process of generation, will by analogy, so to speak, exercise its memory. Whiteread, so to speak, turns to the memory of life, Eisenman to a figurative emulation of that memory in the parallel memory of the architectural object. But it would be a mistake to relegate Whiteread too quickly to the realm of the "realist" as opposed to Eisenman's more abstract procedure. For the Whiteread memorial is after something different from architecture—or at least from that architecture of which the Eisenman project speaks. Her project looks to the always uneasy status of the monument within architecture, its wavering between art and use. As Adolf Loos recognized, and Hegel had theorized, architecture's symbolic role at once constitutes its "essence"—art turned to symbolizing life in three-dimensional form—while its use role entirely undermines this primal symbolism—architecture defined not in terms of idea but of function. Whiteread undermines this binary problem by deliberately confusing sculpture and architecture, and by developing a kind of mutant object that cannot be defined in either set of terms, that asks to be defined indeed by this very refusal.

Lost in Space

Toba Khedoori's Architectural Fragments

In the history of modern art and aesthetics, the fragment has had a double signification. As a reminder of the past once whole but now fractured and broken, as a demonstration of the implacable effects of time and the ravages of nature, it has taken on the connotations of nostalgia and melancholy, even of history itself. As an incomplete piece of a potentially complete whole, it has pointed toward a possible world of harmony in the future, a utopia perhaps, that it both represents and constructs. For the romantics at the beginning of the nineteenth century the fragment combined these two meanings in a highly charged ideal in which, as Schlegel characterized it, the fragment, "like a hedgehog curled up in a ball," was both complete in itself yet pointed Janus-like to the irretrievable past and the unknowable future. Ruins, for example, were invested with all the sadness of destruction, whether of vandalism or natural erosion, and at the same time were seen to comprise the building blocks of restoration and renewal. Whether, following Ruskin, it was argued that there could be no return to the past and therefore no authentic restoration, or, following Viollet-le-Duc, that restoration might once and for all complete the fragment in all its previously unrealized perfection, the postromantic theory of the fragment held its double nature in a precarious balance.

Modernism, however, set out to break what was understood to be the nineteenth century's unhealthy investment in the past, and attempted, not altogether successfully, to deny any nostalgic flavor to the fragment, putting its hopes instead on the notion of incompletion as an intimation of perfection in the future. Thus, in architecture, the work of Le Corbusier, Mies van der Rohe, Wright, and their followers was uneasily set between the geometrically perfect ideal city (the Ville Radieuse, Broadacre City) and whatever unsatisfactory piece it was possible to construct in the present. Objects, rooms, buildings, areas of a city became so many fragments at different scales, incomplete "types" conveying all the force of a dream to be fulfilled, a space to be occupied, a life to be lived. At the same time, the processes of modern reproduction, notably the film and the photograph but also the assembly line and the conveyor belt, implied a technique, if not a technology, of the fragment that allowed for its reidealization in terms of the "real," a literal and material piece of a new constructivist world.

On the level of modernist aesthetics, the idea of the fragment was once again introduced so as to be instrumental in the new forms of representation of film and photography, and was seen as an element of the theory of montage (Eisenstein) or of salutary estrangement and shock (Brecht). The work of art in the age of its "mechanical reproducibility," as Walter Benjamin put it, had the potential not only to be absorbed into the processes of production and consumption but also to resist them, and the fragment, with all its implications of the incomplete and the broken, the allegorical and the melancholic, was a powerful ally in such resistance. That Freud had exposed the unconscious operations of fragmentary memories and dream images only lent force to the claim that the fragment worked secretly to undermine the structures and commonplaces of an increasingly mechanical existence.

Where postmodernism differed from modernism, at least in its treatment of the fragment, was in a return to the historicist, nostalgic and romanticized versions of a past, both lost and retrieved through the reassimilation of pieces of history into a present that at once ironized their effect and banalized their form. No longer an instrument of shock or alienation, the fragment was transformed by postmodernist architecture into a sign of respected tradition, a guarantee of comfort in history, with a mission to ward off or absorb the discomforts of modernity.

In this context of a shifting but interlocking tradition of the fragment, an interpretation of the recent work of Toba Khedoori might be tempted not only to draw comparisons but also to imply historical continuities. At first glance, the pieces of buildings and structures presented in her paintings—railway tunnels, stairs, fences, walls, windows, doors, houses—seem ready to present themselves as the unquestioned heirs of the modern and postmodern tradition of the fragment—incomplete but drawn from a readily understandable repertory of types, broken and uninhabited but perhaps ready for fixing and reinhabitation. The railway paintings might even display a trace of nostalgia for the rapidly disappearing world of tunnels, stations, coaches, and crosswalks constructed out of machine-age steel; the relentless minimalism of the environments implied by the doors, walls, stairs, terraces, and auditoria might equally be understood as implying a return to a purified modernism after the excesses of postmodernism, somewhat along the lines of the neorationalism espoused by Aldo Rossi and his followers in the 1970s.

And yet a closer examination reveals a number of blockages to such an easy, and all too seamless, absorption of Khedoori's work into a historicist narrative of the kind that in the 1820s might have been construed as one of ruination and renewal, that in the 1920s might have been written in terms of loss of aura, and that in the 1980s might have been cast in terms of the resistance to nostalgia. For in many ways, despite their appearance, these portions of architectural environments do not fall into the category of "fragment" at all.

In the first place, a fragment demands a particular scale; whether small or vast, as in Edmund Burke's concepts of the miniature sublime revealed by microscopes or the boundless sublime revealed by telescopes, the fragment took its place in a recognizable world of scaled elements, among which, in true humanist style, the human figure remained the scale of reference. In Khedoori, however, despite the obvious extra-large size of the paintings, there seems to be no humanly dimensioned referent by which to measure their true scale. In the second place, a fragment demands a context, a possible and easily visualized site from which one might imagine it was initially snatched, and to which it might, just as easily, be envisioned as returning. But in the case of Khedoori's elements, there seems no readily identifiable "whole," no former context, in which we might envisage their original state or future restoration. Thirdly, if the common denominator of all historicist fragments was their place in and implications for a narrative of some kind or another, a story, so to speak, of which they formed a part and which they encapsulated in some symbolic or allegorical sense, Khedoori's resist such integration. They seem to stand alone in a world of their own isolation, their origins and endings equally sealed from narrative interpretation. Hermetic and withdrawn, they fail as symbols by the fact of their total alienation from ideal worlds, past, present, or future; they fail as allegories by their stubborn resistance to history and temporality. Neither ideals—their flat depiction destroys all sense of anything but a dry materiality—nor ruins—their near perfection belies any effect of nature or time—they stand alone and complete in themselves.

Perhaps the most striking examples of this double refusal would be the early railway paintings. For if railways and their accouterments signified anything in the nineteenth and twentieth centuries, it was movement, progress, and passage; stations were redolent moments in a narrative of the journey that, more rapid and less romantic than that of an eighteenth-century explorer, nevertheless gained affect from the mechanisms of motion—steam and electricity—if not from the patterns of alternate rhythm and boredom, stopping and starting, so elegantly incorporated into the Proustian narrative of temporality and space. But Khedoori's trains, or rather her coaches, seem to point in no direction, have no end and no beginning; her tunnels are empty and devoid of anticipation (no train-spotting E. E. Nesbit or Reverend Awdry would stand at their mouths, eagerly awaiting the passage of the next express); her crosswalks are without tracks beneath and onlookers above. In short, there is no train story here.

And if Khedoori's paintings reject all appeals to history and narrative, so also do they resist all conventions of representation. Thus while the depictions of railway elements are composed with apparently painstaking accuracy, projected in perspective or axonometric like so many engineering renderings, they are, in reality, supremely nonconstructed, or rather, carefully constructed to look constructed, and a closer inspection reveals many slight distortions and "flaws" in the positioning of viewer and viewpoints. They twist and bend in perspectival space, revealing their impossibilities and responding to a method of painting that, in Khedoori's case, works without setting up, moving across the pieced-together sheets with studied precision but without geometrical or perspectival concern, as if imitating an autodidactic experience of perspective representation, but suppressing all conscious knowledge of its laws and underlying principles.

This is even more true of the more recent paintings, where it seems that a concerted effort is made to block perspective altogether. Thus *Untitled* (*Fence*) is seemingly construed as a continuation of the space of the gallery, with the area it encloses slightly pigmented as if to imply a flow from gallery floor into the space of the painting; but with a trick, or a "mistake," of perspective, the left rail widens slightly toward the viewer and the space is suddenly inverted, so as to form an underside of a plane sliding vertiginously into the floor. Here the strategy has the effect not only of destroying the illusory space of extension "through the window" implied by traditional Albertian perspective theory, but also of removing the traditional vantage point of the viewer, who in this instance feels pressed back from the wall as if expelled from the visual field.

With no space allowed for any hypothetical viewer, and with perspective refusing a conventional window on the world, the space of the gallery itself is put into play. And yet here too one is at an impasse. In one sense there is abundance of space—in the gallery, on the wall, around the architectural element—but in another there is no space left. In the depiction of the *Chainlink Fence,* for example, the enclosure is pressed down into the lower left-hand corner, emphasizing a claustrophobic exclusion of the viewer. Further, the elaborately prepared texturing of the paper surface, or background of the painting, makes of it yet another wall, a filled blank, rejecting entry by the viewer, pushing the subject back in a picture plane rejection of depth. In this sense, what might have been the "ground" ready to receive a positive figure is itself prepared as a figure, with all the imperfections of dust, floor traces, and gray-white pigment, a figure that is definitively not the wall, although posing as and evidently hiding another wall on which the sheets, themselves figures on the figurative field, are ostentatiously hung, with all the evident imperfections of such hanging, buckling, rippling, and slightly bowing so as to distort once more the cool engineering of the perspective. There are here no pristine panels, no seamless backgrounds such as characterized the art of abstraction or of minimalism, nor do we find an echo of the white sublime. The "white" of the vast polar or misty sublime of romanticism—the white of Caspar David Friedrich's or Samuel Taylor Coleridge's "fogs"—is here definitively dirtied, gray-white and freckled with imperfections.

Interpretation is occluded further by the very flatness of the "figures" superimposed on this ground. *Doors,* for example, which presents itself as an endless field of "doors" (cut from a strip of external walkways, as in a sixties apartment dwelling, or perhaps, if an interior facade, like prison access galleries—a "jailhouse rock" no longer rocking), presses toward the viewer through a flatness of view that refuses to open itself up or down in perspective, guardrails pushed against the doors with no space for an entering occupant. Each door, finally, is provided with a conventional peephole or window panel, but behind it there is nothing, except, that is, the ground of the paper itself.

Such a materiality of the ground, joined to the thin and unreal precision of the figures, further closes off the possibility of any abstract reading, and we are returned to the literalness of the paintings, insistent that they do not signify other spaces or objects and content to occupy the field in which they are placed. Thus the *Wall* is not a wall in the normal definition of the term; it has no thickness, nor does it "stand by itself" in space. Rather it is attached relentlessly to the surface of the painting, allowing no movement around it, nor viewer in front of it. Stairs, similarly, which normally would be seen as if situated on a ground or in a field, are presented as if all other architectural elements and the spaces that bind them have been removed, or indeed have never existed; returned to their nature as drawings alone, as distorted depictions of depictions.

Here we might begin to discern a more or less consistent strategy of representation, one that, based on the traditional strategies of three-dimensional depiction, but in an entirely illusory way, nevertheless implies a programmatic place for the contemporary viewer. Whereas throughout the classical and modern periods the viewpoint, and therefore by implication the viewer, have been (distorted or not) essential to the comprehension of the represented idea, now Khedoori seems to pull her objects back from any such participatory involvement. Where even the most radically abstract of modernist and minimalist constructions were in the end deployed with reference to a subject, however effaced and maimed, these images hover in a spaceless place where no one can follow, or more importantly can be situated.

Thus, to take one example, the image of the *House* with its sides taken off can initially be inserted into the tradition of all such views from the nineteenth century on, views imagined in order to bring the private into the public realm, to reveal the complex inner life of private space to the outsider. Thence the celebrated section of an Haussmannian apartment house published by Texier in the 1840s, where each interior level is characterized according to its class occupation, implying a grand Balzacian narrative of mixing and separation; thence, too, in the modern period, the photocollages of Robert Doisneau, where intimate scenes of everyday life are assembled in section, creating a vision of transparency from public to private, or Georges Perec's republication of Saul Steinberg's section of a New York apartment building in *Life, a User's Manual,* intimating a realm of precise description and a discursive space of living. Mondrian's celebrated Paris paintings of 1914–1918, poised between ab-

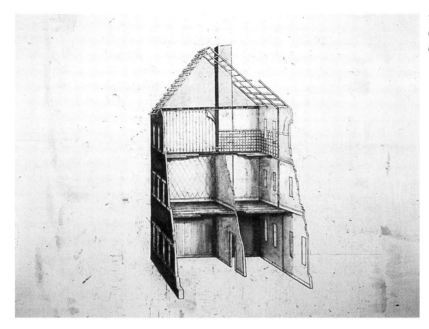

straction and representation, where the section of a partially demolished apartment building revealed on the exposed party walls is used as a literal framework for the working out of an abstract grid of flatter and flatter space, would here be seen as a typical inversion of this tradition.

But in Khedoori's *House* we can descry no such comforting project of realism or abstraction. Indeed it is not even clear that the house has ever been inhabited at all, for it seems, rather, cut away as in the conventions of architectural drawing, to expose the structure. The outer walls are already marked with the implication of endless rows of faceless windows; the party walls and floor structures are only partially shown, with all their materials carefully designated—brick, wood, plaster—as if to some distant specification of an absent engineer.

Perhaps a clue to the place awarded to, or rather withdrawn from, the contemporary subject/viewer in these otherwise silent images would be provided by the recent painting of an *Auditorium,* where the seating is shown from above, without stage or proscenium, and moreover without audience. The rows of seats are viewed from a privileged vantage point, as if hovering in middle distance, so that the chairs seem to be a field or mat covering a patch of warped ground, with the surrounding attributes of theater or cinema erased. The viewing eye is thus distributed across the field of chairs, unevenly, as the rows are not all themselves completely represented, and all conventional reference points for the gaze—stage, proscenium, play, and performance—are displaced into a void, without symmetry of axis or perspectival organization. The eye, which conventionally represents the subject, is thereby freed from bodily connection, wandering aimlessly and disembodied across a field that no longer provides a point of rest or place of entry. And with the dispersal of the eye, all pretense of home, of retrievable places and reconstructed spaces, is gone. In its place a "virtual" subject, bodiless and omniscient, inhabits these abandoned sites that appear to have been assembled, not so long ago, out of the remnants of former nonvirtual sites, but which now are suspended in a nondimensional web, amidst the debris of so many other once active "home pages."

Deep Space/Repressed Memory

Mike Kelley's Educational Complex

The ability of art to construct a critical model for architectural practice has been evident since the Renaissance reinvention of perspectival space. Baroque trompe-l'oeil, nineteenth-century panoramas, and the invention of film have worked to reinforce the especially provocative role of innovations in the representational arts for architecture. The modernist avant-gardes, with their emphasis on movement and aesthetic synthesthesia, filmic montage and cubist rotation, produced their own image of an architecture transformed by spatial performance, the body in space acting as a device by which to undermine the canonical virtues of monumentality. More recently, performances, installations, and land and earth projects have often intersected with and doubled as architectural interventions. All have in some way transformed the space of architectural projection, the manner in which architecture defines its relations with moving and sensing subjects.

On the surface, Mike Kelley's recent "architectural models," evoking his memory of the spaces in which he lived and worked since childhood in the project *Educational Complex,* signal a natural extension of this long tradition of mutual spatial influence between art and architecture. As artworks they seem to comment on the realm of architecture, even taking on the shape of architectural projects, produced and presented in the form of meticulously drawn and measured models. They might even be seen as dealing directly with architectural issues, seemingly concerned, for example, with the nature of housing or of institutions. This is, of course, hardly a new phenomenon in the contemporary art world; from the moment sometime during the 1960s when, to borrow Rosalind Krauss's formulation, sculpture began to play in an "expanded field," art has toyed metaphorically and literally with the architectural dimension. Minimalism, installation art, performance art, land art have all

15. Mike Kelley, *The Educational Complex*, 1995.

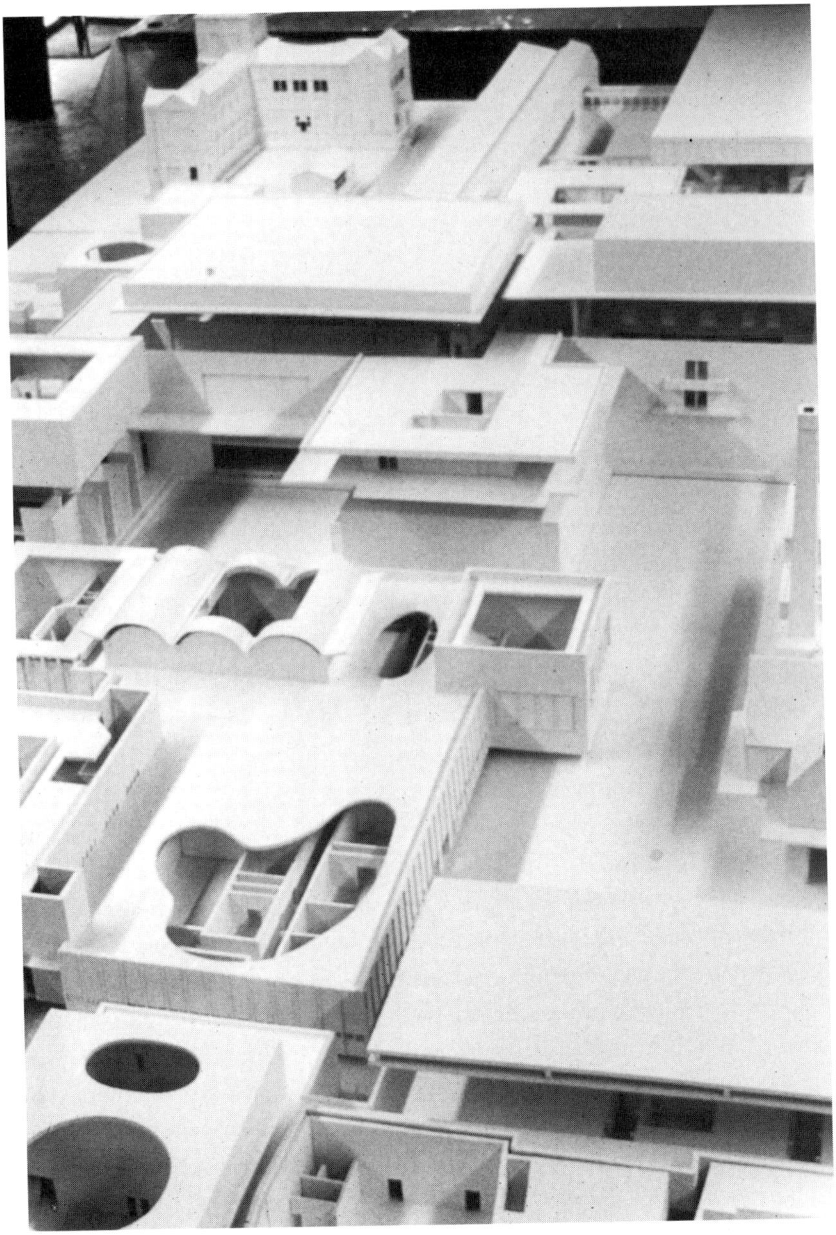

engaged spatial concerns both metaphorically (in the case of discursive en-
quiries, or architectural "ethnographies" as Hal Foster has recently termed
them, such as those of Hans Haacke) and literally (in the case of artists such as
Robert Smithson), often as well directly acting on the architectural object (one
thinks of Gordon Matta-Clark); all by implication critical of received architectural theory and practice.

Kelley's recent work might then be construed as a simple continuation
and elaboration of these preoccupations, especially as Kelley himself, from the
1980s on, was an active performance artist and distributed many of his installations within highly elaborated spatial settings. But the peculiar quality that
marks these new works as different, both in characteristic and kind, from earlier "sculptural" projects is that, in a very self-conscious way, they claim and
take on the status of architecture. Rather than sculptures entering an expanded
field in order, so to speak, to "work on" the limits of sculpture, and testing these
limits as they come into question with ever-expanding spatial dimensions, in
works that are architectural more by implication and analogy than by nature,
these projects have fully entered the architectural discipline; they rely for their
effect precisely on their architectural dimensions, and their messages are coded
in terms that would be incomprehensible outside of architectural discourse.
Which is not to say that they have fully realized themselves as works of architecture; indeed, they stop short precisely at the moment when we would want
to recognize them as "real" projects, and precisely in that momentary ambiguity between the possible and the impossible retain their critical status and their
place in art. Where they are fully architectural is in the questions they raise, and
the special "field" from which those questions have been derived, posing specifically architectural questions about the nature of domestic and institutional
space and its role in the formation of a human subject. More particularly, however, what marks these projects out from their apparent antecedents in the seventies and eighties is their insistent and almost obsessive interest in *memory,*
and at the same time their interrogation of *space* as a primary vehicle for tracing its repression and recovery. Beginning with an interest in contemporary
theories of "repressed memory syndrome," Kelley attempted to recover the
memory of buildings in which he had been educated and to map these memories on their existing plans in order to produce complex models. With a "loss
of memory," and thereby of space, of up to (in his estimate) eighty percent of

the structures, these lost spaces were modeled as solid blocks (blocked memory), while divergences between remembered patterns of use and actual forms were forced in favor of the memory, resulting in complex three-dimensional projects that seemed to Kelley almost utopian in their impossibility. These models, then, emerging as a memory map of the "geography" of his education, as he put it, were also notations of the failure of memory, the unretrievability of past occupations in space: "Buildings that I had occupied almost every day for years could barely be recalled. The teachers, courses, and activities held within them are a vast undifferentiated swamp."[1]

The intersection of memory and space is by no means new in architectural theory: indeed, it informs the ancient construction of memory itself, from the memory arts of classical rhetoricians like Quintillian to the memory theaters of the Renaissance. In this tradition, the names or concepts to be remembered are represented by objects, and the objects in turn deliberately set in a sequence, taking their place within an already remembered plan or architecturally defined path of movement. Quintillian recommended memorizing a palace; Giordano Bruno and the Renaissance theorists preferred that the objects/concepts be arranged within the space of a theater—thence the notion of the "theater of memory," so brilliantly described by the historian Frances Yates. The art of memory, then, is the ability to pass through a series of rooms, or through a specifically defined space, in imagination, each room or position in space providing a place or *topos* for the thing to be remembered. Here, architecture acts as a frame for the object or name, and space acts as a positioning device for locating the desired recollection. In both cases, architectural space is a precondition, an invented and remembered fiction for something else, for something potentially forgotten.

Mike Kelley's buildings, by contrast, are themselves the objects of memory—as institutional structures and frames of the subject's formation in time, buildings remembered in the full, post-Lacanian, post-Foucauldian consciousness that the subject not only develops in, but is developed through, space. Where, in earlier performance or installation projects, Kelley staged the body, inside and out, in all its scatological relations with other bodies and with fetishistic objects, in these buildings it is disembodied memory that attempts to reconstruct a kind of psychic map of early development. Indeed, their production is envisaged as a kind of practical self-analysis, a process of recuperating memorized space through drawing, matching it to "real" space and modeling the difference, so to speak, by forcing the one to adapt to the other. In places, what is remembered, although demonstrably "false" vis-à-vis actuality, is given primacy; this is the case of the entrance to the Catholic Elementary School, remembered on the left of the building though evidently on the right. The maintenance of the left-hand entry produced, as Kelley remarked, "a completely unusable interior architecture, with classrooms much too narrow to be functional and three times the actual number of classrooms." And while memory is here given primacy over reality, what is remembered is treated with the suspicion of the analyst: the "very clarity" of the remembered spaces, Kelley notes, is "too perfect, the scenes are too staged to be real. They must be implanted fictions."[2] The project thus gradually takes shape as a "utopian" fantasy, a wish fulfillment built out of screen memories: "I think the recovered memories are often times wish fulfillment—it's not recovery at all. The past is actually a screen memory, a construction of present desires. Memories and desires are conflated—you can't separate them. As your desire changes, memory changes, and the 'facts' change to suit it."[3]

Freud, in his classic essay "Screen Memories," made much of the fact that, while a number of fragmentary recollections from the earliest years of childhood might be in different ways recalled, and with differing significations, it was only with the onset of maturity, in "many cases only after the tenth year," that memory began to function so as to reproduce the child's life "in memory as a connected chain of events."[4] Freud, here at least, saw memory as a function of time and of the recognition of temporality as a narrative that gave sense to life and the individual biography. Memory was imperfect, that is, as long as history and its temporal structure was absent. Kelley in these projects has reversed this assumption, so to speak, attempting to escape the dominance of time by a retrieval of space. Where Freud was concerned with memories of events that happened in time, Kelley wishes to remember the containers and environments of these events. Where Freud, countering the generally accepted view that a child is more prone to remember "occasions of fear, shame, physical pain, etc., and on the other hand important events such as illnesses, deaths, fires, births of brothers and sisters, etc.,"[5] focuses on the mundane, everyday experiences that seem more likely to be partial, or more precisely screen memories for something else—substitutions or reframings in order to compensate for the blocked, unwanted and repressed memory—Kelley attempts to place significance on the everyday space. Entrances, schoolrooms, passages, and the like become so many substitutes for the "primal scenes" eagerly sought out by psychoanalysis.

In selecting space, rather than event, as the material for his memory analysis, Kelley admits to a certain "failure." Memory has failed to retrieve space in any consistent or complete manner. Indeed it has registered no more than a twenty percent success rate; the deletions that represent what was unremembered take up the bulk of the modeled space. We are reminded of Walter Benjamin's remark, in his essay "The Work of Art in the Age of Mechanical Reproduction," that architecture is experienced in what he calls "a state of distraction,"[6] rendered virtually invisible by the routine of everyday usage and thence hardly registered, at least visually. In this sense, Kelley's models might be considered maps of such distraction, consciously evoking the unconscious in order to construct an oppositional experience of architecture, were it not for the fact that he endows the "blocks" or enclosed areas with more potential significance than places that were simply never registered. These "unremembered blocks," "filled-in" and "inaccessible,"[7] are referred to as "repressed space," a "forgotten architecture" opposed to what he calls the remembered "functional architecture."[8] Further, he posits that what has been forgotten (that is, once experienced, now repressed) may not have simply gone unregistered owing to distraction, but rather represents a transformation of something once "homey" and now rendered by repression "full of potential for the darkness and hostile abuse that we find in these spaces."[9] Where Benjamin would emphasize the positive role of distraction as a kind of "not seeing" that removed architecture from the superficialities of a purely visual experience and opened it up to the deeper sensibilities of a more haptic, intuitive knowledge, Kelley substitutes repression for distraction, revealing what is forgotten as a crucial site of displacement or unconscious unremembering.

But the space thus brought into visuality in model form as "blocked" is not of course necessarily the literal counterpart of an actual space once seen but not remembered. For, as Kelley notes, his memory of spaces has to be seen as potentially false even when more or less complete—as screen memory, which Freud defined as "a recollection . . . whose value lies in the fact that is represents in the memory impressions and thoughts of a later date whose subject-matter is connected with its own by symbolic or similar links."[10] Whether remembered in a (false) clarity or blocked in obscurity, Kelley's spaces follow Freud's understanding that "our childhood memories show us our early years not as they were but as they appeared at the later periods when the memories were revived." The *Educational Complex*, then, would be less a record of past versus present, or even, as supporters of repressed memory syndrome would have us believe, the true past remembered in the present, than something formed now and for its own precise reasons: "In these periods of revival the childhood memories did not, as people are accustomed to say, *emerge;* they were *formed* at that time. And a number of motives, which had no concern with historical accuracy, had their part in forming them as well as in the selection of the memories themselves."[11] This would explain why, in concentrating on spatial memories, with all the implications of space as a fundamental shaper of early identity, Kelley has made a calculated break with Freud, who maintained that screen memories "are extremely well-remembered but that their subject-matter is completely indifferent."[12] Kelley's spatial memories by contrast seem far from indifferent and tied more to the exigencies of his present work than any analysis of his childhood or adolescence might require. Which would not mean that the insistence on memory was simply a convenient intellectual fiction for the generation of this work. Freud insists on the function of displacement and substitution, on the fact that, however arbitrary the apparent connection between a screen memory and its supposed antecedent, however much the suppressed phantasy is "toned down into a childhood scene," this "cannot occur unless there is a memory trace the subject matter of which offers the phantasy a point of contact—comes, as it were, half way to meet it."[13]

Kelley himself offers a few clues as to the possible connections between memory trace and phantasy in his education complex: there is the public identification of the artist with abuse, metonymically constructed with reference to his work with dolls; there is the subsequent ascription of the artistic self as victim, whence follows the association with and search for repressed memory; there is the inevitable working-through of a number of resistances to the artistic conventions of his training. But for our purposes, it will be useful to take at its face value Kelley's statement that "with this project I'm dealing with my bias against architecture,"[14] a statement that places many of the disturbing ambiguities of the project in context. For Kelley is not here construing the work as "against architecture" in the absolute sense developed by Georges Bataille and contemporary artists such as Gordon Matta-Clark: the pure violence of Bataille's conception of spatial destruction, the relentless push toward the *informe* represented for Bataille by anti-architectural matter such as spittle, the clear gestural mark of Matta-Clark's "splitting" are all absent from these elegantly constructed and admittedly "beautiful" objects. Rather, Kelley should be taken at his word that he is "dealing with" a "bias" and not exemplifying a rejection. In this sense the project takes on the aspect of an open-ended exploration of the sources of such a bias, one that touches not only the hidden and "unhomely" but also the utopia of "beauty" and the nostalgia for the "homely."

Here, as he recognizes, Kelley is putting into play the systematic structure of the "uncanny" as outlined by Freud in his 1919 essay "The Uncanny," a structure that understands the relations between what is homely (in German, *heimlich*) and what is unhomely (in German, *unheimlich,* or "uncanny") as a function of the return of the repressed, or more particularly the return of something that was once homely and familiar but which has been repressed, and returns now in an unfamiliar, therefore uncanny guise. In Kelley's spatial terms, following Gaston Bachelard, this structure would be represented by his "forgotten spaces"—under the stairs, in the closet, the bottom drawer—which, once forgotten and now returned through the work of memory, take on an uncanny, mysterious, and threatening aspect. These would be the "blocks" of unremembered space. It is significant that Kelley, while identifying the uncanny nature of these spaces, chooses to keep them blocked off from view, to reveal only what was remembered, as if to underline the impossibility of returning to the homely as well as the untouchable nature of its repression. It is not then accidental that in the process of "dealing with" his "bias against architecture" Kelley produced a result that in many respects sublimates that bias to produce another architecture: his "strategy had the unexpected result of transforming previously mundane institutional buildings into complex and beautiful structures."[15]

An initial attempt to rediscover the roots of victimization (by architecture) had, so to speak, resulted in the overcoming of victimization by the invention of a utopian realm where screen memories were merged with the real, in an architecture that surpassed the real in beauty, and in institutions that not only properly buried the repressed zones of abuse but endowed them with aesthetic significance: something like the operation of the sublime, as described by Freud in the opening passages of his "Uncanny" essay, that worked to cover the discomforting and disturbing sense of lurking horror in the uncanny by a concentration on the overarching beauty of even the most horrifying of spectacles. Kelley, who has explored every dimension of the sublime, from the infinite to the erotic, in performance and exhibit from 1983 on, calls this sublimated architecture "a kind of über-architecture."[16]

But as utopia, the *Educational Complex* is significantly lacking on a number of levels. First, where utopia by definition presents a perfect and totalizing vision of a world outside the world, Kelley's memory map is fundamentally incomplete—like analysis itself, the model, as process, is interminable: "the model is potentially never done."[17] Secondly, the very closure of the unremembered space conceals where utopia would reveal; the transparency vital to utopian existence is denied; the vision of the whole, characteristic of architectural utopias from Filarete to Le Corbusier, is obstructed. And thirdly, a utopia properly speaking would reside out of time and only in space: Kelley's complex transactions between first experience, remembered experience, and reconstructed experience are tightly inserted into the temporal structure of the family romance, in this case a family romance with architecture that began with the exploration of his father's domain—the underworld of the boiler rooms and secret underground spaces beneath the school building for which his father worked as maintenance supervisor. Stopping short of a full-fledged self-analysis, and refusing to complete its apparently utopian aspirations—the sublime as frustrated desire—the limits of the *Educational Complex* might then be drawn around its preoccupation with architecture.

In this context we might consider the *Educational Complex* as an exercise in reconstructing what we might term Mike Kelley's architectural unconscious. What this might be was sketched by Benjamin when, in tandem with his argument around architectural distraction, he sought to describe that particular form of seeing known as photographic. Remarking on the peculiar expansion and contraction of vision made possible by the camera, Benjamin notes that the photograph in some way "intervenes" in our naturalized visionary habits (also distracted by routine) in such a way that "an unconsciously penetrated space is substituted for a space consciously explored by man." "The camera," he concludes in a celebrated phrase, "introduces us to unconscious optics as does psychoanalysis to unconscious impulses."[18] An architectural paraphrase might read something like: "Memory introduces us to unconscious architecture as does psychoanalysis to unconscious impulses," or perhaps, "A precise model of memory introduces us to the architectural unconscious as does psychoanalysis to unconscious impulses."

But what might be the nature of the space revealed by this procedure—the blocked space that to all intents and purposes seems simply closed off to our understanding, resistant forever to any analytical or retrospective inquiry? Kelley himself speaks of a deep space, a space that in some way externalizes and makes visible a space of introjection that mirrors the space of projection characteristic of our first experience of buildings. We might see this sense of "depth" as a resistance to what Walter Benjamin understood as the continuous flattening of modern space, the inevitable transformation, as he put it, of the whole space of Renaissance humanism under the twin forces of modernization and opticality. As we have seen, for Benjamin the *Spielraum* (space of play or elbow room) of the Renaissance had been fundamentally reduced or flattened by the rise of the baroque court, the space of which was pressed against a *tableau,* a superficial wall against which the subterfuges of courtiers and factions alike might be revealed in endless shadow plays. Modernism, with its insistence on the visual spectacle of the film screen or the analogous tableau of the music hall, had simply completed this process. Deep external space had been reduced to a surface. In this context, Benjamin's fight to preserve the haptic realm of introjection was a form of stubborn refusal of this modernity; the Parisian arcades project was one example of his attempt to infuse the already flattened and claustrophobic realm of the real with a depth of mythology and dream that revealed the unconscious structure, so to speak, of the city fabric as a Bergsonian construction in the mind of the subject. Surrealism in this respect had, for Benjamin, only provided a "snapshot" of this potential of the architectural unconscious—a photographic image of an architectural depth.

In Kelley's terms, the spatial exploration of the blocked space of the *Educational Complex* seems to correspond to the imaginary exploration of space itself, and, following his own expressed interests, to space as developed in science fiction writing and space comics. For Kelley, inner space and deep space are the figural equivalents to a visual culture attempting to escape itself. Thus, speaking of the *Educational Complex*'s closures, he noted:

I find myself constantly thinking about the bottled city that Superman keeps safely stored in his Fortress of Solitude. Inside a bell jar is an entire city, filled with living people, from his home planet Krypton—a planet that has exploded. Krypton is the home that can never be revisited, the past that can never be recovered. Yet there it is, shrunken to the size of a doll house—an ageless memento in real time. I wonder if the eternal Man of Steel ever feels the need to smash this city and finally live in the present. That would put a stop to the fear of ending up in the shuttered room.[19]

In this "shuttered room," however, as we have seen, lurk the uncanny revelations that memory itself refuses to give up; to put a stop to the fear would in this sense remove the sources of anxiety and declare the analysis terminated. We might imagine Kelley, by contrast, to relish the intimation of anxious contents, preserving this one realm of unentered space as a potential field for future exploration. Following his own metaphor of the Fortress of Solitude, we might be tempted to draw the analogy to that "fortress" delineated by Lacan in his essay on the mirror stage, the fortified enclosure constructed by the self as it buttresses itself against an inevitable division between inner and outer, paranoia and schizophrenia, what Lacan terms the *Innenwelt* and the *Umwelt:*

The formation of the "I" is symbolized in dreams by a fortified camp, that is to say, a stadium—setting up, from the inner arena to its enclosure, its surroundings of rubbish tips and marshes, two opposed fields of struggle where the subject is enmired in the quest for the high and distant interior castle, the form of which (sometimes juxtaposed in the same scenario) symbolizes the id in a striking way.[20]

That Lacan presents this struggle for the castle as a kind of joust played out in an arena, or stage—consciously holding the double sense of the French *stade,* meaning "stage" of development and "arena"—is significant for our argument here. For Lacan's wordplay has the effect of placing the developmental event of the mirror stage in a spatial field. Thus the first recognition of the self as an image reflected in a mirror, the moment that at once marks the assembling of one's body as totality and forever links this assemblage with a division or split between self and (reflected) image, is set not just within the frame that scales the image in the mirror proportionately to the child but also in the inner space of the self itself: "And similarly, here on the mental plane, we find these structures of a fortified work, the metaphor of which rises up spontaneously, and as if issuing from the symptoms of the subject themselves, to designate the mechanisms of obsessional neurosis: inversion, isolation, reduplication, cancellation, displacement."[21] Within Kelley's blocks of space, then, we might expect to find the discarded and forgotten residues of a self divided from the outset, one for whom the exploration of the "fortress" or "fortified camp" would logically reveal a map of his architectural unconscious, situated and outlined, with the periphery of the enclosure traced in three dimensions.

Here Kelley's own reference to science fiction space provides a clue as to the possible inner shape of this space: a "bottled city" in a jar, but also a variety of abandoned sites that we imagine as so many fragments of once-used and never-revisited three-dimensional websites, those virtual spaces in which the protagonists of William Gibson's recent novel *Idoru* play out their interactions and shelter for refuge from the omniscient web controllers. Sites like Zona's "jungle clearing," complete with birdcalls, bugs, and vegetational music; or the more comforting virtual Venice, furnished by Chia with appropriate companions; or again Zona's "secret place, a country carved out from what once had been a corporate website," a valley scattered with ruined pools, cactus plants, and lizards; or, finally, like a simulation of Lacan's castle, the Walled City with its central black hole that served as a safe haven for Masahiko and his friends.[22] In this latest evocation of the character of cyberspace, Gibson has imagined his former "matrix"—defined with classic clarity in *Neuromancer* as a "consensual hallucination experienced daily by billions. . . . A graphic representation of data abstracted from the banks of every computer in the human system. Unthinkable complexity. Lines of light ranged in the non-space of the mind, clusters and constellations of data. Like city lights, receding . . ."[23]—now littered with the remains of once-populated virtual worlds to infinity.

In this ascription of deep space, the classical model of perspectival depth has been inverted or rather folded in on itself, as the screen, once a window onto the world of three-dimensional play, remains closed and flat—rather like, to use Gibson's telling analogy, "the color of television tuned to a dead channel." Real space in Gibson's novels is rendered as flat—as in "the sky over Burbank was perfectly blank, like a sky-blue paint chip submitted by the contractor of the universe,"[24] in contrast to the projected depth, inner and outer, of the subject exploring that space. Deep space is "jacked into," through an inner port that transforms flat space into a multidimensional experience by means of a rapid oscillation between projection and introjection that expands into "a 3D chessboard extending to infinity."[25] The Hacker/flâneur Laney worked this space: it was said that he had "a peculiar knack with data-collection architectures, and a medically documented concentration deficit that he could toggle, under certain conditions, into a state of pathological hyperfocus." He was "an intuitive fisher of patterns of information. . . . A natural channel-zapper, shifting from program to program, from database to database, from platform to platform," as he sought the important and hidden "nodal points" that represented the spatial connections of knowledge.[26]

It would not be difficult to imagine memory taking on such a form, and to understand Kelley's *Educational Complex* in this light as a virtual landscape of former milieux and spatial matrices that, in working through his "bias" against architecture, sets out to rehabilitate these abandoned rooms for present occupation; were it not for the fact that the cuts opened in the walls of his new institutional utopia reveal only what is remembered and close off from our contemplation, at least, what is not. Superman may have an occasional urge to smash the bell jar; Kelley has resisted such analytical violence, preferring to work up to the borders of the enclosure, leaving well alone what might be inside.

Terminal Transfer

Martha Rosler's Passages

Construction Ahead

The building of the Autobahn and the completion of the New Jersey Turnpike in the 1930s gave rise to a genre of road photo that celebrated the motorway as the way to the future now, as a futurist route of progress, if not of violence and force, that emblematized the convergence of automobile and the ideology of speed. As late as the 1950s, with the extension of the U.S. federal highway network, the freeway was still seen as both escape and arrival: escape from a postwar mundanity of suburbia and family values, arrival at the exotic and sometimes forbidden sites and sights of the park-strewn, vista-filled, *National Geographic*–framed continent. There were traffic snarls, of course—dramatically illustrated, as Edward Dimendberg has noted, by the B movie *Plunder Road* where the newly completed Harbor Freeway was to have offered an open route to the fleeing bank robbers, all the way to San Diego, a freighter, and freedom, but which was in the event jammed from on-ramp to off-ramp, catching the criminals in their own form of escape—but the message was still clear.[1] The modernist parkways and turnpikes of the twenties and thirties, the civil-defense infrastructural highways of the fifties, the beat-biker roads of the sixties, the Los Angeles freeways of the seventies were, despite all evidence to the contrary, seen as "open roads," of the type to which, with vorticist-inspired passion, Mr. Toad of Toad Hall was so much addicted.

In Martha Rosler's *Rights of Passage* series, all such freedom of movement, real or conceptual, is blocked: by traffic, by the endless process of roadwork, by deteriorating surfaces and margins, by the inexorable sameness of the modern highway landscape that turns all travel into arrival at the same destination. Temporary concrete lane dividers, lined up to constrict the flow into single lanes, or piled up in simulacra of industrial buildings; highway signs, bill-boards, bridge and tunnel details, trailers (anonymous in white or tarpaulins, advertising donuts, Wal-Marts, and hauling cars in their turn), all act to screen out any sense of position (are we in Brooklyn or New Jersey now?) and instead, as Rosler has remarked, "[demolish] place and time in favor of space."

Already, in the mid-1950s, the planner Kevin Lynch had pointed to the consequences of such a loss of orientation in the contemporary urban land-scape, among the elements of which the freeway was perhaps the most "funda-mentally disorienting."[2] Basing his research on psychological studies, such as the Automotive Safety Foundation's 1958 *Driver Needs in Freeway Signing*,[3] Lynch tried to identify a set of markers, of positioning elements, that might transform urban experience into a modern version of the traditional small town, with its squares, towers, identifiable monuments, and memorable street patterns. Echoing Camillo Sitte's complaints against the agoraphobic Ring-strasse of Vienna in 1898, Lynch cited psychologists, including Pierre Jaccard, H. A. Witkin, and Alfred Binet, in support of his position that "orientation" in the "overt chaos of the modern city" was a fundamental constituent of good city planning:

> Jaccard quotes an incident of native Africans who became disoriented. They were stricken with panic and plunged wildly into the bush. Witkin tells of an experienced pilot who lost his orientation to the vertical and who described it as the most terrifying experience of his life. Many other writers, in describing the phenomenon of temporary disorientation in the modern city, speak of the accompanying emotions of distress. Binet mentions a man who took care to arrive at one particular railroad depot in Lyons when coming from Paris, because, although it was less conve-nient, it concurred with his (mistaken) image of the side of Lyons which lay toward Paris.[4]

Evidently, for Lynch, to be lost in the city was to be both psychically and bod-ily disoriented: "The terror of being lost comes from the necessity that a mo-bile organism be oriented in its surroundings."[5] Significantly enough, part of his research was carried out in Jersey City, in a landscape, as seen in one of Rosler's photographs, separated from the New York skyline by parking lots and junk-filled marshes. As Lynch put it: "Much of the characteristic feeling for Jersey City seemed to be that it was a place on the edge of something else." A resident of Jersey City succinctly stated: "How would I recognize Fairview Avenue when I come to it? By the street sign."[6]

Despite this obvious loss of "place," Lynch was confident that a new symbolic order might be created, a new "image of the city" that, responding to movement and speed with appropriate forms and signage, might once more orient the modern citizen of the highway. Rosler's "images," however, assert precisely the opposite; that, indeed, not only is no orientation possible in the technically determined scheme of road and vehicle, but that no amount of image proliferation will restore orientation. Images, that is, are not monuments, nor are they memorable. Thus we have no way of knowing which way through the Lincoln Tunnel we are traveling, where on the Turnpike we are. What signs *are* legible, in the moments of distraction from the road, explicitly deny all place: "Your Ad Here" states one, with a phone number unreadable at any speed; "Keep Left" another; and "Dip" as the camera suddenly lurches to one side.

But in Rosler's series the explicit loss of orientation with regard to the landscapes of the highway outside the car is doubled and reinforced by the projected vision of the highway implied by the framing mechanism of the panoramic shot. The vision of the early freeway photos—Germaine Krull's travelogues, Hitler's official photographers of the Autobahn—was perspectival. There the vanishing point resonated as the point at which a moving object was directed, at which it disappeared, and which, at any speed, could never be reached. Wrecked vision was mimicked by the auto accident itself, as in the crash that broke up the endless perspectives of poplars in Godard's movie *Weekend.* The view then was forward, preferably from the driver's seat; the format was square, the sides of the scene only important for framing the center. The Renaissance, which had utilized perspective to frame as well as engender streets, the baroque, which used it to construe its radiating streets as the objectives of pilgrimage and traffic, the Enlightenment, which used it to depict the regularity of reason, and finally the modern period from Haussmann to Le Corbusier, who understood perspective as a tool of planning and a route to what the latter termed "infinite space," all these "objectives" were brought together in the perspective view of the endless highway. Even the picturesque parkway, which framed its gently winding vistas with carefully set clumps of trees and bushes and folding greenswards, adopted the scene of the early modern landscape painting, itself propelled by perspective, as the viewer's eye was led by diminishing meanders to the center of the horizon, the vanishing point of the spatial sublime.

Rosler's panoramic frames, by contrast, reject the central vanishing point of perspective; their vanishing points are conceptually ranged around a 180-degree curve, drawing the eye from side to side, impeding its flight into the picture, and constructing a flattened surface where there should be depth. Apparently taken from the driver's seat (although certain images, such as that of the tunnel, are obviously taken from the rear, and some from the side), the

16. Martha Rosler, *Under the B.Q.E., Brooklyn,* 1994. From the series *Rights of Passage.*

photographs do not in any way replicate the driver's vision. We are presented with an impossibly widened scopic scene, invited to linger as no driver could, to take in the sides and edges of the route, a kind of vision, walleyed and distorted, mirrored by the looming side of the Wal-Mart truck in one of Rosler's panoramas. Further, while the driver's view in fact alternates between frontal and rear, rearview mirror, side rearview mirror, and windshield taken in at regular intervals, Rosler's panoramas compress all views into one, and even, at moments, occlude the one with the other, in an (impossible) backward/forward, in-focus/out-of-focus collapse and reversal of perspective. In one image, an out-of-focus scene outside the right-hand window of the car is redoubled by a side rearview mirror reflecting blurred and blinding headlights. This tendency toward spatial reversal, to a closed loop return, is dramatically demonstrated in the photograph of a night scene on the Turnpike, an accident or breakdown illuminating the center of the image in a red glow, radiating from the wet surface of the pavement, and, in the center of the frame, as in the center of the road, a single figure walking back toward the traffic as if to stop it in a futile gesture of resistance and supplication. Perhaps it is the mortality of this figure, erect for an instant in the horizontal flow of the automobiles, that is figured in the ghostly reflection in the windshield of a skeleton seemingly hovering above the New Jersey meadows between Rosler's car and New York City, an image that returns us to the underlying theme of all of these photographs: that of the "Road Closed" whose interminable psychic and physical repairs signal an end to our twentieth-century ideology of the freeway.

Flight Delayed

The associations provoked by the "texts" originally displayed above Rosler's photographs, in an exhibition of photographs taken over a number of years in different American and European air terminals,[7] would not be out of place in a book of modernist architectural theory. Offering a range of observations and critical intersections with the images, Rosler's aphoristic fragments, reinforce our first impression that the photographs, whether positively or ironically, are set pieces of modernist high-tech architecture, displayed dispassionately, as if by the original architects, to encourage our appreciation of the transparency and elegance of their impeccable spaces.

Thus her notation "Boulevard or intestine?" might refer to the modern image of a city or building as a biological organism. For Le Corbusier it would signify the transformation of Haussmann's Parisian arteries into intestinal canals for the efficient flow of commerce; he illustrated the premise with biological diagrams in *Urbanisme*. Similarly, "Simplify and minimize" might well have been Adolf Loos's refrain; "Containment and control" would be the desire of any urban or social planner of the twenties and thirties; "Hospital regime" and "Brightly lit atrium" echo the polemics for "white space" in the same period; while "Total surveillance" resonates with Benthamite hunger for power.

And it is not entirely clear that the photographs themselves do not display these ideals with equal fidelity. Materials, lighting, structures, smooth flows and mechanical systems, media technologies, all would have been close to the dreams of an El Lissitzky or a Norman Bel Geddes, and were in fact, as designed, the direct heirs of modernist ideology. Even the absence of people, in spaces obviously crowded in real use, would be explained by architects' predilections for photographing their work empty and clear of untidy human intrusion. The polished tubes of walkways, moving sidewalks, and broad concourses; the curving ramps and soaring roofs; the steel mechanisms for baggage handling; the screened images of news and directions; all would mark these photographs as potential advertisements for the best in airport architecture, icons of the triumph of modernism after the modern movement. Their self-conscious emulation of "the modern" would, in this context, be emphasized by their relentless fascination with the space of flow, with the passage (never clearly marked as one way or the other) from ground to flight or vice versa, with the *machine à voler* as the epitome of a functionalist architecture suited to the second machine age.

For, from the inception of air travel, modernist architects made the metaphorical connection between air flow, air speed, the streamlined section of the wing, and the determinants of functional design. Le Corbusier, in *Vers une architecture* extolled the characteristics of the plane and its aerodynamic struts, adopting their forms for the entrances to villas (the Villa Stein at Garches) and the legs of dining tables. For the early functionalists there was an unbroken path between the precise contour of a flight machine and the aesthetics of modernity. The journal *L'Esprit Nouveau* between 1918 and 1923 published articles on houses built by the Voisin aircraft factory, houses conceived like airplanes, built on assembly lines like airplanes, moved to their sites like airplanes, and that were, in Le Corbusier's terms, fit for the upbringing of tomorrow's engineers and technocrats. Airplanes were, after all, simply "houses that fly."

And similarly, for the modernist architect nothing should interfere with the joyful experience of infinite space in flight and the transfer from ground to air. Airports were no longer terminals, like railroad stations and seaports; Richard Neutra characterized his project for an airport in his imaginary Rush City as a "through station," a "junction," a "belt-line," or better an "air-transfer." "Terminals? Transfers?" was the title of his article illustrated by a perfect example of "flow" transferred into spatial organization—a prototype of airport that has been built in multiple iterations since 1930: tubes and ramps connect, on one side to the auto park and on the other to the arriving and de-parting planes. Between these two stages is an upper-level grand concourse, hovering above the field, with its "broad well-illuminated shopping arcades" running "in one direction toward the promenade overlooking the field, the café, the amusement park and the hotel, and in the other direction toward the aircraft display hall and the street bridge which connects this concession avenue with the spacious auto park."[8] Neutra calculated that the optimum turnaround time between landing and takeoff, with passengers let off and new passengers taken on, was fifteen minutes.

For Le Corbusier, fifteen years later triumphantly presiding over the "in-frastructure" section of the first postwar Congress of French Aviation, even this interruption between ground and air was too static: in a paragraph on "Archi-tecture and Modern Airports" he claimed:

> Once on the ground, only one kind of architecture seems tolerable and perfectly admissible: that of the magnificent airplanes which have brought you or will take you away, and which in front of you occupy the visible space. Their biology is such, their form such an expression of harmony, that no architecture seems reasonable beside them, no other building possible. An airport then seems to have to be naked, entirely open to the sky, full in the center of the field, with the concrete runways.

The necessary functions would thus be underground, shielded by a six-foot wall: "The beauty of an airport," he cried, "is the splendor of space!"[9]

Such an ideology of flows, of rush, of transfer, of space opposed to place—for what had the airplane brought about if it were not a submission of all places, all borders, for universal space, for one world?—entered into the postwar formulation of airports by government fiat and with expressionist vengeance. Regularized in the U.S. Department of Commerce's *Airport Ter-minal Buildings* (1953) by the definition of the airport as "primarily the ser-vice center for the transfer of passengers and their property between surface vehicles and aircraft,"[10] the premise found its formal apotheosis in Eero Saari-nen's TWA Terminal of 1960. Citing the architect, a critic in 1960 found the rationale of his biomorphic design in his concern for "the flow of people through the terminal," "both to aid and to express his flowing forms."[11] As the British architectural critic Lionel Brett soliloquized in an essay of 1955, "the essence of travel, symbol of our journey through life, is drama, and the role of the architect is to heighten the drama by the way he sets and shifts the scene."[12]

As Le Corbusier had realized, of course, the ultimate fate of airport buildings designed with such efficiencies of flow in mind was their eventual disappearance. Michael Brawne, writing in 1962 and noting that Saarinen's terminal was "designed to emphasize and facilitate passenger flow," observed: "It may well be that the architecture of passenger-handling buildings will then become more rational, perhaps less memorable or possibly, except for a vestigial space, disappear altogether."[13]

Here, Rosler's images of the passages and ramps of the TWA building take on another significance, however. For clearly we cannot leave their interpretation within the discourse from which they were designed. The evident irony of Rosler's labels, and the critical postmodernity of observations like "white-noise hiss" or "trace odors of stress and hustle," with their own echoes of Georges Bataille and more recently of Bernard Tschumi, would indicate that the apparent "straight" reading of a self-referential modernism might be complicated by a late twentieth-century sense of betrayal. The realization of modernism's "abstract space," as Henri Lefebvre observed and Rosler recalled, was tied up with "capital costs," "mergers and acquisitions"; and what modernism called for as a Nietzschean overcoming of social and cultural difference through technological development was, in the event, realized as an "explosion" of history, and thence of the city. As Lefebvre put it, implicitly contesting Sigfried Giedion's ecstatic embrace of "space, time and architecture," and in a text also displayed and cited by Rosler, "Abstract space reveals its oppressive and repressive capacities in relation to time. It rejects time as an abstraction—except when it concerns work, the producer of things and of surplus value. Time is reduced to constraints of space: schedules, runs, crossing, loads."[14] In this context, Rosler's photographs take on the air of pictorial revelations of the underbelly of capitalism, its spaces manifested as empty, sterile non-places, determined more by mathematical calculation of times of arrival and departure than by any regard for the human subjects subjected to this version of total control and surveillance. Humans would be absent from the photographs, then, not for aesthetic reasons but to mark their real nonexistence for spaces occupied by their transient bodies, moved through as quickly as possible. Bleakness would be seen in the place of modernist fulfillment; anomie and estrangement in the place of a truly public realm. Spaces, that is, have been substituted for places; airport spaces now take the "place of the public."

We are reminded of another, earlier modernist space that was not a place, one forensically examined by Siegfried Kracauer in a now celebrated essay analyzing the spatial conditions of "official poverty" in late Weimar Berlin, where his attention was drawn to the "construction" of a new spatial building type: the employment agency.[15] Forged by the necessities of the depression and the ensuing mass unemployment, these "exchanges" were "constructed," as Kracauer put it, "unconsciously," without the help of architects, and as such were the perfect representations of class space. In the same way as the *neue Sachlichkeit* office was associated with the managing director, or suburbs were "the characteristic location" of the lower middle classes, so the employment agency was the epitome of a space suitable for the unemployed—"more generously proportioned" than the suburban house, but "as a result . . . the opposite of a home and certainly not a living space."[16] Rather, the employment agency was more like an arcade, a place of passage and waiting, where, indeed, the activity of waiting fruitlessly for one's name to be called for possible employment became "almost an end in itself." "I do not know of a spatial location," Kracauer concluded, "in which the activity of waiting is so demoralizing."[17] For Kracauer, the upper- and middle-class equivalent of such waiting rooms would be found in the "hotel lobby," a space of individual anonymity, where only the detective would find solace in the activity of observing the passage of the crowd from the relative security of a club chair.

For Rosler some seventy years later, the space of the contemporary airport seems to offer the combined discomfort of demoralized waiting and anonymous passage. And if the class divisions of mass travel are less apparent in the late twentieth century, the apparatus of "security," ostensibly on behalf of the passenger, ensures that the airport, like the shopping mall, the theme park, and the new gaming palaces of multimedia combines, will remain free of the disturbing presence of the truly homeless, leaving them open to the vicarious and temporary homelessness of privileged nomadism. The realization of Neutra's dream of a consumer concourse in the ever-expanding retail activities of the bigger airports gives a similar edge to Kracauer's evocation of the arcade. Here Rosler captures the absolute spatial void of the terminal, in photographs such as *JFK* (1990) with its broad panoramic view of a waiting area, empty save for two standing figures, or *Minneapolis* (1991), another panoramic view, this time outside the waiting area, showing the spread of the tarmac and two planes, themselves laconically waiting at the gates.

17. Martha Rosler, *Untitled* (*Los Angeles*), 1985. From the series *In the Place of the Public.*

But, beyond this sense of generalized estrangement and anomie, Rosler's photographs intimate another aspect of the airport that is, at least in crime-free areas, absent from the shopping mall: the latent and always suppressed anxiety that anticipates the event of flight itself. No doubt the brilliantly lit and multi-reflective interiors, womblike passages and carefully framed views of the airfield are all calculated by designers to occlude this patently present angst, but for Rosler they are so many traces of repression, tell-tale images of a barely hidden fear. Indeed, the very framing of the photographs, with their insistent, centered, one-point perspective leading to almost literally conceived "vanishing" points, exacerbates this sense of phobic tension, suspended somewhere between the claustrophobia of the tunnel and the agoraphobia of the takeoff.

What Walter Benjamin had noted as the "suffocating perspective" of the nineteenth-century arcade interior now becomes a mechanism for the stimulation of phobia under the guise of its postponement.

The psychological implications of flight for a mass public were noted from the outset. The program for the Lehigh Airports Competition of 1928–1929, the first such comprehensive public design enterprise, observed the need to prevent passengers from being "jolted or inconvenienced while preparing for take-off or immediately after landing." "It is recognized," the report of the jury concluded, "that passengers unfamiliar with flying operation are most nervous during the preliminary period before the plane is in the air and, if they are then subjected to rather rough treatment, their timorousness is enhanced rather than abated."[18] And while Freud was hardly a frequent flyer, his investigation into anxiety neuroses stimulated widespread psychoanalytical inquiry into the fear of flying; "locomotion anxiety" (from which Freud himself self-avowedly suffered), "vertigo," and "disorientation" became the watchwords of designers concerned to buffer the masses from the shock that inevitably attended radical spatial dislocation of any kind. And yet, as Rosler's images of subjective alienation in transit relentlessly emphasize, the palliative of design, the propaedeutic formulas of modernism, generated, as Manfredo Tafuri has observed, "to ward off shock," have succeeded only in engendering its effects. It is as if the very premises of functionalism, bound to the solution of physical and mental problems, have turned on themselves, in some way to reproduce them.

In an evocative poem written at the inception of the era of flight, Stephen Spender characterized the surroundings of the modern airport, with its sprawl of huts and huddled suburbs, as a "landscape of hysteria," a landscape on "the outskirts," seen from the passenger windows of a large airplane:

Beyond the winking masthead light
And the landing ground, they observe the outposts
Of work: chimneys like lank black fingers
Or figures, frightening and mad: and squat buildings
With their strange air behind the trees, like women's faces
Shattered by grief. Here where few houses

Moan with faint light behind their blinds
They remark the unhomely sense of complaint, like a dog
Shut out, and shivering at the foreign moon.[19]

It would seem that, even as this exterior landscape has become increasingly sophisticated technologically in its ability to signal and survey, gridded with landing lights and spotted by radar dishes, fenced and secure against terrorism, so the "hysteria" of the airport landscape has now been internalized, brought into the realm of the phobic subject waiting for flight, there to be channeled and directed according to the abstract laws of flow and consumer demand. Rosler's photographs stand as veritable imagos of this subject, a subject no doubt surrounded by crowds but, in Rosler's perspectives, utterly alone, pressed forward into the picture, as if projected mechanically towards an unknown goal.

These subjects are, it seems, deliberately *uninformed* by messages appearing on flickering screens, messages so ambiguously suspended between admonition and information, solicitation and surveillance, that a kind of vertigo of knowledge is produced, corresponding to the psychic and bodily vertigo of the subject itself. Thus the slogan, "Imminent Departure. For these people there is no return. You can stop the destruction of the rain forest and its inhabitants by calling Cultural Survival. Join Cultural Survival Join the Human Race," with a life-sized photograph of the starving children of the rain forest, greets the passenger about to embark on her own flight whose "imminent departure" has just been announced, and whose "return" is at least worthy of a moment of anxiety. More sinister still, and in the cause of generously updating the passenger with all the news that counts—"For all the reasons in the world, CNN"—is the screened message, "Jet crash/126 passengers/5 crew members/Lost contact 7 miles from airport/Body parts hanging from trees/Black box removed."

For today's nomadic subjects, subjected to "news" of this kind, caught in the interstices of a spatial matrix that recognizes them merely as "contents" of flights to be announced, the airport is little more than a temporary container, neither a grand terminal nor a functional transfer but simply a state of terminal transfer to destinations signaled, but not entirely revealed, in the acid blue maps of the world, etched in neon (*Boise*, 1986), or tantalizingly framed in the tourist posters of Germany, Italy, and London (*Philadelphia*, 1992). "Maybe there is a substitute for experience" hopefully opines a wall poster in the *United Terminal, O'Hare* of 1991.

The difference between the "transfer" supplanting the terminal in Neutra's modernist dream and the "terminal transfer" of today is nowhere so marked as in Rosler's images of empty polished corridors that seem to go nowhere, or at least in no particular direction (*Madrid*, 1990), or the polished gridded floors of *O'Hare* (1986), or Helmut Jahn's twisted neon ceilings above the connector passages at the same airport, or, finally, the seemingly endlessly repeated curving tubes of the TWA Terminal's ramps, lit in a ghostly red glow, like some voyage inside the body, all shot at *JFK* in 1990. And, once through these twisted cords, only the implacable impetus of the fixed one-point perspective pressing the passenger toward the entrance to the plane through the telescopic gate provides relief (*Untitled*, 1990); a relief hardly reinforced by the tube of the plane interior itself (*Trump Shuttle*, 1990), a tube for which the passenger has been prepared and which, embellished with the continuing saga of the "news," offers the discomfortingly ghostly image of President Reagan flickering on yet another screen (*Untitled*, 1983).

In this way Rosler's images of the airport, transcontinental and ubiquitous in their uniformity, stand at once as figures of the triumph of modernist spatial concepts and of the forces that have supported this triumph. As in Kracauer's employment agency, where "the concepts governing it ooze through all pores," so in the modern airport all travelers are for a moment subject to the powerlessness of the unemployed, and a once excited thrill of spatial exploration has been regularized into a controlled mechanism of calculated flows and uneasy, unwanted delays.

Angelus Novus

Coop Himmelblau's Expressionist Utopia

Our architecture has no
physical plan, but a
psychic plan.
There are no walls. Our
spaces are pulsating
balloons. Our heart beats become
space, and our face the
facade of an apartment house.

Coop Himmelblau, 1968

To practice architecture *against* architecture has been the repeated dream of many avant-garde groups in the twentieth century. Rejecting academic formulas and historical styles, expressionists and technological futurists alike have sought to return architecture to fundamental conditions of structure and shelter, while exploring the possibilities of entirely new languages of form. Rejecting the traditional split between technology and nature, architects have experimented with sometimes monstrous mergings of both, whether, as in the early work of Bruno Taut, fusing the geological forms of mountains with the postcubist and crystalline potentials of glass, or, as in the intrauterine homes imagined by the surrealists, bringing together biology and psychoanalysis to emulate the original conditions of life.

The renewal of avant-garde utopianism following the political and social struggles of the mid-sixties, and guided by the theoretical insights of poststructuralism, was accompanied in architecture by a revival, if not a continuation, of these bio-, psycho-, and geomorphic themes, many of which, as in the case of the Situationist International, owed their initial framing to still active surrealist and Lettrist tendencies. Such continuities were reinforced by the presence of those whose careers spanned the two generations: Frederick Kiesler, Konrad Wachsmann, Buckminster Fuller, and, important in the Viennese context, Hundertwasser. In retrospect, indeed, it is tempting to agree with the notion of a permanent twentieth-century avant-garde in architecture, especially between the years 1918 and 1968.

From the standpoint of the nineties, there is no group founded in the radical and oppositional climate of the late sixties that so contributes to the continuing permanence of this avant-garde in the present fin-de-siècle than the Viennese "cooperative" Coop Himmelblau, which has survived as the only such practice still dedicated to an uncompromising attack on the architectural status quo, its traditions, and its academic formulas. Their work from the outset proposed a radical departure from classical humanism, a fundamental break from all theories of architecture that pretended to accommodation and domestic harmony. Standing against "Palladian" humanism and Corbusian modernism alike, their architecture no longer served to center, to fix, or to stabilize.

But we don't want to build
Biedermeier. Not now and at
no other time.
We are tired of seeing Palladio
and other historical masks.
Because we don't want
architecture to exclude everything that is disquieting.[1]

In the context of a consumer-oriented historicism, this aggressive and uncompromising delineation of what we might define as a posthumanist architecture has taken on the allure of the "pure and hard" last stand, a final gesture against the too easily embraced "return" to the simulacra of classicism in commercial postmodernism. As Himmelblau affirmed in "Die härtere Architektur" (1980), a poem that anticipated the socially disastrous outcome of the Reagan/Thatcher eighties: "Je härter die Zeiten, umso härter die Architektur."

Beginning with projects that explored the possibilities of technology as a "natural" extension of the body, such as the "Michelin Man" pneumatic Villa Rosa of 1968, their work has consistently put into question the received "wisdom" of architecture, while at the same time proposing increasingly elegant structural solutions for its replacement. Coop Himmelblau was not yet well enough known outside Vienna to merit a mention in Charles Jencks's essay in futurology *Architecture 2000,* published in 1971; but, in retrospect, the most prescient of Jencks's predictions was the final double-page illustration of the book, comparing the homologous bone structures of a bird's wing, a horse's leg, a reptile's claw, and a man's arm, all following the same basic pattern of bones. Against the stylistic evolution illustrated by traditional architectural encyclopedias, this diagram of structural evolution might well be taken for the hidden manifesto behind all of Coop Himmelblau's work, obsessed since the House with Wings of 1973 with the notion of an architecture of flight, of wing structure, of skin and bones. If architecture won't be found in an encyclopedia ("Wir finden Architektur nicht in einem Lexikon"), it might, on the other hand, be found in a biological textbook.

This pervasive motif of the "wing" in Himmelblau's architecture—whether blazing in the Hot Flat (1983), or temporarily immobilized in the Red Angel Bar (1983), or simply resting lightly and ready for flight, as in the Icarian project for the Open House (1983–1988) on the Malibu cliffs, or perched as if caught in an invisible net on the top of a Viennese apartment house, as in the rooftop remodeling at Falkestrasse 6, Vienna 1 (1978–1988)—this motif seems at once to echo angelic hopes and recognize historical catastrophe. Suspended as it were between Paul Klee's *Angelus Novus* and Walter Benjamin's Angel of History, these giant wingspans, like so many grounded pterodactyls, shelter a population estranged from their once comfortable houses and seeking shelter beneath less historically determined roofs. Roofs that enfold and gently offer space for a moment's respite from the storm wind of progress that, in Benjamin's words, "blows from Paradise." Himmelblau, likewise, speaks of the "wind-inflated white sails" that replace the wreckage of ships (or of history), and the "wingspans" of an architecture that replaces those of eagles or birds ("On the Edge," 1989). In their mythology, even whales fly, as "thirty tons of flying weight" launch themselves in the air as if Jonas had been swallowed by a Zeppelin. But while offering temporary shelter, and modeling a form of structure no doubt only seen in Heaven, these wings have their sinister sponsor in the "Todesengel," as if the realm of *Paradise Lost* were to be rebuilt by the fallen angel as architect.

If there is a poetry of desolation
then it is the aesthetic of the
architecture of death in white
sheets. Death in tiled
hospital rooms. The architecture
of sudden death on the pavement.
Death from a rib-cage pierced
by a steering-shaft. The path
of the bullet through
a dealer's head on 42nd street.[2]

It is a world to be entered with eyes closed. Himmelblau's trembling hand, guided only by the unconscious resonance of the void, inscribes the paths of yet unexplored energies in an automatic writing that bears the traces of panic and anxiety. Himmelblau has consistently worked to return to the innerscape of the mind—treating drawing as a kind of seismographic exercise. Out of this apparently unreadable "scribble," to be interpreted as a form of psychic hieroglyphics of space, emerges a structure lightly touching the ground, floating above a space that is marked by its struts and ribs, a space that encloses the unfortunate Jonahs of the late twentieth century within the beached rib cage of the modernist Moby Dick.

In this way the persistence of spatial warping as a contemporary signal of modernist aspirations has been marked in the work of Coop Himmelblau since the late 1960s, work in which the uncanny visions of expressionism have found a peculiarly appropriate "home" in a space of canted planes, intersecting angles, pyramids of light, shifting floors, and tilted walls. With evident reference to the vocabulary of the original expressionists, Himmelblau formulated an environment that went beyond imitation to construct an entirely contemporary world of disquiet and unease, estrangement and distance, from the insistent world of the modern "real." As they wrote as early as 1968: "Our architecture has no physical plan, but a psychic plan."[3] It was especially appropriate, then, that Himmelblau was called on to install the exhibit "Expressionist Utopias" for the Los Angeles County Museum of Art in 1994. In this installation, the "psychic plan" was doubled in a tantalizing way. It was at once an archaeological reference to an imaginary scene long buried—that of expressionist utopia

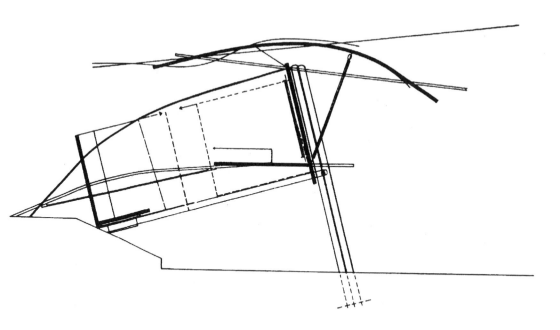

before World War I—and a contemporary scene of deliberate distortion and displacement. Freud once remarked that it would be impossible to conceive of the same space containing two different contents at the same time—he was speaking of the series of monumental constructions over the centuries built one on top of the other in Rome. Only in the mind, he argued, was the retention of two "places" in the same space possible. But it is a peculiar property of some architecture to resonate with double meaning, in such a way as to approximate the imaginary of Freud, and in this afterimage of expressionism such a double exposure was evident.

18. Coop Himmelblau, Video Clip Folly, Groningen, Netherlands, 1990. "Video presentation space in a moving box for 40 viewers." *6 Projects for 6 Cities* (Vienna: Jürgen Häusser, 1990).

Nowhere was this more apparent than in the most dramatic event of the installation, in a thick "slice" of light, so to speak, cut at an angle from one side to the other. Captured between sheets of Plexiglas, this slice had an obviously material dimension; but, as light, it was as if a negative fault line had cracked open the solid fabric of the interior, displaying its inner substance. Earlier projects of Himmelblau had played with the metaphor of skin peeled back to reveal the flayed flesh of building beneath; now the building overcame its organic attachment to the human body and was revealed as pure desire. In a kind of

Rosicrucian metaphor of "light from within," this crack of luminosity lured at the same time as it closed itself off from accessibility.

For the light was in a real sense captured, sliced as if between the two glass slides of a microscopic specimen: light that no longer served its function of lighting, as for example in Bruno Taut's Glass pavillion of 1914, but was now deprived of all function, simply to be looked at as an exhibit in a museum. Fetishized light then, cut uncomfortably close to our own bodies as we moved carefully through these uncertain spaces. Where previously Himmelblau's images of desire were figured in the many semiangelic wings that hovered, soared, and blazed through the space of their projects, in this slice of light any material reference to structure is abandoned. The "angel" was dissolved, as if in the navel of the dream, into an umbilicum of searing nothingness that hurt our eyes.

Commentary on expressionist dreams and fabrication of our own, this installation fittingly ended up displaying them in the museum as if to offer a cabinet of curiosities dedicated to the exploration of our own spatial warpings. No longer can we be satisfied with the comforting distance that separates us, as spectators, from the implications of Dr. Caligari's cabinet; we are literally entered into a scene populated by our doubles, and constructed like our psyche. And, inevitably, the moment we feel we are arriving at the center of this strangely comforting experience, we are suddenly and cruelly cut off from any access to what we want most: trapped light. As if to imply that the essential characteristic of modernism's psychic "utopia" was not so much the happy and transparent dream of wish fulfillment, but the anxious dream of blocked desire.

Beyond Baroque

Eric Owen Moss in Culver City

> The earlier work investigated overlapping of geometrical entities. Then the interior space—Western. Now it's the space between inside and outside where geometries dance. The space in between is flexing. The inside of the outside and the outside of the inside.
>
> —Eric Owen Moss

Rejecting the ascription "jeweler of junk" bestowed on him early on by Philip Johnson, and distancing himself from a too pervasive "deconstructivism," Eric Owen Moss now stakes out a ground originally prepared by modernist theory and practice—that of "space"—as a starting point for his own increasingly complex geometrical explorations. In the context of postmodernism and deconstruction, this claimed filiation might have a nostalgic, even retro air—reminding one of Bruno Zevi, Christian Norberg-Schulz, postwar smugness, and fifties comfortable shoes—were it not so elegant in its tactical simplicity. "Space," "geometry," "structure": the three themes that resonate through this iteration of Moss's persistent incursions into Culver City and elsewhere bypass entirely almost every question of style and cutting-edge theory of the last decades, referring instead to the supposed fundamentals of architecture, and especially modern architecture. For the idea of space and the image of modernism have been intimately connected since the turn of the century, in historical theory as in architectural practice. If the aesthetic psychology and sociology of Lipps and Simmel, and the historical studies of Schmarsow and Frankl, confirmed the essential place of space in the analysis of architectural history—"space, protagonist of architecture," as Bruno Zevi put it in 1948—the polemics of Le Corbusier and Mies van der Rohe and their followers dramatically attested to its essential place in a truly modern architecture.

There has been, of course, no lack of contenders for a "return" to, or a "continuity" with, modernism in the last quarter of a century: from "late" modernists like Richard Meier and "endless avant-gardists" like Peter Eisenman to those more or less self-consciously implicated in deconstruction, the refrain has been persistent of a modernist century that refuses to hide beneath the excesses of postmodern eclecticism. But in the case of Moss, the need to distinguish himself from neomodernist architects on the one hand and expressionist deconstructionists on the other has generated a different note, and one that perhaps signals a slight shift in the framing of fin-de-siècle apologetics.

For Moss assays his critical return to the basics of modernity in relation to principles of space and structure expounded in that by now canonical text, Sigfried Giedion's *Space, Time and Architecture.* Not, of course, that we are expected to read Giedion as trustingly as before; a half-century of countermodernist critique and debased modern practice has given the lie to space, geometry, and structure as virtues in themselves, and Giedion's structural and spatial determinism seem quaintly out of place in a poststructuralist universe. Rather, Moss explicitly sets up Giedion as a structural reductionist who left out the most important architectural ingredient of all in neglecting the "content," whether spiritual or artistic.

Implicitly, *Space, Time and Architecture*'s attempt to trace the "growth of a new tradition" sets up the coordinates for Moss's own retelling of an old story. We are, by inference at least, asked to place Moss's own self-constructed itinerary, from "geometrical entities" and "Western" interiority to his more recent experimentation with inside and outside, in the context of the strong narratives of Giedion's historicism. And certainly, Moss provides an account that bears some resemblance to Giedion's own biography of modernism, from the Renaissance, through the baroque, to the structural innovations of the nineteenth century, and thence to the "new space-time synthesis." But with the significant difference that, where Giedion's book attempted to establish its thesis firmly on the assumed congruence of modernism and historical progress, Moss is forced to avoid any simplistic reduction of terms like structure and space that seem to evince the very opposite of stability. Moss's "space," like his geometry, is conceived as shifting, "flexing," and jumping, described in gerundive terms that would have delighted the romantics of the early nineteenth century and given him a place among the organicists of architecture.

But the parallels with Giedion go further, and perhaps throw a new light on the particular character of Moss's work from the outset—that insistence on the distortion, reformulation, and mutation of pure geometries (the circle, the cube, the cone) that has been generally uncharacteristic of recent radical attempts to "deconstruct" tradition (whether by Frank Gehry or Coop Himmelblau). If for a moment we were to escape from the theoretical prejudices of the present, we might find it instructive to read Moss's oeuvre not in the light of junk or constructivism, but as an extended and intensely worked meditation on the formal predilections and pathological insights of Giedion and his generation—Emil Kaufmann, for example, or Hans Sedlmayr. We might thus be able to construe a kind of formal evolution, as these historicists would have put it, from the rational cylindrical and conical geometries of the Pin Ball House and the Fun House, to the more broken and shattered forms of the 708 House, the Petal House, and Houses X and Y, to the narrative *architecture parlante* of the Reservoir House, to the imbricated overlapping geometries of the Uehara House. These geometries would then be the starting point for more public work, such as the Lower East Side Housing for the Indigent Pavilion, the Escondido Civic Center, and the Tokyo Opera House. This would be the moment where all these formal experiments found an ideal home, so to speak, in what has become Moss's own little utopian community, the Frederick Smith developments in Culver City.

In such an imaginary "history" we would be presented not with deconstruction, and certainly not with postmodernism nor even modernism as it was adumbrated by the "masters" of the twenties and thirties. Moss would be seen to be reflecting on an even more foundational route—that described in Kaufmann's title of 1933, *Von Ledoux bis Le Corbusier.* This little book, published in Vienna on the very eve of the Nazi putsch in Berlin and just before Kaufmann's own exile, intriguingly joins the generation of the 1730s (Ledoux, Boullée, Lequeu) to that of the 1930s (Le Corbusier, Walter Gropius) in an argument that rests on a direct connection drawn by Kaufmann between form (independent, rational) and the rise of bourgeois society (freedom of the individual, social democracy), with Ledoux and Le Corbusier as the heroes. A similar argument, with differences in heroes and villains, was to be made by Giedion and Sedlmayr.

Whether or not Moss's own "history" refers self-consciously to such obviously oversimplified historical genealogies, the reference to the formal and

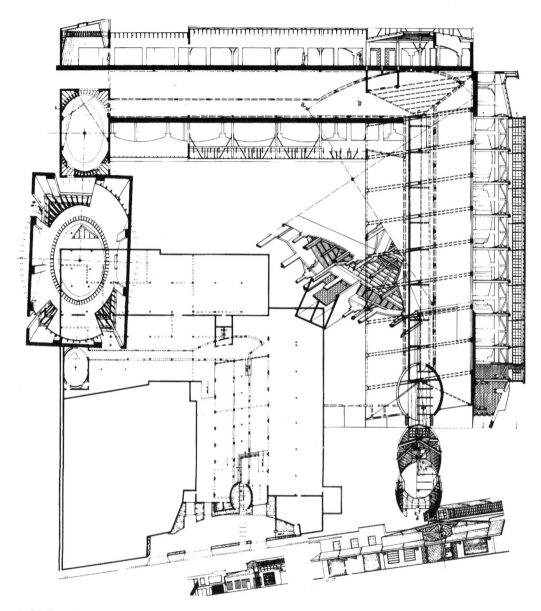

19. Eric Owen Moss,
8522 National Boulevard
complex, office building,
Culver City. Plan and
projection.

spatial "origins" of modernism is nevertheless revealing on two counts. First, it definitively separates Moss from the rationalism of the neorationalists and the pastiche rationalism of the postmoderns, neither of which was fundamentally concerned with geometry as the basis of architectural invention. And second, it puts him in the context of an alternative "modernism" to that of the functionalists and structural determinists, one represented interestingly enough by the last "hero" cited by Kaufmann—Richard Neutra, whose statement from California rings hauntingly from the last page of *Von Ledoux bis Le Corbusier,* and which seems tellingly to anticipate Moss's own critique of Giedion's structural determinism. "It is a long way from the plastic formalism of the Greek world to the swelling facades of the baroque, but this route is not illogical, it always traverses, so to speak, the same region: that of a certain spiritual attitude towards architectural creation."[1] And the form of this "spirituality" was, in Neutra's and Kaufmann's terms, geometrical, dominated by the "predilection for simple forms."

Here, of course, we are presented with a tantalizing nexus of further imaginary associations. It is tempting, for example, to raise the possibility of a "California" modernism, forged by Neutra and now transformed and permutated a half-century later; this might well be an exilic practice, driven to geometry in its search for stability in movement. We might also, paradoxically enough, find ourselves crossing paths with Philip Johnson in the 1930s and 1940s, intersecting his very different "modern" trajectory at the moment when Kaufmann himself introduced Johnson to the forms of Ledoux, in his first Harvard seance of 1943.

Johnson himself, in his concise introduction to the first volume of *Eric Owen Moss: Buildings and Projects,* preferred a genealogy for the work that operated by generation: the fathers (Mies, Corb, et al.); the emulators and first sons (Johnson et al.); the "kids" (Gehry, Eisenman, et al.); and the children of the "kids" (Morphosis, Moss, et al.). And with a twist of the family tree that shifted the responsibility for these last children away from the grandfathers and fathers to another paternity altogether (Sullivan through Scarpa), Johnson neatly proclaimed them both orphans and bastards, characterized by their transgression against modernist spatial planning and their fundamentally ornamental preoccupation. In this way, Johnson was able to characterize Moss as the "jeweler of junk," at once complimenting his skill (as a diamond peddler?)

and implying the marginality of his practice: the jeweler/peddler, at home in the wasteland of LA but denied the spatial pedigree of truly Western architecture.

Inevitably, Johnson was following the continuing modernist ploy of affirming the authenticity of "space" against the inauthenticity of "ornament," if not as crime, at least as superfluity and therefore lesser. From Giedion to Hitchcock, Zevi, and Johnson himself, "space" has been the litmus test of true architecture, in its long history from volumetric solidity to ineffable fluidity—as Giedion had it, from rock temple to Le Corbusier, or, in Johnson's terms, from Greece to Mies. And, as the Greco-Roman cultural tradition had, for nationalist reasons, to be welded to Gothic political roots, so this "space" was itself joined to the morality of structure (whether Puginesque or Choisyesque) that determined precisely the limits of the ornamental. Space and structure were endowed in turn with socially ethical ends in order to construct the well-known ideological complex known as "morality in architecture." In this context, Johnson's description of a new generation's work as ornamental and not spatial was hardly innocent.

At the same time, however, and in the context of Moss's own assertion of his spatial identity, one would have to admit, with Johnson, that if space were indeed a central characteristic of Moss's work, it would certainly not be the clear, open, and ineffable space of modernism. Structural complexity, apparently unnecessary and often gratuitous, if not ironically redundant, joined to geometrical combinations and hybrid forms, render space, if present, difficult to identify, at least in the traditional ways. To see space at work here, one would have to reformulate its very qualities, its roles, and even its representational modes.

And yet, there is a way in which we might see Moss's spatial complexities in direct lineage from modernism, and especially from Giedion's own formulation of modernist space as distinctively cubist in nature. As Giedion summarized it in his description of Le Corbusier's Villa Savoye, "It is impossible to comprehend the Savoie house by a view from a single point; quite literally, it is a construction in space-time. The body of the house has been hollowed out in every direction: from above and below, within and without. A cross section at any point shows inner and outer space penetrating each other inextricably."[2] Such interpenetration and multiple-point perspective was, as we have seen, integral to the utopian vision that Giedion had of the "baroque"—joining space and structure in such a way as to liberate the one from the other. Giedion formulated a baroque that was both triumphant and prospective. For him, the baroque, and its complex questioning of Renaissance perspective stability and realist representation, its combination of perspectival multiplicity and illusion, found in its most developed form in the work of Borromini and Guarini, seemed, in retrospect, to prefigure cubism. When joined to the spatial interpenetration exhibited in the engineering structures of the late nineteenth century, the potential of the baroque was turned into constructive possibility: "this possibility was latent in the skeleton system of construction, but the skeleton had to be used as Le Corbusier uses it," concluded Giedion, "in the service of a new conception of space."[3] In this model of spatial history, the role played by structure became pivotal; Giedion's pairing of Borromini's lantern of Sant'Ivo and Tatlin's project for a Monument to the Third International has itself become a commonplace, as has his analysis of Guarini's cupola of San Lorenzo, where "the impression of unlimited space has been achieved not through the employment of perspective illusions or of a painted sky but through exclusively architectural means" that go "to the very end of constructional resources."[4] It remained only for modern construction methods to overcome these limits, and for modern architects to imagine modern space, and the equation *spatial imagination + structural invention = progress* would be confirmed. The dynamics of baroque spatial interpenetration were further pressed to their modernist fulfillment, so to speak, by such a return of temporality, but this time in an antihistoricist guise. Long before the popularization of Einstein, the calibration of space to time preoccupied philosophers and aestheticians, writers, painters, and architects to the extent that "space-time" became a dominant leitmotiv of modernism.[5]

It is in relation to this "baroque tradition" that Moss's own geometrical work begins to take on a certain significance beyond the merely incidental and perhaps accidental filiations with the more general historiography of modernism. For there is much evidence in Moss's own projects that a modern "baroque" of some kind is at work, at the level of overt formal similarities as well as in theoretical inference. On the visual level alone, there are many parallels that would have fascinated a latter-day Giedion: she might, for example, have chosen to pair the dome of San Lorenzo with the Culver City conference room, or with the vault to the Gary Group entrance lobby; or even to the elliptical insertions in the Uehara House. There are no doubt comparisons to be drawn between Gropius's *Totaltheater* project and that for the Ince Theater in the extension of the notion of a "many-sided spectacle." The complex reworkings of spherical geometry in, say, the Aronoff House might be considered a "baroque" reworking of Ledoux's Spherical House Project; similarly, parallels may be drawn between neoclassical geometrics and their refashion in, for example, the Lawsen/Westen House, or, in more public modes, in the R3 "Theater," the Plaza Vieja, or the Contemporary Art Center. Equally, the complex eroded, leaning, and warped planes and facades of Samitaur, and Stealth, or earlier the facades of the Gary Group, might be seen in relation to the undulating and pressured walls of Borromini and Guarini. On the urban level, and according to the formal comparisons deployed by Giedion himself, we might, finally, look to the bridge infrastructure of S.P.A.R. City as it moves "serpentining through east Culver City," in relation to the precedents for such serpentine moves in the Nash terraces of Bath.

In each case, structure is put in play to articulate geometry, which in turn pushes the boundaries of a succession of intersecting and overlapping spatial entities, leading to the delineation of a complex warped space, ambiguously balanced between "inside" and "outside." Space itself is "folded" somewhat in the manner described by Gilles Deleuze in his explication of Leibniz's elaboration of baroque mathematics, a mathematics of variability, inflection, and tangent curves.[6]

Here, however, we have reached the limits of a "baroque" that is legitimately filiated to any recognizable "modernism," whether cubist or purist. By contrast, we are precipitated into a world of half-ruins and fragments, shattered wholes and disseminated entities, of a violence expressed through and even against geometry. Such a topos, indeed, seems to echo that other, *negative* baroque, identified throughout the modern period as the sign of ending, of melancholy, and of the empty frames of allegorical rhetoric. In the context of this admittedly imaginary plot, where the ascription "baroque" refers more to modernist fantasies of spatial explosion than to any seventeenth-century historical condition, Moss's recent work seems positioned at the intersection between Giedion's progressive hope and Benjamin's melancholic pathology. In its formal experimentation and exploration of spatial ambiguity, not to speak of its evident commitment to a renewed public realm, it continues, albeit with conscious dislocation, a long modernist tradition; in its assertion of a narrative comprised of allegorically redolent fragments, it fittingly represents a new fin-de-siècle condition where the utopian symbols of modernity have lost their former allure.

Whether or not one chooses to follow this trail of analogy to the present fin-de-siècle and its own formal and social disruptions, it is clear that those of Moss, at least, cannot be read without reference to this alternative pathology, one that admits the incongruity, if not the impossibility, of artistic achievement conceived according to laws of harmony and autonomy, and, for better or worse, understands a perpetually unfixed manner of expression as the representation of a work that attempts to infuse new life, perforce with violence, into the shells of forsaken dwellings, sites, and landscapes.

Death Cube "K"

The Neoformations of Morphosis

> It seems that the most modern functionalism more or less voluntarily re-
> activated the most archaic or mythical forms. There, too, there is a mu-
> tual penetration of two bureaucracies, that of the past and that of the
> future (we're still at this stage today). Realizing this mixture, we can only
> distinguish the following as the two poles: *archaisms with a contemporary*
> *function* and *neoformations*. It seems to us that Kafka was one of the first
> to recognize this historical problem.
>
> Deleuze and Guattari, *Kafka*[1]

William Gibson, in his novel *Idoru,* describes what he calls a "Franz Kafka
theme bar," on the upper floors of a self-healing, bio-active building in the
epoch after the postmillennial great Tokyo earthquake. Its first room, a "Metamorphosis" bar constructed out of "acid-etched metal . . . of artfully corroded
steel," sets the tone, with chairs molded from "some brown and chitinous resin"
emulating insect backs, and sharp mandibles hovering over the heads of the
drinkers. The light too is brown—"roach-light"—illuminating translucent
walls that evoke wing cases and "bulbous abdomens." Beyond, a stair, itself in
the form of "glossy brown carapaces," leads to a disco—"The Penal Colony"—
lit by "pulses of silent red lightning." Suspended from the ceiling is a machine
with articulated arms, "suggestive of antique dental equipment" and "tipped
with sharp steel," the "pens" with which to engrave the sentence of guilt on the
condemned victim's body. Finally a second stair led to the "Trial" room, with
its low ceilings and "walls the color of anthracite."[2] In this description of the
"Death Cube K" bar, Gibson neatly intersects the postapocalyptic tones of the
cyberpunk "zone city" and the anticipation of catastrophe built into the modernist canon of the twenties. Kafka, the ironic peddler of counterbureaucratic

insects, is himself metamorphosed into a creature of millennialist consumption for the citizens of a world beyond hope, in an architecture of deconstructive decay. Corroded metal, sharp steel, prosthetic instruments mimicking dental tools, insectlike interiors, dead-end black holes for judgment beyond the law, all seem images drawn directly from the recent past of 1980s architecture. While overpictorial and obviously undertheorized, "Death Cube K" could stand for any of a number of metallic, postcyber, and counter-postmodern environments of the last few years. On a purely imagistic level, indeed, one might think of connections to the restaurant interiors of Morphosis, with their steel, clockwork-like contraptions and sharp-edged details, like so many "Penal Colony" writing machines. The literal evocation of "Metamorphosis" in Morphosis is hard to resist, and surely was not far from Gibson's own mind. And while the caricatural level of Gibson's architecture works against any sustained elaboration of the analogy with the elegant and abstract work of Morphosis, it would be wrong to dismiss out of hand what seems to be an intuitive association of "K" with their work. Morphosis was obviously not the architect of "Death Cube K," but in more ways than one Kafka's own architectural and spatial formulations of modern life might be brought to bear on an interpretation of their recent urban and institutional projects.

Scapelands

Certainly from the air, as models are inevitably viewed, represented like so many frames from "Flight Controller 98," angled and zoomed, these projects seem to be conceived as extensions of a William Gibson zonescape: fragmented, broken, twisted and scored lines on the earth, perhaps marking the passage of multiple civilizations and the death throes of the last. From a lower perspective, Stealth-like and racing close to the contours, the models seem to meld with the earth's crust itself, heaving and breaking, splitting and opening up with seismic precision, as if mapping the fault lines of a once hot, now cooling culture. Inside, if we are allowed entry, the forms are all-enclosing, elliptical, ovoid, womblike, as if half-encased within the shell of some long-broken dinosaur egg. Projected along endless, Klein-bottle-shaped corridors, the eye's perspective is canted with the planes that everywhere refuse the vertical, nowhere come to rest in the horizontal. The body, or rather its introjected projection, is relentlessly impelled forward at warp speed, as if suspended in the virtual frames of "Doom," with gravity-bending contortions that seem to defy Nietzsche's aphoristic invocation of the end of perspective: "we cannot see around our own corner."

At least, this would be one construction of the world constituted by Morphosis in its second iteration, a world no longer confined to the intricate filigrees of steel and concrete that mirrored the interior clockwork of the psyche in so many private restaurants and houses, but now, like the "Difference Engine" in Gibson and Bruce Sterling's image, exploded from the mechanical to the digital, and thus taking over the public realm by virtue of its conquest of matter as a whole, merging at once with the temporal moves of the population and the spatial shifts of the earth. The result can only be compared to a "landscape" with all the characteristics invoked by Jean-François Lyotard to describe what he calls a "scapeland": displacement, estrangement, and, most importantly with regard to its implications for modern architecture, a kind of *dépaysement,* a shifting of location and judgment from the stable conventions of inside and outside to a realm where a kind of "systematic madness" reigns supreme. Not insanity but *versanity,* where, as Kant (cited by Lyotard) notes, "the soul is transferred to a quite different standpoint, so to speak, and from it sees all objects differently . . . just as a mountainous landscape sketched from an aerial perspective calls forth a quite different judgment when it is viewed from the plain."[3]

And yet, while Lyotard extends Kant's characterization of the distantiation implied by the visualization of the sublime in landscape form, to meditate upon the virtuality of all matter transformed into "landscape" by melancholic introjection, there is nothing virtual about the morphosis accomplished by Morphosis. For the space that is transformed into a kind of landscape in these recent projects is not just any space but a direct commentary on that kind of space peculiar to modernity, and, in particular, to modern architecture's rendering of modernity. And what is being exploded from inside to outside is not simply a representation, Caligari-like, of a fin-de-siècle soul in torment, an expressionist visualization of the neurotic psyche revamped for the end of the millennium, but a conscious reworking of a set of modern architectural prototypes, developed in the twenties on behalf of a Taylorized and Fordized mass society, rendered lifeless from long complicity with corporate capital, but now seen as potential material out of which to shape a regenerated late twentieth-century modernism.

Here, Morphosis is enacting a complicated form of formal redemption. For, rather than jettisoning "modern architecture" in favor either of an ideological critique from the left or a nostalgic revival of "traditional" motifs from the right, Morphosis has chosen to identify a fundamental difference between "modernity" (and the spaces and socioeconomic forces that have supported its global extensions) and "modernism," with its sometimes critical, sometimes utopian architecture that has attempted, spasmodically throughout the century, to offer alternative spaces, other realms, through which the posttechnological, postbureaucratic life might be framed and lived. That a critique of modernity might give rise to an architecture of modernism, that, in the words of Ibsen's master builder Solness, "castles in the air" might paradoxically be built on "firm ground," has ever been an aspiration of the avant-gardes—an aspiration that has often enough fallen into the unthinking service of modernity. But it is nevertheless on the basis of this sustained hope that Morphosis has attempted its own reframing of modernity's absorption of modernism, working with the language of the latter to construe a critique of the former.

Men in Black

The notion that a modernist critique of modernity might also harbor the premises of another kind of modernism has been a verity of avant-garde practice since the futurists. And yet the terms of this critique have often simply reduplicated the premises of modernity in avant-garde guise—hence the substitution of "war" and "violence" for bourgeois "accommodation" in futurism, the substitution of "rationalization" and "efficiency" for the uneven forms of capital development in the work of Le Corbusier and his contemporaries, the aesthetic idealization of manufacturing processes in the work of constructivists, and so on. From the turn of the century, what might in retrospect be called "mainstream modernism" responded to the bureaucratic state with a rationalizing vigor and an implacable will to systematic downsizing that would have done honor to a late twentieth-century venture capitalist. For every item on the corporatist agenda, modern architecture eagerly supplied a corresponding aesthetic alibi. What Max Weber saw as a loss of individual "charisma" was countered by an optimistic acceptance of what Walter Benjamin termed "loss of aura"; the economics of mass architecture were furthered by a rejection of ornament; the prison surveillance of a Bentham was extended onto the factory floor and thence to the secretarial pool with the techniques of Taylor; the drive for time and motion efficiency was sustained by a futurist ideology of speed, which also buoyed the inextricable relations of industrialization and war. Individual aspirations were contained within a rigid separation of private and public realms. The "men in black" of the turn of the century, overcoated and bowler-hatted, every bit as faceless as their contemporary, digitally virtual counterparts, shuttled between their apartments and the elevators of Metropolis in anonymous silence. From Otto Wagner through Walter Gropius, Mies van der Rohe, and Ludwig Hilberseimer, the new, endless and all-encompassing city was stamped out in anonymous "bar buildings"—rows of minimal offices served by double-loaded corridors cut with precision from seemingly endless strips like so many steel rails that became the leitmotiv of modernist space.

Against this relentless production of rational space there was little resistance, save for the "charismatic" excesses of fascism on the one hand or the individual psychic revolts of expressionism and Dada on the other. And, as Siegfried Kracauer noted, the complicity between the world of *Dr. Caligari* and that of *Metropolis* was hard to miss. Despite the formal explosions of film and theater, the stage sets of psychological disturbance were easily dismissed, and the traumas they expressed all-too-easily pushed back underground, hunted, like the murderer of *M,* off the streets and lynched in secret underground trials by the "normal" mob. The psychic life of modernism, despite the efforts of psychoanalysis, was abandoned to the unconscious. Kafka's early nightmares of what he called "the horror in the merely schematic"[4] and Huxley's dystopian projections were no more than the parentheses within which the entire apparatus of twentieth-century shock, trauma, phobia, and neurosis was seen as the wastelands and *îlots insalubres* of the metropole, ripe for demolition and redevelopment rather than for architectural exploration.

The dream of a potentially liberating "space," more representative of the psychic and social fractures of modern life, has, however, been hard to resist: surrealists, situationists, and lately deconstructivists have cultivated the notion of an oppositional realm, part introjected, part projected, that through the force of its ruptures and disjunctions will force open the hermetically sealed vacuum of corporatism. The experiments of expressionism and constructivism, the biomorphisms of surrealism, the radical *informe* conceived by Bataille (recently revived under the sign of the amorphous "blob") have all offered formal vocabularies with which to counter the hermetically sealed realm of business. Theoreticians of space have at the same time attempted to envisage a realm that might potentially be taken back by the public—or at least afford shelter from the pervasive forces of institutionalized capital. Lefebvre's call for the social "right to the city," Foucault's "heterotopias," Deleuze and Guattari's "nomadisms" have sought in different ways to characterize "other spaces," not least in realms of gender and identity studies unthought of by the early modernists.

Morphing the Type

These various oppositional stances have led to much experimentation with architectural languages, either in the extension of modernist forms or in the invention of "other" forms. But, and despite the intense interest in the nature of institutional and formal "types" and "typologies" in the 1970s, sustained by the early studies of Foucault and his followers into the discursive structures of medical and penal institutions, few architects have sought to revise the structures of the fundamental building blocks of modernism—the office building, the apartment house, and their ancillary urban functions. Indeed, the word "type" itself has, in the late 1980s and early 1990s, become an almost extinct term, as interest in expressive vocabularies and high technologies has displaced questions of urban and architectural typo-morphologies. On the one hand this is explicable as a result of the quick absorption of typological concerns in the decorated sheds of postmodernism—a movement itself now revealed to be no more than the cosmetic pastellization of the corporate image. On the other hand, the waning of interest in type is paradoxical in the light of the present reaction against postmodern excesses, for the concept of type, emerging in the work of Giulio Carlo Argan in the 1960s and advanced by Joseph Rykwert, Alan Colquhoun, and Aldo Rossi, among others, was, at least initially, deliberately posed as a critique of the reductive containers of modernity, the empty shells that, in postwar development, had become the emblems of *anomie,* the visible frameworks of what Max Weber had understood as the "iron cage" of the bureaucratic state. Typology in this sense was an attempt to admit the macrostructure of the city into the microstructure of the individual building, at the same time recognizing the individual building as a member of a "family" of types to which it, in general, belonged. While too quickly immersed in the postmodern fashion for stylistic traditionalism and aesthetic contextualism, typology at its best represented a hope for the continuation of the utopian and countercorporate ambitions of avant-garde modernism, couched in terms that remained committed to modernity and rejecting nostalgia.

It is precisely here, in this conjuncture of resistance and utopia, that Morphosis has returned to typological concerns. Initially identified with an aesthetic of expressive force and individual momentum that, in its embrace of the machine, of industrial materials and forms, of the broken and the fractured, exemplified the language of resistance to postmodern style in the 1980s, the work seems now to have gained in intellectual and formal strength, by virtue of its contestation not only of corporate modern and postmodern style but also of its basic organizing structures.

Thus, at a small scale, in the Friedland Jacobs Communications building, Morphosis introduces what it terms a "transformation of generic office space" by inserting a "radius wall" to form an "embryonic shell." This principle of enclosure and individuation was also followed in the design for the Ove Arup offices in Los Angeles, where Morphosis developed an "organic language within the office interior" as a means of providing a degree of specificity—"the definition of a specific interior place" that dispensed with "the ubiquitous office syntax in normative work environments." Similarly, the ASE Design Center in Tokyo is constructed of "elliptical territories" delineated by curved primary walls, forming a "biomorphic planar shell system" crossed through and striated with structure and linear volumes. At a larger scale, the Frankfurt Waste Management Facility, conceived as a kind of efficient "disposal campus," houses its administrative offices in an administrative "ribbon" adjacent to the repair workshops. The American Business Center, located, ironically enough, at the site of the original Checkpoint Charlie, transforms the perimeter block into a high-density office space with a hollow, semipublic court within.

Ellipses

In what way, however, would these obvious formal metamorphoses of modern types be at once critical and prospective? Here we might return to our first model, that of a third architectural term between the utopian and the realist, the modernist and the modern, one sketched most evocatively by Walter Benjamin in his remarks on Kafka. In a letter to Gershom Scholem, written from Paris on 12 June 1938, Benjamin compared Kafka's work to "an ellipse" with its two foci far apart, the one "determined . . . by mystical experience (which is above all the experience of tradition)" and the other "by the experience of the modern city-dweller."[5] To Benjamin, himself ever caught between the same two foci, Kafka's prescience for the postapocalyptic century was that his understanding of modernity, of the plight of the modern city-dweller, was precisely filtered through the lens of a traditional sense of disaster and redemption signaled by the "mystical." On one side Benjamin poses Kafka's "modern citizen, who knows he is at the mercy of vast bureaucratic machinery, whose functioning is steered by authorities who remain nebulous even to the executive organs themselves, let alone the people they deal with," a figure well exemplified in *The Trial,* and on the other, Kafka's equally powerful inner world "frequently so serene and so dense with angels," through the frame of which he looked out at modernity. Kafka's "ellipse," then, was for Benjamin a kind of vertigo machine, drawing together worlds that could in no way be commensurate either on the level of reality or of dream. Rather, Benjamin cites the poetic evocation of "reality" posed by the contemporary physicist Sir Arthur Eddington, whose book *The Nature of the Physical World* seemed uncannily to prefigure Kafka's vision:

> I am standing on the threshold about to enter a room. It is a complicated business. In the first place I must shove against an atmosphere pressing with a force of fourteen pounds on every square inch of my body. I must make sure of landing on a plank traveling at twenty miles a second around the sun—a fraction of a second too early or too late, the plank would be miles away. I must do this while hanging from a round planet heading outward into space, and with a wind of ether blowing at no one knows how many miles a second through every interstice of my body.

The plank has no solidity or substance. To step on it is like stepping on a swarm of flies. Shall I not slip through? No, if I make the venture one of the flies hits me and gives a boost up again; I fall again and am knocked upward by another fly; and so on. I may hope that the net result will be that I remain about steady; but if unfortunately I should slip through the floor or be boosted too violently up to the ceiling, the occurrence would be, not a violation of the laws of Nature, but a rare coincidence. . . . Verily, it is easier for a camel to pass through the eye of a needle than for a scientific man to pass through a door. And whether the door be barn door or church door it might be wiser that he should consent to be an ordinary man and walk in rather than wait till all the scientific difficulties involved in a really scientific ingress are resolved.[6]

Out of similar components, Kafka constructed what Benjamin sees as a kind of "complementary world," one that "is the exact complement of his epoch, an epoch that is preparing itself to annihilate the inhabitants of this planet on a massive scale." Only Paul Klee, of Kafka's contemporaries, had construed his life in so "solitary" a manner. Benjamin concludes: "The experience that corresponds to that of Kafka as a private individual will probably first become accessible to the masses at such time as they are about to be annihilated."[7]

Leaving on one side for a moment the significance of this last observation for our own fin-de-siècle epoch, what is interesting in Benjamin's observations is the spatial character he ascribes to Kafka's vision, and not so much that posited by the analogical ellipse (although the elliptical has often enough figured in countermodern formalisms under the sign of Klein and Lacan) as that of the precarious atomistic, fault-ridden universe posed by modern physics, with its slippages and unexpected empty spaces (also linked in atomic diagrams of the period, we should remember, in intersecting elliptical trajectories). Here, Benjamin's model of Kafkaesque space finds a contemporary echo in the schema traced by Deleuze and Guattari, who distinguish between two "states" of Kafka's architecture, the one linked to the old, traditional world of power, imperial and despotic—the world of the story "The Great Wall of China"— and the other to the new capitalist or socialist bureaucracy—the world of *The Trial*. In formal terms, these two states are complementary: Deleuze and Guattari identify them as (1) "infinite-limited-discontinuous-close and distant" and

(2) "unlimited-continuous-finite-faraway and contiguous."[8] The first state takes its model from the the Great Wall of China itself, imagined by Kafka as a structure of discontinuous blocks, a "system of piecemeal construction," as Kafka terms it, that would, according to Kafka's "scholar," provide the most secure foundations for a new Tower of Babel.[9] Deleuze and Guattari diagram this form as a sequence of broken arcs in a circle surrounding a spiral tower at the center. The second state, taking its cue from the spatial complexities of the bureaucratic and legal offices in *The Trial*, situates its furthest distances—those spaces that are furthest away from each other—in close contiguity. Thus, to cite Deleuze's example, K. will drive to see the painter Tintorelli, "in a suburb which was almost at the diametrically opposite end of the town from the offices of the Court," only to find that a second door leads from the studio into the Judge's quarters.[10] Perhaps the most important aspect of Deleuze and Guattari's model, however, is not simply the formal identification of these two states, and their parallel to the "two foci" of Benjamin's elliptical model, but the assertion that the states are not only complementary but also essentially coexistent—that indeed they interpenetrate despite their distinct qualities. Deleuze and Guattari compare such intersection to that of the tower of Tatlin's Monument to the Third International, with its tipped and dynamic openwork spiral enclosing the traditional cubes, pyramids, and spheres that nevertheless are put into movement as they house the new bureaucracies of the Soviet state in mobilized forms of the old traditional orders: "the most modern functionalism more or less voluntarily reactivated the most archaic or mythical forms" in the "mutual penetration of two bureaucracies, that of the past and that of the future," in what Deleuze defines as a combination of the "infinite paranoiac spiral and the unlimited schizoid line."[11] An ascription that precisely describes the spatiality of *The Castle* (height, hierarchy/contiguity of offices with moving boundaries) and not incidentally recalls the space of the paranoid/schizoid subject as delineated in Lacan's "The Mirror Stage," a virtually inaccessible "fortified keep" set in an arena of struggle, surrounded by "marshes and rubbish tips."

In this combination of avant-garde aspiration to invent the new and the inevitable reliance on the form of the old, Kafka precisely outlined the spatial dilemmas of modernity as a whole, at the same time as pointing toward a possible form, not of their reconciliation or synthetic resolution, but of their uneasy, interpenetrating, and always broken coexistence. It is in this sense that we can see in the fractured blocks and arclike forms of Morphosis's office complexes, and in the ovoid enclosures of their interior alignments, a bringing together of the distant and the close, and the faraway and the contiguous, in a setting that describes as it deconstructs the bureaucratic infinities and closures of modern life.

Thus the Spreebogen project for the Berlin Parliament competition establishes a symbolic "center" by setting up a symbolic periphery—a "large Platonic circle" that is then, like the Great Wall, "fractured and disjointed," its

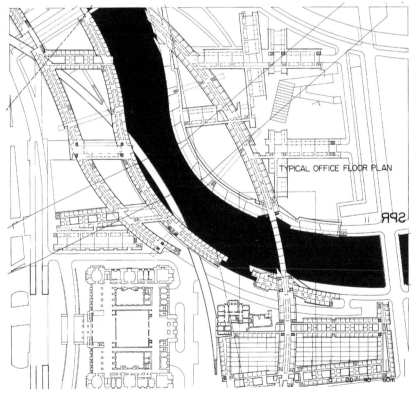

20. Morphosis, Internationaler Stadtbaulicher Ideenwettbewerb Spreebogen (Spreebogen Urban Design Competition), Berlin, 1992. Plan showing office floors.

fragments reformulated to serve the different functions of the complex. Here the reference is evidently to the already demolished Berlin Wall, now standing only in "memorial" fragments, and its reassimilation into the fabric of a unified city. Morphosis's "piecemeal construction" operates on the level of memory (the memory of the Berlin Wall is transformed into walls of memory) but also on the level of symbolic power. For even as the ambiguities of Kafka's China Wall allow for multiple hypotheses as to the Government's intentions—the Wall was in fact meant to be piecemeal, and therefore "inexpedient"; the Wall was the foundation for a new Tower of Babel; it symbolized the all-pervasive yet necessarily incomplete power of the vast Empire—so the breaks in Morphosis's Wall of Government register a fact and a desire: that, in their words, "government is now seen as dispersed and integrated into the urban fabric . . . it is fluid, open, transformable, and symbolic of the diverse culture it represents." Its form, however, however fragmented, has to be "coherent and rational in order for its constituents to know it." On another scale, the serpentine, fragmented "wall" of interior offices in the SHR Perceptual Management building functions in the same way to play individual location against collective identification.

Tipping the Wall

If Kafka's Great Wall of China was in some way a metaphor for a modernist Babel structure, its fragmented and piecemeal character anticipating in some way the discontinuities later to be celebrated in deconstructivism, the walls of Morphosis refuse even this stability. As if, following the visual laws of Kafkaesque space, they literally enact the forced perspective of the paranoid subject, always sloped and canted, fractured and broken. And while this has become a common signature for a certain school of post-postmodern form, in Morphosis the canted wall takes on a polemical quality, self-consciously posed against the "right angle" of modernity, the horizontality and verticality announced by the Maison Domino prototype. Perhaps, with *The Castle* in mind, we might see in these slopes an echo of the traditional fortification, the glacis, the pyramid; and yet, more often than not, the wall, again polemically, is removed from its support, floating in space, detached from any but a screening function. Canted walls were, it is true, a leitmotiv of expressionism, where the complexes of a Freudian generation were exaggerated in perspective and shadow as so many psychic eruptions breaking the calm serenity of modern rationalism, itself dedicated, as Robin Evans has observed of Mies, to a resistance against such "seismic" events.[12] But where the exploding walls of Coop Himmelblau might warrant such comparisons, the canted walls of Morphosis should rather be understood as an extension of their reflection on modernism.

Construing the complex formal gesture of the entrance wall at La Tourette, and observing its obvious departure from the transparent screens and horizontal ribbons characteristic of the earlier Domino model, Colin Rowe seized on an apparently innocent remark in Le Corbusier's text, one ostensibly directed to an explanation of the effect of the interior of the Pompeii houses: "the floor, which is really a horizontal wall."[13] This deceptively simple formulation, as Rowe points out, began to explain the apparent contradiction between the horizontally sliced space of Domino—the "sandwich"—and the vertically walled enclosures of the megaron volumes that appeared first in the Citrohan House and later in the chapel at La Tourette. As Rowe noted, "if floors are horizontal walls, then, presumably, walls are vertical floors; . . . elevations become plans, and the building a form of dice."[14] Here we are presented with a far more complex condition of "wall" than simply the dialectical "return of the wall" characteristic of much post- and countermodernism in the late twentieth century. Where this movement has insisted on the return of the wall, of the bounded space, of the recognizable place, in the face of the infinite horizontality of the modernist *espace indicible* and its pretensions to universality, the dialectic proposed by Le Corbusier between the horizontal and vertical elements of containment is completely lost. Further, the wall at La Tourette acts both as a surrogate "facade" and as a parallel container to the megaron volume of the chapel. This double function, itself mediated by the implied twisting of the wall, an illusion set up by the nonparallelism of the marks left by the "horizontal" shuttering, takes on a new significance in the light of the canted walls of Morphosis's modernist reprise. Here, the dictum "the floors are horizontal walls" would be reflected back in order to produce the interesting result, "the walls are really canted floors," leading to the conclusion that all enclosing surfaces are destabilized, "sheared," and "fractured," to use Morphosis's own terms.

In this instability we approach the condition implied by Kafka himself, of a spatiality that refuses gravity, that dissolves into a cosmic flux, at once microcosmic and macrocosmic, ceaselessly shifting from moment to moment according to the psychological drives and impusions of the moving and sensing subject; a space that, in the words of Javier Navarro de Zuvillaga, replicates a "cosmic space" that exhibits nothing but scorn for the concept of gravity: "K in all his characters moves in a cosmic space the fundamental characteristics of which are shown in the confrontation of various levels: the human level, the level of infinity and the absence of laws of gravity which . . . consequently produce a disorienting space on which Kafka's architecture is based."[15] This sense of cosmic anxiety, already noted by Benjamin, creates a virtual architecture in Kafka's novels and short stories that varies constantly "according to the mood of the character," that "changes together with the physiological momentum of the character": "one recalls the endless corridors which offered K an ever-longed-for escape but simultaneously one notices that these long corridors could never be contained within the limits of perspective."[16] Such spaces would, in these terms, be perceived less through sight or even the senses than through the anxious states of mind of the character—"eminently functional spaces," as Navarro de Zuvillaga notes, that stretch and shrink according to the character that moves within them. In this ascription, all Kafka's spaces, as described, are banal and normal enough—offices, corridors, bedrooms, and the like—but are transformed into a frightening abnormality by the projections and introjections of their inhabitants.

The canted walls of Morphosis that slope and curve into infinity along canted floors that seem to allow no access but which reveal ever-receding horizons with the movements, actual and psychological, of the subject, would be in this sense the analog to Kafka's sense of space. New, sloped screens, as in the Salick Health Center Headquarters, or the Village Fashion Building in Seoul, Korea, are set up to break the rigid frames of existing buildings, creating interstitial spaces, impossible to inhabit save by visual projection; these new "walls" are often visually permeable, translucent, and themselves ambiguous. Angled walls frame the interconnecting spaces of the Friedland Jacobs Communications offices and the Ove Arup and Partners Corporate Offices, giving rise to perspectival distortions that "zoom" in from one zone to another.

The Burrow

And if canted walls could be construed as so many sloped floors transposed into the "vertical," then the floors themselves would be so many slanted and inclined planes without vertical closure—above and below. Like the "mole" in

Kafka's "The Burrow," Morphosis digs into the ground as if to imply that if there is no limit to height nor to depth. Thus the Berlin projects are seen as so many "landscapes"; in the Mack residence importance is given to the integration of the landscape into the house; in the Diamond Ranch High School the building itself is conceived as a kind of "sitework," combining "reshaped topographies" and architecture to form a "primary space made with the earth and in the earth." The architects write of "folds," "plates," and display topographic folded grids in projects such as the M. A.S.H. (Mobile Assisted Shelter for the Homeless), a school and childcare facility that features a "reconfigured" earth; the Junipero Serra Shrine is formed of an embracing wall, an earthen mound, a shrine below ground, all set within a planted landscape. The project for the Prado Museum extension figures a sunken, artificial landscape, while the scheme for the Rockledge offices of Dan Logan and Medical Planning Associates in Malibu has turf roofs as if to camouflage its architectural nature.[17] Architecture indeed has here gone to ground, if not underground; the "burrow" has been literalized, but not, however, in an entirely Kafkaesque sense. For, as Siegfried Kracauer noted of Kafka's conception of architecture,

> the building that one generation erects after another is sinister, because this structure is to guarantee a security that men cannot attain. The more systematically they plan it, the less they are able to breathe in it; the more seamlessly they try to erect it, the more inevitably it becomes a dungeon. It rears up like a nightmare in the story "The Burrow" . . . the cave-like construction built by "perhaps a mole or a hamster" "out of fear of an invasion by all conceivable forces." Since this fear wants to eliminate those insecurities, inherent to creaturely existence, the burrow is a work of self-deception. It is no accident that its labyrinthine passageways and squares extend through subterranean night.[18]

Morphosis, on the other hand, seems to celebrate the underground as simply another dimension of gravity-free space, moving at will around ground zero without recognizing the transition, without the sense of constriction given by the canonical modes of modernism and postmodernism.

In Morphosis, indeed, the paranoid "burrow" is recast as sanctuary: most notably in the Junipero Serra Shrine, where an angled, enclosing wall bounding a "sacred" mound finds its resolution in an underground shrine, forming a complex that is neither above nor below, a "hybrid" spatiality that is reinforced by the shafts of light that are calculated to touch the interiors at certain marked times of the year. Similarly, in the more secular context of the private dwelling, the projects for the Mack House and the Blades House, in particular, dig and reform the earth as if the "datum" of ground is entirely removed, forming a gravity-free space in which the various domestic functions are resited and staged in relation to already dramatic landscape sites. The public analog to these small "burrows" is found in the roofscapes of the Hypothenkenbank projects I and II, where the buildings rise up in great shallow curves, "mnemonic," as Morphosis puts it, "of the rural topography" and creating a new, artificial landscape within the city intersecting with the old in broken and fragmented ellipses. The building-as-garden theme is continued in the Science Museum School; while in the crystalline cuts and fills of the Diamond Ranch High School, with its "folded surface" that moves easily above and below ground, the topography seems to respond to Deleuze's characterization of a Leibnizian space that refuses vertical and horizontal striation in favor of the continuous, folded, and Klein-bottle curves of monadic movement.

With these "earth moves," as Bernard Cache would term them,[19] Morphosis has completed the morphological transition from modernism to a form of late twentieth-century practice that, while recognizing the legitimacy of critical theory in its attacks on the bureaucratic modern state, nevertheless refuses to abandon the quasi-utopian stance of the modernist avant-gardes. In the wake of what we might call the "Kafka effect," and the attempt to reconstrue the terms of judgment for a modernity that has exceeded its own self-constructed rationales in its postnational and posthistorical conditions, Morphosis's "neoformations" begin to open up the territory of deterritorialization, without nostalgia and also without false promises. In this space there is freedom of movement, even if of a nomadic and fluid kind, for an architectural practice of global, but not globalizing, aspirations.

Skin and Bones

Folded Forms from Leibniz to Lynn

The House of Folds

In his exploration of the spatial characteristics of Leibniz's philosophy considered as "baroque," Gilles Deleuze introduced what has proved to be a provocative formal theme for contemporary architects: that of the "fold" or *pli,* registered both as a material phenomenon—as in the folds of Bernini's sculpture of Santa Teresa, for example—and as a metaphysical idea—as in the "fold" that joins the soul to the mind without division. As Deleuze expands on the implications for the fold, and its cognates the pleat and the crease, it gains an almost ontological status as the defining characteristic of baroque space and thought; its place in the theoretical and design culture of the 1990s is almost equally secure. In Deleuze's terms, as derived from an exceedingly original reading of Leibniz, the fold is at once abstract, disseminated as a trait of all matter, and specific, embodied in objects and spaces; immaterial, and elusive in its capacities to join and divide at the same time, and physical and formal in its ability to produce shapes, and especially curved and involuted shapes. This last characteristic has been of especial interest to architects, always searching for the tangible attribute of an abstract thought; but it is not at all clear that folds, in the sense of folded forms, correspond in any way to Deleuze's concept, or even less to Leibniz's model. For Leibniz, and also for Deleuze, to say that folds are manifested in "pleats of matter" is not simply to refer to a crease in a piece of cloth; matter is, in these terms, everywhere, in the void as well as in the solid and subject to the same forces. Folds then exist in space and in time, in things and in ideas, and among their unique properties is the ability to join all these levels and categories at the same moment.

To clarify this difficult concept Deleuze sketches what he calls an "allegory" of these relations, figured in what he sees as the "Baroque House"

21. Gilles Deleuze, "La maison baroque (allégorie)," *Le pli. Leibniz et la baroque* (Paris: Editions de Minuit, 1988), p. 7.

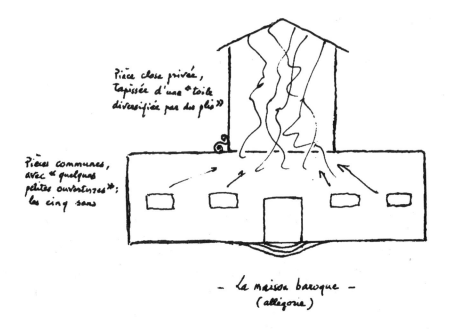

imagined by Leibniz. It consists of a ground floor, four windows and a door wide, the door approached by a flight of three curved steps. Above is a second story composed of a closed room, with five small openings in its floor to let in emanations from below. This room, in Deleuze's drawing, is hung with five curtains, "a drapery diversified by folds" that fall loosely through the openings below. Evidently, the five openings below represent the five senses, the five curtains their receptors, and the closed upper room a kind of mental space, based solidly on the lower physical body. In a nice touch, Deleuze lightly joins the two stories with a baroque scrolled motif on one side—the tie between body and head, so to speak.

This house is, for Deleuze, an image of Leibniz's "great Baroque montage that moves between the lower floor, pierced with windows, and the upper floor, blind and closed, but on the other hand resonating as if it were a musical salon translating the visible movements below into sounds up above."[1] Or, put in Leibnizian terms, a figure of the relations between the material, sensing body on the ground and its "monad" or soul, to which it transmits the knowledge given by its senses. Itself without senses, the monad nevertheless registers the impulse of the outside world as it does the inner and innate knowledge with which it is endowed from birth.

Deleuze matches this image with others drawn from studies of baroque architecture, and especially the formal analysis of Wölfflin, whence he derives the idea that the baroque

> is marked by a certain number of material traits: horizontal widening of the lower floor, flattening of the pediment, low and curved stairs that push into space; matter handled in masses or aggregates, with the rounding of angles and avoidance of perpendiculars . . . spongy cavernous shapes, or to constitute a vortical form always put into motion by renewed turbulence . . . matter tends to spill over in space, to be reconciled with fluidity at the same time fluids themselves are divided into masses.[2]

In other words, an architecture of endless folds. Here the abstract formalism of Wölfflin has been used to advantage in order to delineate an architecture of substances and masses, a curved architecture always in virtual motion, an architecture of waves and infinite spatial extension. Such a "baroque" had, as we have seen, a powerful influence on the spatial imagery of modernism, and it is not surprising that a digital decade has seen in Deleuze a prophet of the morphing, warping, and complicated curvatures of virtual space.[3] Constructed in this way "through" a Wölfflinian perspective, translated into architecture through the late nineteenth-century reading of a baroque that was, in retrospect, more a fiction of the new psychology of the body than a historical account, Deleuze's Leibniz emerges as a more complex entity than the seamless textual ecstasy of *The Fold* leads us to suspect. And indeed, a return to the Leibnizian texts from which Deleuze derived his "House" seems to introduce an unexpected rupture in the kinds of transactions intimated by the Deleuzean fold—a different and perhaps more analytically precise model through which we might begin to measure the special *effet du pli* of the last decade.

Deleuze formulated his Leibnizian model from a combination of readings, two of which were primary. The first, Leibniz's celebrated essay the *Monadology*, described the characteristics and forms of the monad; the second, a response in the form of an imaginary dialogue with the British philosopher John Locke entitled *New Essays on Human Understanding*, includes an important modification of Locke's image of the brain as a camera obscura. This second text, which provides so to speak the architectural structure for the *pli*-House, is couched in terms of an extended clarification of Locke's dark room metaphor for discernment. Locke's assertion seemed rational enough: "The understanding is not much unlike a small room [*un cabinet entièrement obscur* in Leibniz's French] wholly shut from light, with only some little openings left, to let in external and visible images; would the images coming into such a dark room but stay there, and lie so orderly as to be found upon occasion, it would very much resemble the understanding of a man."⁴ The spatial setting of the understanding is thus a pinhole camera, only with more than one opening for the purpose of transmitting images (Locke says "pictures" in the original) from the outside, and there seems to be an ordering principle within the box, ready to line up the images in what Locke would term a chain, ready for the associations, thence ideas and reflections, that constituted the understanding.⁵ Locke's camera, like that of perspective artists since Alberti, was assumed to transmit reality, clearly and in focus, undistorted and ready for its transformation into representation. Leibniz accepted this space, but extended and adapted it to his own purposes:

> To increase the resemblance we should have to postulate that there is a screen/canvas/curtain/membrane [*toile*] in the darkened room [*la chambre obscure*] to receive the species [*les espèces,* or beings, sensible species] and that it is not uniform but is diversified by folds [*diversifiée par des plis*] representing items of innate knowledge; and what is more, that this screen/canvas/curtain/membrane, being under tension, has a kind of elasticity or active force, and indeed that it acts (or reacts) in ways that are adapted both to past folds and to new ones coming from impressions of the species. This action would consist in certain vibrations or oscillations, like those we see when a cord under tension is plucked and gives off something of a musical sound. For not only do we receive images and traces in the brain, but we form new ones from them when we bring "complex ideas" to mind; and so the screen which represents our brain must be active and elastic. This analogy would explain reasonably well what goes on in the brain.⁶

Leibniz has, in this way, considerably complicated the picture space. Rather than accepting the back surface of the camera as a receiving surface, standing in, so to speak, for the painter's canvas, he has himself stretched a canvas in the space, as a receptor of the images. This screen, moreover, is not the flat picture plane of classical representation; it is from the start ridged and folded, in ways that depict already innate ideas. Locke's tabula rasa, or white sheet of paper, has no place in this box of miracles. Further, this canvas is in no way a passive instrument of the "real"; rather it moves or "oscillates" like a plucked string, according to the nature of the images coming in from outside. These movements in turn create new folds in the surface of the screen, turning it into something like a diaphragm, elastic and mobile, a two-dimensional oscilloscope responding to the activity of the brain. The brain, meanwhile, is itself no static collector of pictures, but acts to construct new images out of combinations of those already received.

Locke's camera has here been transformed into a kind of wheezing, churning barrel organ furnished internally with stretched diaphragms that give out a sound in pictures, a tone played out so to speak across the scarred surface of a canvas that has been riven by every picture it has held, and accessible only to the "inhabitant" of the dark room—our brain but also our soul. Or rather than a simple "inhabitant" of this little house, the soul would *be* the dark room, somewhat like a monad: "As for the soul, which is a simple substance or 'monad': without being extended it represents these various extended masses and has perceptions of them."[7] In the *Monadology* Leibniz clarified the formal nature of the monad as entirely internalized: "monads," he writes, "have no windows through which something could enter or leave." So the closed room, itself a soul, has no windows. Its only furnishing, to use Bernard Cache's term, is that of the screen, which represents the brain, a pulsating, organic substance, "active and elastic," "not unified, but diversified by folds."

Hence of course Deleuze's need to provide a lower story for this unlivable house without windows, one which, with five openings to let in the five sense impressions, operates as a kind of bodily anteroom to the monadic soul, a filtered way in for the brain, already innately active, to be fed and renewed from the outside. But this is not necessarily the Leibnizian solution, which rather than building a baroque house according to the rules of Wölfflinian architectonics, themselves derived from a psychology of bodily projection, prefers to set its monads free in space, unified on the outside, folded on the inside. The entryway by which impressions reach the screen of the brain is no simple opening; for the "space" in which Leibniz sets his monads is itself a thick and full substance, one that at once fills the dark room and constitutes its impregnability: "We should think of space as full of matter which is inherently fluid, capable of every sort of division and indeed actually divided and subdivided to infinity." Finally, this fluid space, like the screen in the dark room, is never uniform; it too "varies from place to place, because of variations in the extent to which the movements in it run the same way."[8]

In this viscous universe, two points of distinction between Leibniz and Deleuze emerge. The first is that Leibniz posits no necessary connection between the folded screen and the room in which it is placed. He simply notes that "it must be supposed that in the dark room there is a screen to receive the species." The canvas, screen, or membrane stretched like a musical string is thus independent of its container. There is a box without openings, and inside this box an elastic membrane the folding of which is continuously shifting according to new combinations of received and innate images. Secondly, the characteristic of the "fold" precipitated by these forces is at once less ambiguous than Deleuze would want and more extensively connected to the relationships between inside and out. If the membrane is stretched, and not simply hanging as Deleuze depicts it (and as a "curtain" and not a membrane, it is hard to see how it might oscillate as if being plucked like a stringed instrument), then the folds appear and disappear on its two-dimensional surface like the striations of a geological map thrust into three dimensions. The *toile* is an interior function, working as a receptor of vectors from outside and as a condenser of traces generated from inside.

The consequences of these distinctions for "folded" architecture are significant, especially as designers and theorists have tended to see the Deleuzean model as an invitation for a rather literal folding of the envelope, a complex curving of the skin, that tends to ignore rather than privilege the interior. According to Leibniz, a fold could in no way be replicated simply by the curved surface of a tentlike or bloblike structure, and not only because of its external qualities. The Leibnizian fold is in continuous movement, enveloping former folds and creating new ones on the surface of the diaphragm. Secondly, the

Leibnizian fold, as an interior mechanism which at once reflects the outside and represents the forces of the inside, is more of a mediating device, a spatial instrument, than an object acted on from one side or another. Here the nature of Leibnizian space is crucial; thick and full, container and contained, it recognizes no distinctions between the solid and the void, and thence no real division between the inside of a fold and its outside; the matter out of which a fold is constituted is after all the same matter as forms the space in the pleat, under the pleat, and between pleats.

Animistic Architecture

> To construct our city we have utilized elements directly taken from human anatomy, on one side, and on the other "mathematical objects": plastic figurations, in three dimensions, of sometimes three-dimensional mathematical problems. . . . Humane or totally cast off—and by this finding again their humanity—these are allegorical forms with which we propose to construct the architecture of tomorrow. . . . Perhaps these new cities will palliate, to a certain degree, psychological catastrophes and others that prepare humanity for a miserable "reconstruction" in its spirit as in its material means.
>
> Marcel Jean, "Allegorical Architecture," 1946[9]

Surrealists, save for the occasional flights of fancy of a Matta or a Dalí, generally eschewed concrete expressions of an architecture that might better remain insubstantial to retain its psychic dimensions, its alliance with dreams and drives. In the complex intersection of the animal psychology explored by Roger Caillois and Jacques Lacan and the structural investigations of biomorphic theorists such as Raoul Francé and Robert Le Ricolais, however, there emerged a form of architectural utopianism that, just before the Second World War, proposed a form of "allegorical surrealism" built up out of mathematical topology and psychological fantasy. Such was the project of Marcel Jean, the sur-realist sympathizer and friend of Man Ray, who first published his "mathematical objects" in 1936.[10] After the war, in a direct and amusing critique of Le Corbusier's geometrical metropolis, Jean proposed a hallucinatory landscape of mathematically and anthropomorphically derived forms for a "Plan of Reconstruction for a European Capital," and detailed plans for an office block (the models of which were photographed by Man Ray), a public monument, and an apartment building.

His city, he acknowledges, might well be termed a "Ville Surréaliste," suitable for Picasso's frescoes and in which Marcel Duchamp would be in charge of the interior design of the apartments—he had, noted Jean, already invented "a door at the same time open and closed."[11] The design of the office block was built up out of elliptical formulas (P1 (U) for G2 = 0 and G3 = 4) and responded to what Jean understood as the functional requirements of orientation, light, and air, while the city as a whole was developed according to a plan that inscribed its name in letters formed by the lines of office blocks (lit up at night), and that included a labyrinth and gigantic symbolic structures in the form of horses and bodies. "One notes," he writes, "bridges without any precise destination, cupolas, spiral pyramids, a mathematical monument ('constant negative curved surface of Euneper, derived from the pseudo-sphere')." Buildings composed of huge folded planes, emulating tissue; freeways transforming themselves into buildings; a monumental national library (or a union headquarters) built up in the form of a kneeling female nude, as if in emulation of the nineteenth-century vision of the Saint-Simonians, completed the picture of a riotous assemblage of biomorphic and mathematical forms that would achieve, at last, the "non-Euclidean" city. When juxtaposed in the same number of *L'Architecture d'Aujord'hui* with the following articles on "Formes imaginées. Formes concrètes" by the structural theorist Robert Le Ricolais, and on "L'architecture naturelle" by Jacques Couëlle, Jean's allegories took on all the force of a manifesto for a bioarchitecture. Informed by the Bergsonian doctrine of "spiritual energy," and controlled by a precise and meticulous three-dimensional analysis of biological and mathematical form, this new architecture merged the psychological with the evolutionary, in such a way as to give the ancient biological analogy scientific support and realization. Such experiments were thrown into sharper relief to the prevailing modernist doctrines as they formed the sequel to Le Corbusier's own introductory article in the same number, "L'espace indicible."

Marcel Jean's fantasies seem to anticipate, in form and philosophy, a number of more recent projects by architects who have sought to develop a new alliance between spatial theory and biotectonics, utilizing the potentials of digital modeling and drawing on the observations of Deleuze and Cache, among others, as a way of sidestepping the traditional modernist and postmodernist polarities of simplicity/complexity, harmony/opposition, form/*informe*, and, of course, construction/deconstruction. Admittedly somewhat literalized versions of Deleuze's theory of the "fold" in philosophic discourse have interested those searching for a formal method that, as Greg Lynn has reiterated in a number of essays, might go beyond the degree zero–sum game of the Wittkower/Rowe nine-square grid.[12] Such "reductive typologies" are replaced in Lynn's practice by an open-ended set of mathematical/topological experiments that disturb if not replace the formal paradigms of postmodernism. In a series of essays that add up to a mapping of the discursive field of the architectural *informe*, Lynn deploys the investigations of nineteenth- and twentieth-century biologists, morphologists, and mathematicians against the static geometries of modern and postmodern typologies. Forms are now "proto-geometric," "anexact," "bloblike," "pliable," "viscous." Form is no longer conceived of as a geometric "original" distorted or broken to incorporate complexity or represent conflict, but rather as seamlessly countercontradictory, a topological surface the movements of which register the synthetic result of forces applied by computer models, as if organically generating new species in a speedup of Darwinian evolution. Here the metaphorical relations between animation as a digital technique and animate as a biological state are, by a process of conscious literalization, deployed in the service of an architecture that takes its authority from the inherent "vitalism" of the computer-generated series.

This biotechnological *informe* differs from the *informe* of Bataille, however, on at least three levels. In the first place, where Bataille's quasi-Darwinian evolutionary explanation of the architectural monument—that "morphological progress" in which the human stood somewhere as an intermediary stage between "monkeys and great edifices"—was a deliberate provocation to the humanist theorists of the monument as analogically proportional to the body, merging the two into their third logically consistent "simian" form as an attempt to close the evolution of both the human species and architecture, Lynn's spatial morphologies are generated to offer potential evolution to architecture if not to the species; they seize on the metaphor not to end monumentality but to change its formal nature. Secondly, while for Bataille the *informe* was precisely that—a phenomenon entirely resisting any formal categorization—

Lynn's *informe* is in fact highly formalized. The almost obsessive return to Rowe's application of Wittkower's Palladian schema to Le Corbusier's villas seems to admit that what is being sought is not so much a nonformal outlet to this perceived geometrical closure, but more a rejection of the formal-dialectical method on which the analogy rests, in favor of an all-subsuming "solution" in formal continuity. Thirdly, the psychodynamics of Bataille's post-surrealist shock tactics, with all the counterhumanist overtones of the *informe* imaged as a "gob of spit" or illustrated as a mess of blood on the floor of an abattoir, and "space" understood as an all-devouring force, breaking down the walls of prisons and cannibalistically envisaged as a process wherein "one big fish eats a smaller," is transformed in Lynn's technobiologism into the elegant play of topological mutation according to the "natural" permutations of models that indeed "model" nature. Certainly, there is a moment of shock in the assimilation to architecture of "blobs" "that threaten to overrun a terrorized and deterritorialized tectonics like a science fiction horror movie," but that shock is inevitably blunted by the technical details of blob construction, or the sheer hyperbeauty of the bloblike iterations of force fields and topographic mappings on the screen.

But if there is little trace of avant-garde shock left in these surface permutations, even as talk of an "anarchitecture" derived from the passionate and violent performance acts of Gordon Matta-Clark seems little more than the intellectual domestication of a previously unthinkable event, the notion of an architecture developed out of topologies rather than typologies nevertheless introduces a fundamental rupture into theory if not into practice. For the generation of form from the outside, as envelope or skin, subjected to mathematically generated "force fields," removes the humanistic subject definitively from all individual consideration. If the "human" is introduced as a force, it is as movement—crowd or swarm—and not as a generative instrument in itself; indeed where the eye, and its mental corollary, visual abstraction, stood at the vision point of generative perspective, and thence of classical space, now all trace of optical or bodily accommodation is removed in favor of "an abstraction based on process and movement"; and not the process and movement inherent to either the eye or the body, but rather one that is genetic, so to speak, to machine dynamics.

The "inside" of architecture, then, to return to an early theme of Lynn, would not be shaped by occupation or by any other attribute than its profoundly *residual* character—like the fortuitous insides produced, say, by the external necessity to fashion a shape like that of the Statue of Liberty. In this sense, the notion of the "death of the subject" takes on a positive role in the rejection of all pretense to conventional functionalism. If form could never have been precisely calibrated to function according to the first biological analogy, and with the variously derived cultural-symbolic-spatial substitutes in postmodernism degenerating into mere stylistic bickering, as Lynn would have it, then only abstract, mechanical authority can hold. The ethical imperative shifts from sociopolitical authenticity to formal impartiality. And with the imputation of animate life to inanimate animation, our own participation in, if not imperial domination of, the biological process of evolution is assured.

Such an interiority for architecture, one "without windows," to paraphrase Kracauer paraphrasing Leibniz, would be perhaps like that described more than a century ago by Victor Hugo in his image of the monumental elephant built of wood and plaster at the Place de la Bastille during the Napoleonic era. This forty-foot-high "monster," "blackened by wind and weather," a "ponderous, uncouth, almost misshapen monument . . . endowed with a sort of savage and magnificent gravity," served as shelter to the street urchins of Paris. An elephant from the outside, inside it looked like a great wine barrel, or perhaps the whale of Jonah: "a huge skeleton."[13]

> A long beam overhead, to which massive side-members were attached at regular intervals, represented the back-bone and ribs, with plaster stalactites hanging from them like entrails; and everywhere there were great spiders' webs like dusty diaphragms. Here and there in the corners were patches of black that seemed to be alive and had changed their position with sudden, startled movements. The litter fallen from the back of the elephant on to its stomach had evened out the concavity of the latter, so that one could walk on it as though on a floor.[14]

The space inside, then, residual, entirely formed by the dictates of the outer skin, and structured according to the needs of that skin's support, was occupiable, indeed served a conjuncturally useful purpose—almost functional, in Hugo's detailed description; but it was a space that, like a cave or a burrow, was only incidentally for human occupation. Of it Hugo observed: "The unforeseen usefulness of the superfluous!"[15]

This "superfluous" characteristic of space, a direct resultant of the abstract generative process, should not be mistaken as evidence for an indictment along traditional humanistic-functionalist lines. This is rather the implacable and inevitable space of the contemporary, post-political, post-psychoanalytical subject, a somewhat fluid character of the kind outlined in the preceding chapter. Formed by the nonreflectivity of screens, immersed in the indeterminate depth of their spatial opacity and semitranslucency, this subject no doubt feels entirely at home inside the elephant, the dinosaur, the anthill, or the viscous blob: as if the subject itself were at one with the surfaces of its enclosure, its body no longer imitated, dissected, or deconstructed by its environment, but now enveloped and dispersed at one and the same time, its own surfaces, inner and outer, mapped by the same processes that generate its multiple outer skins, if any "outer" or "inner" may any longer be distinguished. Perhaps this would be the logical, evolutionary trajectory of the Nietzschean/Corbusian aerobic subject of modernism, first merging with the infinities of ineffable space, then synesthetized by the multimedia play on the warped surfaces of the Philips Pavilion, now finally at one with its surroundings. One retroactive interpretation of the modernist-functionalist fiction would be, after all, that, architecturally speaking and despite the claims of humanist perspective, we have been "here," in the elephant, so to speak, all along.

But in fact we do not have to search for extra-architectural examples to make this point in terms of built form. Gilles Deleuze reminds us that this forced separation between inside and outside, this "severing," was a property of the baroque: "Baroque architecture can be defined by this severing of the facade from the inside, of the interior from the exterior, and the autonomy of the interior from the independence of the exterior, but in such conditions that each of the two terms thrusts the other forward."[16] Working out from Wölfflin, Deleuze wants the baroque to construct what he sees as an entirely new kind of link/nonlink between inner and outer, upper and lower, that corresponds to the structure of the Leibnizian monad, "the autonomy of the inside, an inside without an outside," with "as its correlative the independence of the facade, an outside without an inside."[17] The outside may have windows, but they open only to the outside; the inside is lit, but in such a way that nothing can be seen through the "orifices" that bring light in. Joining the two, as we have seen, is the *fold,* a device that both separates and brings together, even as it articulates divisions acting as invisible go-between and visible matter: "the fold affects all materials," it "becomes expressive matter, with different scales, speeds, and different vectors (mountains and waters, papers, fabrics, living tissues, the brain)," and thus "determines and materializes Form." Here again the architectural metaphor serves philosophy: "the facade-matter goes down below, while the soul-room goes up above. The infinite fold then moves between the two levels."[18] The fold is here a stair, but one with a complicated kind of reduplicative perspectivity—that of the perspective conundrums of Desargues, a favorite of Deleuze.

But philosophy, as Bernard Cache and others have registered, also serves art and architecture; the ever-expanding delimitation of Leibniz by the equally disseminated notion of the baroque emerges in Deleuze's writing as a new model of architecture, one that moves beyond the traditional antinomies of modernism—the implied conflict between the "bearing principle" and the "covering principle," between, as Deleuze hazards, Gropius and Loos—and establishes a post-Leibnizian house for a new "harmony" of inside and outside. But where the modernist "baroque" drew on the spatial ambiguities of its seventeenth-century antecedent on behalf of a synthesis between space and time, for Deleuze the new baroque house exists to join animate and inanimate, to fold the one into the other with insistent force. Where once was a "closed chapel with imperceptible openings," now we have the model "invoked by Tony Smith, the sealed car speeding down the dark highway."[19]

In generating form by means of digital animation software, Lynn has explored the potential image of such an architecture in evocative ways.[20] Thus "House Prototype in Long Island" begins by a multiple-level site analysis that takes account of visual obstacles and destinations, physical forces, movement forces, and the like to produce a composite fieldscape of attractions and repulsions into which certain prototypical "house" organizations are inserted and warped accordingly. Different values ascribed to different levels of forces produce different distortions; different structures and coverings are tested against interior forces and exterior vectors; the resulting forms are gridded and

22. Greg Lynn, Cardiff Bay Opera House competition, 1994. Computer-generated bird's-eye view.

simplified into skeletal systems; the "prototypes" thus produced reveal, like the plastic forms of animated cartoon characters, all the deformations of pressure and release. On a larger scale, the Cardiff Bay Opera House project literalizes the site as an empty insect shell, a "chrysalis," out of which the new construction emerges. This construction is figured as a "hull," the voided space of former waterfront hulks, with ribs and casing turned over and merged into a system of ovoid forms that, animated as "polyps," in the final iteration house the functions of the Opera House. Not unexpectedly, the plan of the complex resembles a section through an insect carcass, with head, tail, extensions, and attached young, while the model realizes this image in three dimensions, with raised head, pincers, feelers, and the like. In both of these projects, and in others such as the larvalike Yokohama Port Terminal, or the pupalike Henie Onstad Kunstsenter installation, the serial implications of "animate" form are described in ways that demonstrate the potential for producing a "counter-architectural" morphology that materializes, in a way unattainable throughout the modernist period, all the phantoms of the biological analogy.

In these terms, the apparent "destination" of animate form would be to construct not so much the folded skin, the severed facade or twisted bodywork, nor the all-enclosing interior as an independent and windowless entity, but rather the fold itself. No literal interpretation of "folding" or of material folds, whether of fabric, facade, or space, can perform the Deleuzean/Leibnizian function; it would not be so much a question of illustrating complex folds, with all the geometrical rigor of computer-generated images, as it would be of discovering the equivalent "form" that might join the two floors of the material and immaterial. Deleuze is clear on this: our monads are no longer closed interiors that contain the entire world; they are opened up, prised open "as if by a pair of pliers," penetrating other monads, rupturing the previous distinctions between private and public like a Cage or Stockhausen performance, a Dubuffet "plastic habitat." Deleuze's example is musical (the baroque, he states, is the abstract art par excellence) in the formulation "Music has stayed at home; what has changed now is the organization of the home and its nature,"[21] but if we substitute "architecture" for "music" the point is clear. The baroque house that Leibniz/Deleuze designed possessed an inside and an outside, the one torn away from the other, each independent of the other, and with two stories, the one material, the other spiritual, joined by a stair of infinite folds. A neo-Leibnizian house would not, however, replicate this construction, but would expand beyond it with partial and intersecting velocities, into the city. In the new baroque, "the same construction of the point of view over the city continues to be developed, but now it is neither the same point of view nor the same city, now that both the figure and the ground are in movement in space."[22] In this new framing of the neo-baroque house, both the modernist solution to the monad (Deleuze gives the example of Le Corbusier's chapel at La Tourette) and the postmodernist (one might imagine the gestalt of Rowe's Collage City, with its stable interplay of figure and ground) are supplanted by a folded city, one where above-ground and below-ground, private inside and public outside are forced into each other, "overtaking," in Deleuze's terms, "monadology with a 'nomadology.'"[23]

Building in Empty Spaces

Daniel Libeskind and the Postspatial Void

Even as we experienced a severe nostalgia for time and history at the beginning of the modern period, a nostalgia resurrected from time to time throughout the century in order to counter the uncertainties of spatial modernism, we are now in the throes of an equally strong nostalgia for space, in both theory and practice. The rereading of spatial theories from the 1970s, now in translation; the interest in the history of spatial thought from the nineteenth century; the readoption of spatial models by other disciplines from literary criticism to geography; the potentialities of three-dimensional digital manipulation, all seem to have endowed spatial thought with a new energy at the end of the century.

And yet, despite the obviously positive virtues of such rereadings of spatial theory, the sense of nostalgia that pervades them—for politics, for the subject, for identity, for gender—intimates that the spatial world heralded by modernism might be already lost to us. Where Foucault was able to proclaim the supersession of humanism by a posthumanist science of man that finally lost the human subject as an object of study, now science and information have apparently constructed a world that has little need of the human in the first place.

Perhaps, following an era of spatial supremacy, which itself followed one of temporal hegemony, we are approaching a state in which neither time nor space holds primacy; a condition of "no-space," or that horrifying condition, unthinkable for the Cartesian subject, referred to by Pascal as a "vacuum," as it has reemerged in the contemporary discourse of cybernetics. While this paradigm has been couched until now for obvious reasons in spatial terms—"virtual" space or "cyberspace"—I would contend that these terms are generated in order to think the hitherto unthinkable (or rather the unthinkable within the frame of modernism) conditions of life without space, of the spaceless, or of the absolute "void." Even to describe them this way is to engage analogies with our own conventions, conventions that force us, against the grain, to understand the spaceless in spatial terms. Thus a term like "cyberspace" may well, I think, be a hybrid coined out of nostalgia, an attempt to ward off the difficult notion of the spatially absent. Perhaps even as the notion of space-time seemed to have been constructed at the very moment when time itself was an endangered species, a way of thinking through the new spatial conditions by way of the old, "lost" time, so now cyberworlds are being construed in spatial terms at the moment when space as we know it no longer holds as a frame for thought.

For what is spatial, after all, about an endless string of 0's and 1's, a string that for the purposes of display has to be looped around a screen; an endless line, without direction, displayed on a screen without depth? While the *representation* of information might well have spatial cognates, information itself seems to have no inherent spatiality. Nor can we return to the comforting terms of a temporal discourse, the authorities of narrative, of beginnings, middles, and ends, of pasts, presents, and futures, that so controlled our thinking in the nineteenth century and that have reappeared consistently in the nostalgic counterspatial moves of the twentieth. For narrative itself, temporality itself, has been collapsed, like space, into no-time and no-space. Which might be why speculative thought about the cyberworld since the 1980s, and especially in the genre of novel pioneered by William Gibson (and that today seems itself so comforting and almost archaic in its formulations), has been couched almost entirely in dystopian terms—not only no-space and no-time, but bad-no-space and bad-no-time.

In this context, and to return to an example touched on in this book, we can see how the vituperative attacks on Rachel Whiteread's *House* might have been stimulated not only by the politics and aesthetics of "resistance" to avant-garde art, but by her shockingly simple gesture of shutting space out, or rather, shutting us out of space. There is not only no room for us in *House,* there is no space left either. Space is both denied and destroyed; filled, where a modernist or postmodernist sensibility would demand that it be opened. Equally, it is precisely in terms of this space-filling move that we might read the project by Daniel Libeskind for the Victoria and Albert Museum's "Boilerhouse" addition (and how comforting it is to feel that we are in the process of replacing a boilerhouse, a first-machine-age structure, with a second-machine-age structure

that, however avant-garde its guise, is still recognizably avant-garde in form).
For Libeskind's project, despite its radical justifications and the suitably horrified reactions of some critics (themselves equally comforting as confirming the
possibility of a contemporary avant-garde), takes its place in a long line of
counterspatial projects, all conceived within the spatial paradigm to cut against
the normalizing tendencies of modernist, universal, hygienic space. For, as we
have seen, from the very emergence of space in architectural theory, counter-
space, or rather counterrational space, has been a necessary antinomy for the
support of the entire discourse. Thus, Wölfflin's terrifying baroque versus
Giedion's progressive baroque; the surrealists' "intrauterine" space against Corbusian transparent space; tent and tensile space against gridded space; moving
space against static space; psychogeographic space as against sociological, planning, and urbanist space; nomadological versus state space as Deleuze and
Guattari would have it; rhizomic space versus network space; Bataille's *informe*
versus modernist form.

This last concept—one that has also been revived in critical thought in
the last decade, culminating in Rosalind Krauss and Yve-Alain Bois's 1996 exhibition at the Centre Pompidou—is one that I would cite as informing the
Victoria and Albert design. It is fundamentally a "space-eating" project; it sets
out to image the consumption of space by a substance that is not quite solid,
not quite liquid. It might be linked to the recent interest in "blobs"—substances that have no fixed form but that devour as they fill, and spill over un-
controllably into realms previously sheltered and defended from their power.
Alien substances, of course, but ones that have been around in movie form for
a long time.

On one level the architectural consequences of this spatial appetite
emerge as one version of traditional interstitiality, the in-between, first theorized by gestalt theorists and made into a leitmotiv of collage city planning by
Colin Rowe and his followers. Such a nostalgic appeal to the spatial might almost seem reassuring in itself, if, however, something else was not lurking behind this and other similar schemes—Frank Gehry's Bilbao Museum has been
mentioned, but we might equally cite Peter Eisenman's project for the competition for the Vienna Holocaust Memorial, or even the new South Bank project by Richard Rogers. These are schemes that, in their nostalgia for modernist
space, positive or negative, are in a way all-consuming artifacts; even as they

contain intimations of the new cyberworld figured in spatial terms, they nevertheless almost literally devour the old spatial world as they go. They thus enact literally what many theorists of modernism from Bataille on have known for a long time: that space, as well as time, is destructive of the object; that space in the abstract is all-pervasive; that transparency once accomplished is at the same time monumental oblivion.

But on another level, the recent work of Libeskind both registers this propensity of modernism to devour its own children and at the same time offers another kind of "exhausted" space. The new Jewish Museum in Berlin is instructive in this regard. In the making of this *Raum* for memory and reflection, Libeskind has very consciously reinterpreted the founding premises of "space architecture," to use R. M. Schindler's term, in such a way as to create an architecture that does not simply construct space or shape space, but that is almost literally built out of space. Certainly, Libeskind pays formal homage to modernism. The echoes and traces of Le Corbusier are evident everywhere in the work, not least in the transformation of the spiral museum (from the Mundaneum project to the National Museum of Western Art in Tokyo) and the reinvention of the wall (as at Ronchamp), as well as in the deeper epistemological attitude to the city and its inhabitants registered in the spatial movements of the urban projects. The powerful imagery of the avant-gardes is ever present, transformed and displaced, reformed and replaced, with no apologies necessary to Tatlin, Lissitzky, Moholy-Nagy, or, perhaps most strongly of all, Kandinsky.

Beyond this, however, when confronted by the withdrawn exteriors and disturbing interiors of the Jewish Museum or the Victoria and Albert extension, we find ourselves in a phenomenological world in which both Heidegger and Sartre would find themselves, if not exactly "at home" (for that was not their preferred place), certainly in bodily and mental crisis, with any trite classical homologies between the body and the building upset by unstable axes, walls and skins torn, ripped and dangerously slashed, rooms empty of content and with uncertain or no exits and entrances. What Heidegger liked to call "falling into" the uncanny, and what for Sartre was the dangerous instrumentality of objects in the world as they threatened the body and its extensions, is for Libeskind the stuff of the architectural experience.

And yet, admitting Libeskind's obvious debt to phenomenology, there is in the Jewish Museum an implied architectural rereading of Benjamin. Indeed,

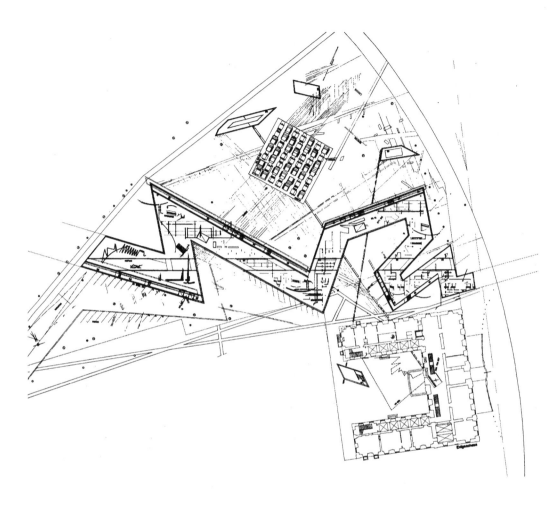

the half-sunken enclosure offers many potential connections to the Berlin of Benjamin's "childhood" and maturity. Not so much in any simplistic reference to the arcades or to a crude interpretation of Klee's *Angelus Novus*—although these may both be found lurking not far from the garden of the museum, and sometimes a "crude" reading, as Libeskind has himself noted, is entirely adequate for an observer—but rather in the profound effort that Benjamin himself made to reread the city and its artifacts in a way that was not trapped within a sterile neo-Kantian formalism or Hegelian historicism. In a way that eschewed the traditional perspectival "optical" framing of the city and its

23. Daniel Libeskind, Jewish Museum, extension to the Berlin Museum. Site plan, competition stage.

monuments, and that recognized the loss of perspective characteristic of modernity, the collapse of depth, the premium of the surface, the irreducible flat space of the modern image, Benjamin, following Riegl and other theorists of modern space, found solace in the haptic. For him, the modern experience was, as Nietzsche had already proposed, "labyrinthine"; not clear and transparent like the Heideggerian temple, but obscure and ambiguous as to both its figure and its ground. In this condition, as we have seen, Benjamin preferred to lose his way in the city, experience it in absentmindedness, stumbling along without the help of the Ariadne's thread provided by the modern guidebook, only to bump into a dwelling whose facade could not be picked out from any other, detached from any other, but whose interior might provide at least temporary sanctuary for the wanderer and the stranger (those haunting characters from Georg Simmel's metropolitan sociology), or at least substitute dark spaces for those of dreams, liminal places for the confrontation of the psyche. The unrecognizable exterior of Libeskind's museum (in the sense that its shape and form cannot be understood from any privileged vantage point) and the unmappable spaces of the interior (in the sense that only a "film," in Benjamin's terms, might provide the mechanisms of montage sufficient for its interpretation) all tend toward a haptic model of architectural experience, pushed back from the normal distance of vision, in a collapse or multiplication of the point of view that seems coordinated to a parallel collapse of perspective in the world.[1] Here Libeskind joins the modern and the mystical, as in what Benjamin referred to as Kafka's "ellipse," whose two incommensurate worlds were yet rendered joint, and immutably modern, through the very fact of their contemporaneity in Kafka's imaginary.

Perhaps it is in this way that we might begin to comprehend the precise attention of Libeskind to every detail of the museum's "program," as if pressing the modernist fetish for function to its limits and beyond. For Libeskind such a program, stemming from every potential move of the material and subjective fabric of the institution or urban quarter under examination, really does represent the fundament of contemporaneity, its reason for being. Never mind that the dizzying possibilities of this program, if examined under the rationalist's microscope, might lead to the bizarre consequences of a program apparently madly and incontinently out of true with its assumed rationality. Never mind that the surreal is closely stalking the real; if this is the program, then so be it. On the other hand, if there can be no "logic" on earth that explains each subject's experience of light and dark, form and space, vertical and horizontal (for in such a logic, as Goya pointed out long ago, lies certain madness), then we might at least leap straight up to the so-called "mystical" experience that, as Benjamin understood so well, could be no more nor less than collective tradition, the collective memory of the past, that weighs so strongly on the present and controls in ways unknown our imagination of the future. In such a world, Libeskind's ellipses, his wandering paths and warped spaces without perspective and ending blindly, can only be seen as so many tests of our own abilities to endure the vertigo experience of the labyrinths that make up our modernity. If, for the historian Manfredo Tafuri, the unavoidable choice was between the (false) sphere of reason and this uncertain labyrinth, for Libeskind one senses another way out; not from the labyrinth, for that would be too much to ask, but within the labyrinth—a provisional path that he calls a void, which through habitual and piecemeal encounters, by unexpected and suddenly revealed shocks, and through touch and feel in the dark as much as by clear vision in the light, might in some way domesticate what for Pascal, as for us, has been a rather stern, uncompromising, and certainly terrifying *horror vacui* in a world of apparently endless space and no place. Thus domesticated, who knows, we may learn to inhabit it, or at least pitch our tents there for a moment.

It was Ernst Bloch who, writing in 1932, characterized the landscape of Berlin as without foundation, giving to the city the continuous impression of "groundlessness," of having sprung into existence overnight, to disappear equally easily. Based on "the swamp in which Berlin is immersed" and the "sand upon which it is built," this landscape was one for which "the ground had not yet settled," an "especially abstract ground."[2] As if anticipating the new and rapidly redeveloped Berlin of the postunification era, he wrote of the "unstable, probabilistic ground" of Berlin and the "colonial exhibition character of the always new City of Hollow Space."[3] Libeskind's construction of inner space, hunkered down in the land, patched over with tin, and with narrow slits for its eyes, seems peculiarly appropriate for this provisional site. If, as Bloch quotes Karl Ritter, "man is spatially and bodily the mirror of his place on earth," then it is as reflected in this striated metal siding, hearing the rattling echoes of the tin cups of Celan's beggars, that a memory of man should be traced.[4]

If what Nietzsche implied for Le Corbusier was the image of superman in ineffable space—one who could overcome the void by virtue of superhuman power—for Libeskind he implies a less comfortable but at least an imaginable treaty: that between an irreducible void in time and in space, rendered the more horrifying by its human and inhuman contents, and an uncertain but at least receptive subject, whose being is tied to the void but who has need of a few walls for shelter and guidance. Then the business of the architect would not be to arrest the tempo of history, nor to return to a better time, but to deploy space in a historical way that recognizes its own temporality at the same time as it provides a momentary fusing of the two, a temporary respite for reflection and experience, and thus a momentary point of reference for the modern psyche: a "postspatial void," so to speak.[5]

Planets, Comets, Dinosaurs (and Bugs)

Prehistoric Subjects/Posthistoric Identities

> With neurotics it is as though we were in a pre-historic landscape—for
> instance in the Jurassic. The great saurians are still running about; the
> horsetails grow as high as palms.
> Sigmund Freud, 12 July 1938[1]

Digital Identity

The relation between space and identity has always been linked to representation. The humanistic subject in perspectival space, the modern subject in montage space: these tropes of interpretation have, with many variations, come to
stand for historically defined identities if not experiences—the point of view
standing in for the viewer, the image of a space representing its apparent effect.
The effects of digital representation, however, despite claims of its revolutionary impact, have been less clearly joined to a new construction of subjectivity.
Cyberpunk has given us the image of the hacker, but the hacker seems to dif-
fer little from the modernist/humanist subject. Screens, after all, are readily
construed as windows, and the now commonplace images of virtual space seem
closer to wire-frame emulations of traditional perspective than to any more
radical or explosive forms. And yet the infinite mutability, the seemingly endless permutations and rotations of digital constructions, the speed of virtual
travel within the image, not to mention the complexity of the networks of
communication themselves, all lead to the suspicion that some transformation
in subjecthood is under way. Even if we are not yet at the point where the interpenetration of mind, matter, and matrix is as complete as imaged by Gibson, the relations between image and experience have nevertheless been
changed beyond recognition within the processes, if not the outer forms, of

spatial design. In this concluding chapter I want to explore some possible models of what might have become of the modernist subject within these processes, and more especially what might be the effect of these processes on the architectural projects for which they are increasingly used. Here Freud's comparison of neurotic space to a prehistoric landscape inhabited by giant dinosaurs, however unwittingly, opens up the question of digital identity in the late twentieth century, as it has itself been framed by a veritable cult of the saurian.

There is no lack of evidence for a contemporary fascination, if not obsession, with galactic, apocalyptic, prehistoric and posthistoric life—to the extent that one might descry the emergence of a kind of "new galacticism" over the last few years. Movies like the *Star Wars* series, *Jurassic Park, The Lost World,* and *The Land Before Time,* Parts I through V; scientific works debating the reasons for dinosaur extinction, most recently exemplified by Walter Alvarez's *T. Rex and the Crater of Doom;* the fashion for cuddly purple dinos singing earnest moralizing songs to hypnotized children; the mania for mutant turtles engaged in bloody battles to the delight of the same, less moralized, younger set; the recent appearance of the Hale-Bopp comet dangerously close to our horizon, and the resulting tragic and hysterical reaction of World Wide Web–surfing cults; not to mention the emergence of dinosaur-like RVs consuming enormous amounts of fossil fuels; or, finally, the auction at Sotheby's of "Sue," the most completely preserved *T. rex* specimen yet found (with 99 percent of her bones in place) with a starting price of $1 million and a final sale price of more than $8 million: these alone should indicate to us that dinos have not just arrived but are true works of art—modern totems, as W. J. T. Mitchell argues in his recent cultural history of the modern dinosaur.[2]

This current interest in dinos and galaxies is of course not new; nor is it a simple function of our millennium-driven decade. Its history goes back to Cuvier's time, or at least to the 1820s, when the newly discovered dinosaur remains first began to haunt the romantic imaginary. But our own mania seems to bear a special relationship to the dino fever of the more recent past—that of the 1950s and 1960s—of which it appears in many respects to be a survival, and in other respects a revival. One might point not only to the survival of *Star Trek* and NASA in their various incarnations, but also to the reruns of *The Jetsons* and *The Flintstones* (playing back to back on the Time-Warner Cartoon Channel and now apparently about to be morphed into a new series, *The Jet-*

stones). Indeed, many of the dinosaur exhibits now being reinstalled in museums to reflect current scientific wisdom and to capitalize on film-rights linkage and consumer franchising were those originally refurbished from their nineteenth- and early twentieth-century incarnations in the sixties.

Between the 1960s and now, however, there has emerged the great divide of the digital, which, I would argue, has had results that go beyond a simple change in representational techniques, to imply a profound shift in the nature of our subjectivity with regard to architectural space. Here I am not only speaking of the way in which digital software has allowed us to re-represent things in the same way we used to represent them: the enormous efforts of CAD, for example to replicate perspective, or that of so-called virtual reality simulators to throw this perspective into a felt three dimensions—the well-known wire frame that with great effort manages to caricature what the Renaissance painter took for granted as reality. Rather I am concerned to characterize, if not interpret, the peculiar kind of subject, the *I,* as Lacan would have it, that has been unconsciously constructed by its confrontation with a "mirror" entirely different from that which faced the 1930s psychoanalyst and his child-subjects. This new mirror, which is more of a screen than a reflective surface, is, I believe, in the process of creating an imago that was hardly imaginable when Lacan first drafted his mirror stage talk in 1936.[3]

It reflects and produces a stage at once of refusal—a refusal of reflection, of transparency, of extension—and of resignation—resignation that the grand narratives of introjection and projection that characterized historicist and modernist space/time models no longer hold. It is a space of absolute self-consciousness of prehistory and posthistory, as if the baby, now held firmly by a dedicated caregiver of any age and gender, knows all the tricks; is aware somehow that in looking at itself, and denied its desire to capture the face of the Mother, it is committed to a split identity, not only as between imago and *I,* but as between two imagos, so to speak, blurred and morphed into a distorted physiognomy that is far from transparent or clear, but rather opaque and translucent. It would be as if this subject were truly lost in space, wandering vaguely in a state of continuous psychasthenia, disguising itself as space in space, ready to be devoured by the very object of its fear. It would be, finally, that we were dealing with a subject whose imago was screened and projected back to it, not as reflection but as scanned image. In an initial, historical moment of digitalization, one would have imagined this image to be in black and white—a surveillance camera image banded and spotted with video inter- ference; now we are more likely to be asked to assume a hyperreal, 3D image, or even a holographic lasergram. I imagine that the socialized version of this subject is caught somewhere between the lobby of Fredric Jameson's Hotel Bonaventure and William Gibson's grayed-out, neuromantic computer screen; in a matrix, that is, where introjection and projection are merged in a timeless state of warped and intersecting planes: what Gibson calls "a 3D chessboard ex- tending to infinity."[4] Leading to the discomforting conclusion that this, the subject of our mirror stage, would be something between a television addict and a hacker, which in architectural terms might situate it somewhere in the space between multiple screens.

Posthistoric Prehistory

Perhaps the critical difference between this subject and that of modernism lies in this sense of being caught in a matrix, a web, a space of no time and no place, with a corresponding intimation of historical impasse, of the blockage of modernist progress. For it is clear that its space—translucent, screened, scanned—has no history properly speaking—it implies no way forward and no way back—and is thus suspended out of time, or rather at the place where pre- history and posthistory meet. This would not be easily construed as postmod- ern, at least in the way that either Jameson or more literal revivalists of historical motifs have used the term. Indeed it bears closer comparison with an earlier notion, that of *posthistoire* or posthistory advanced in the 1940s and 1950s, a concept whose history has recently been studied by Lutz Nietham- mer.[5] Posthistory was espoused by those who, like the German anthropologist Arnold Gehlen, sought to characterize post–World War II disillusion with the failure of the great nineteenth-century narratives of historical progress—the moment, as Gehlen says, "when progress becomes routine." Following Gehlen, and returning the concept of *posthistoire* to the thought of the nineteenth- century mathematician and historian Alexandre Cournot, the Belgian social thinker and former labor activist Hendrick de Man, in his posthumously pub- lished and portentously entitled "The Age of Doom," wrote in 1950:

The term posthistorical seems adequate to describe what happens when an institution or a cultural achievement ceases to be historically active and productive of new qualities, and becomes purely receptive or eclectically imitative. Thus understood, Cournot's notion of the posthistorical would . . . fit the cultural phase that, following a "fulfillment of sense," has become "devoid of sense." The alternative then is, in biological terms, either death or mutation.[6]

Gianni Vattimo has extended this idea of *posthistoire* to coincide with what he sees as an all-embracing technological postmodernism of the present. Taking his cue from Gehlen, Vattimo characterizes what he calls "the experience of the end of history" as exemplified in the routinization of production and in the developments of technology and consumerism that, while continuously renewed, nevertheless stay the same:

> There is a profound "immobility" in the technological world which science fiction writers have often portrayed as the reduction of every experience of reality to an experience of images (no one ever really meets anyone else; instead, everyone watches everything on a television screen while alone at home). This same phenomenon can already be sensed in the air-conditioned, muffled silence in which computers work.[7]

Flattened out, simultaneous, the world appears dehistoricized. What made us "modern"—that is, the experience of living every day in a narrative history of progress and development reinforced by the daily newspaper—now comes to a halt. The master narrative, once a secularization of religious salvation, now fails, and multiple other possible narratives rise up. In this argument, Vattimo extends Gehlen in order to "prove" postmodernism: "What legitimates postmodernist theories and makes them worthy of discussion is the fact that their claim of a radical 'break' with modernity does not seem unfounded as long as these observations on the post-historical character of contemporary existence are valid."[8]

And yet the space of our digital mirror stage does not seem to be entirely "posthistorical" in this way; its future orientation, or rather its vision of the future-in-the-present implied by the galactic sensibility, and its search for the past-in-the-present, characteristic of its need to unearth prehistoric precedent, precisely delineate it as staged at the intersection of the pre- and the posthistorical and belonging to neither. In visual and spatial terms, this intersection is closely tied to that parallel and complementary intersection between the galactic and the prehistoric that, as I noted, has been a continuing preoccupation since the sixties, and which perhaps received its most innovative and radical treatment in the work of the artist Robert Smithson between 1966 and 1973.

In the context of our enquiry into the digital effect, Smithson's works are interesting precisely because of his prescient recognition of a galactic, dinosaurian space that potentially displayed the characteristics of our own. For Smithson, it was all to be found, literally on display, in microcosm in the American Museum of Natural History, to which he had paid many visits as a child, and in the adjacent Hayden Planetarium. In a piece coauthored with Mel Bochner and suggestively entitled "The Domain of the Great Bear," Smithson imagined the Planetarium as a model of infinite space: "For some, infinity is the planetarium, a frozen whirlpool at the end of the world, a vast structure of concentric circles."[9] In the murals and panoramas of the Planetarium and the Museum, Smithson was fascinated by the recurrent images of "catastrophe and remote times," which seemed to him to portray a world where the normal boundaries between space and time had been dissolved into a "bad boy's dream of obliteration, where galaxies are smashed like toys."[10] But rather than producing a repetition of modernist fantasies of space/time merging, or time warp in the present, the cumulative effect was one of "dimensions beyond the walls of time," a coming together of the two dimensions to produce the effect of stasis. As he wrote, a "sense of extreme past and future" was engendered by the fact that "there the 'cave-man' and the 'space-man' may be seen under one roof,"[11] or, as he put it in a reminiscence of Charles Knight's panoramas, "Space Age and Stone Age attitudes overlap to form the Zero-Zone, wher[e]in the space-man meets the brontosaurus in a Jurassic swamp on Mars."[12] In this environment Smithson found the realization of his childhood interest in dinosaurs and reptiles, and his later fascination with the space fictions of writers like Peter Hutchinson (*Creation of the Humanoids; The Planet of the Vampires; The Thing*) and William Burroughs (*Nova Express*).

In these and many other similar formulations from Smithson's writings and projects in the late 1960s, we find all the ingredients of a conception of space/time that recognizes the end of progressive modernist space and its dissolution—its fading, Smithson would call it—into a kind of entropic stasis. History, the conventional vehicle of progress, has come to a full and empty stop; indeed it has returned on itself to join its origins; prehistory has finally joined posthistory.

The architectural effect of this entropic fatalism was sketched in Smithson's celebrated essay on "Entropy and the New Monuments" from 1966. Here the works of Robert Morris, Donald Judd, Sol LeWitt, and Dan Flavin were seen as so many forms of "inactive history," of "entropy" and of an "Ice Age" rather than a "Golden Age." As if suspended in some prehistoric landscape, "they stop time, decay and evolution" in a way that joins "past and future . . . [in] an objective present."[13] Presciently enough, Smithson finds the architectural parallel to this work in what he calls an "architecture of entropy" (one that lines the new Park Avenue and pervades the work of Philip Johnson) which is characteristic of the "bland and empty" objects of contemporary commercial life. This is the side of modernism that puts the idealist and dynamic abstraction of the 1920s to work on behalf of commerce, bringing the avant-garde explosion of movement and speed to a full stop. Here the "City of the Future" (an evident reference of Le Corbusier's "Ville Contemporaine" of the mid-1920s) is realized in the present, transforming, as Smithson notes, the promise of Malevich's "nonobjective world" into a real as opposed to an imaginary desert.

> For many of today's artists this "desert" is a "City of the Future" made of null structures and surfaces. This "City" performs no natural function, it simply exists between mind and matter, detached from both representing neither. It is in fact devoid of all classical ideals of space and process. It is brought into focus by a strict condition of perception . . . as a deprivation of action and reaction.[14]

For Smithson, the entropic universe tends increasingly toward the crystalline, but again not in the sense evoked by the expressionist devotees of the crystal after Scheerbart. Smithson's crystals are static and all-enclosing, like the lattices described in Damon Knight's "Beyond the Barrier": "Part of the scene before them seemed to expand. Where one of the flotation machines had been, there was a dim lattice of crystals, growing more shadowy and insubstantial as it swelled; then darkness; then a dazzle of faint prismatic light—tiny complexes in a vast three-dimensional array, growing steadily bigger."[15] In these kinds of science fiction environments, Smithson finds that the traditional evolutionary and progressive thrust of future worlds has been forced into reverse, so to speak, paralleled in art by works such as what he calls LeWitt's monumental "obstructions," Morris's imaging of "a backwardlooking future" with lead cast erections and vaginas, or, more directly, Claes Oldenburg's prehistoric "ray-guns."

For Smithson, one might say, the interest of the dinosaur/space man, of the geological galactic, was that it opened up precisely where history had closed; posthistory was in this sense simply a blockage erected by history that, to be cleared, had to be joined to prehistory. Here Smithson's tactical and disruptive introduction of "extreme past and future" potentially destabilizes both historicism and its complement, posthistoricism. Smithson's purpose was, with the limited means available to him as an artist, to break into and shatter the pervasive and all-dominating rule of the spectacle, to reflect or deflect vision (mirror play) to reassert the power of space in the epoch of the "fading of space." Hence his various photo and mapping projects, conducted with instamatic and graph paper; hence also his varied installations of mirror planes from the salt mines of Cornell to the Yucatan, reflecting and deflecting the sites in which they are installed, preventing framing, picturesque fixing, or even subjective, narcissistic identification. His "mirror stages" set deep in the earth, scattered across its surface, reflecting its entropic, geological, and industrially wasted landscapes, threw the subject definitively out of the stadium once and for all, condemned to wander in the marshlands and rubbish tips of the "outside," perhaps catching glimpses of its preorthopedic body in the shards of mirror thrown down like so much jetsam—but only if crawling close to the ground. Here we might find an anticipation of the way Michel Foucault was to define "heterotopia," with reference to the mirror. At once a utopia, because entirely unreal, a "placeless place," the mirror was also fundamentally joined to the real, the place where it exists and the context it reflects: "The mirror functions as a heterotopia in this respect: it makes this place that I occupy at the moment when I look at myself in the glass at once absolutely real, connected with all the space that surrounds it, and absolutely unreal, since in order to be perceived it has to pass through this virtual point which is over there."[16]

These themes were brought together most effectively in the earthwork and movie of *Spiral Jetty* (1972),[17] where Smithson draws the by now obvious comparisons from the spiral of the sculpture to outer space galactic nebulae and magma, and to the inner space of the "spiral ear." The movie self-consciously tried to map this space/time interpenetration, both in its techniques of fabrication—Smithson likened the movie editor to a paleontologist "sorting out glimpses of a world not yet together, a land that has yet to come to completion, a span of time unfinished, a spaceless limbo on some spiral reels"—and its medium, itself seen as "archaic," with the movieola envisaged as "time machine" that transforms "trucks into dinosaurs." In a string of carefully juxtaposed images, Smithson crafted a map of the prehistoric world seen "as coextensive with the world [he] lived in," where the continents of the Jurassic period were merged with the continents of today. Perhaps the most graphic evidence of Smithson's consciousness of the end of history and the space of time are the blank spaces between the images, absent and lurking with uncanny potential for the return of the past in the future or vice versa: "One must be careful of the hypothetical monsters that lurk between the map's latitudes. . . . In the emptiness one sees no Stegosaurus . . . not a trace of the Brontosaurus."[18] The final endpoint of the long pan from left to right that comprises the movie is, inevitably, the desert of Utah and *Spiral Jetty* itself, drawing all time and space together into the vortex of its virtual funnel.

In order to bring these considerations back to architecture, where they began and where, I am implying, they have been transformed, first under the influence of conceptual art and then under the more extreme impact of digitalization, I want to take two examples of recent projects and buildings that have tried in their own way to exorcise the demons of space and time by reference to wider spatial and temporal spheres, deploying what we might now call the "galactic analogy" as justification, authorization, and even form-giver to the works in question. Most striking was the eruption of this analogy in the recent preliminary competition for an architect to develop the expanding site of the Museum of Modern Art in New York, and especially in two projects for that competition by Rem Koolhaas and Bernard Tschumi respectively: Koolhaas with his elegantly carved and gemlike model of the site, with MoMA at its center preserved like a fly in amber and the setbacks cut like diamonds in Hugh Ferriss style, and Tschumi with notes reminiscent of the *Manhattan Transcripts,* here developed science-fiction-style as if a Manhattan Project, complete with the MoMA site described as a giant magma.

Koolhaas, with his precise deployment of biological and geological metaphors, cast in precious materials and evoking the cities of cryptonite and interstellar luminosity that have held sway in the popular imagination since the birth of Superman, has found a medium that transcends the now equally popular revival of fifties style, and intersects with current technological and computer-generated images of contemporary fantasies of lost worlds. At the same time, his commitment to the translucent over the transparent endows his especially ironic kind of functionalism with a poetic materialism—one also evident in his contribution to the competition for the French National Library.

Tschumi, on the other hand, with equal elegance but with a firm avoidance of the physical object, picked his way through the labyrinth of MoMA's site with situationist aplomb, tracing the expansion of the museum as if retracing the moments of an asteroid impact, dissolving the existing buildings in

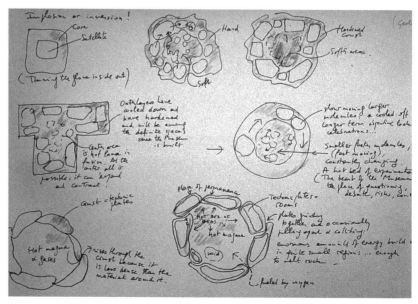

24. Bernard Tschumi, project for the Museum of Modern Art expansion, New York, 1997. Sketch of "magma" idea.

a magma of light and matter, and recombining their atoms in the process. It was perhaps no accident that during the last week of the first phase of the limited competition, at the very moment of the first "charette" (homely word for these stirring visions of galactic mutation!), the portentous Hale-Bopp comet was hovering over the clear skies of New York, provoking hysteria and suicide among the cultists of the World Wide Web, but evidently evoking an image of the MoMA site as a potential "crater of doom."

Galacticism, although in a different key, is present in Frank Gehry's new Guggenheim Museum in Bilbao. Now, this structure is not "galactic" in the way I have been using the word: as far as I know, it does not rely on any dinosaurian or space metaphor for its form. Rather, it is galactic in a new way, one that is becoming entirely ubiquitous in architectural conception and production, in the sense that it is almost entirely and necessarily the product of software, much of it similar to if not the same as that employed by Spielberg and his collaborators. To generate the complex and shifting forms of the museum, forms that could not have been even envisaged in plan, section, or static model, Gehry used a combination of software drawn from aerospace, auto, and medical usage to digitally map his sketch models in three dimensions, transform the digital model, and return it back to quick 3D mapping models, in preparation for the final stages of design. The production of the building was equally dependent on these programs, allowing the entirely nonstandard sections of titanium, steel, and glass to be cut directly "from disk to product," so to speak. Here, of course, the very notion of modern standardization begins to break down.

But, more importantly from our point of view, any formal reliance on traditional perspectival space, or for that matter on the traditional subject, is abandoned. This subject is now embedded within the "gaze" not of a hypothetical viewer but of a scanning system; it is as if, by some means, the subject might be able to "see" through the 3D lens of the CAT scan machine as it maps the observing brain and measures its responses. From this admittedly problematic point of view, whether or not we can enter the building and walk around inside it, or whether or not we can snatch traces of the old perspectivism in the new folded spaces, or whether or not we can trace its outer forms to early expressionist precedent, Bilbao remains *in the process of its conception* profoundly indifferent to our presence. I mean this in the sense that while of course it is possible to construct perspectival and humanistically traditional space through the use of software—virtual reality engines are doing this all the time—the way in which this software is used, and the increasing reliance on its subtle internal and programmatically defined determinants, gradually moves toward a state in which the building begins to construct its own identity like some revived dinosaur, finding solace in its own self-absorption.

Historically, of course, the successive introductions of perspectival, then axonometric modes of representation also transformed their own objects of projection in parallel with complementary new systems of production. Digital representation, however, has introduced a decisive difference. Where perspective and other geometrical projections were controlled, so to speak, by the ruling metaphor of the primacy of the viewing subject, digital projection has its own internal logic. This reversal can be dramatically illustrated once more in the realm of the dinosaurs. If, as W. J. T. Mitchell notes, "the early dinosaur . . . was primarily an architectural construction," utilizing the newest technology of iron and reinforced-concrete construction for its realization (as in the case of Benjamin Waterhouse Hawkins's 1854 proposal for the reconstruction of the Crystal Palace),[19] now the tables have been turned. It is now the advanced technology of dinosaur reconstruction that serves as a model and process for architecture.

Postscript: It's a Bug's Life

Dinosaurs may have provided a more or less continuing and convenient metaphor for the modernist project, which, since the Crystal Palace, has always been a "skin and bones" affair, but as identity surrogates they have always lacked a certain humanoid affect. In this context it might be instructive to return to Lacan's original mirror stage meditations of the late thirties and forties. For while in the first iterations of the essay (1936, 1938) the mirror stage seems to have been derived from the studies of Bühler and others on apes—"the chimpanzee stage"—by 1949 the pervasive model is the insect: the praying mantis, the stick and leaf insects that were, so to speak, the major protagonists in the early versions of the essay. In later examples drawn from the studies of Caillois into what he called "legendary psychasthenia," these insects suffered from a self-devouring, self-destructive, hypermimetic impulse that forced them to disguise themselves as twigs and leaves, ostensibly to avoid the birds but in reality placing them in direct danger from the leaf and twig eaters. What Lacan described as "morphological mimicry" was pressed in these species to the point of obsession, a "spatial obsession" that had a "derealizing" effect—no doubt the insect version of Freud's experience on the Acropolis. Two years later, in a paper read to the British Psychoanalytical Society on 2 May 1951, Lacan extended this insectology to include an account of the behavior of the migratory locust, "commonly known as a grasshopper," by the entomologist Chauvin. The reasons for this shift in analogy are not entirely clear, but is seems that for the postwar Lacan the ape would too simply (and comfortably) support an evolutionary psychology of the developmental ego; the insects, on the other hand, would represent the more dangerous tendencies to schizophrenia, and thence to paranoia, that were the inevitable marks of an imago constructed through a reflection, distant, reversed, scaled down, and never to be internalized. Indeed, what interested Lacan in 1951 about the migratory locust was the natural switching mechanism, so to speak, that determined whether, after birth, the insect would become solitary or move with the swarm, according to whether or not it was exposed to the vision of a female of its own kind. Chauvin had gone further, investigating the effects of light and dark on grasshoppers. He had discovered that crickets, when subjected to bright light in a crowd, fled in confusion, knocking into each other. This was particularly evident in the case of the field cricket, which, he noted, "was driven mad by the presence of members of its own species." "Thus, in a movie house, when a panic occurs, the spectators try without order to find shelter, and the scrambling counters the general movement to the exit."[20]

The study of crowd panic in insects must, for Lacan, have provided a convenient analogical mirror for the socio-psychological conditions of the 1941–1945 period, and it is tempting to see the various iterations of the essay as a miniature fable of the psychoanalyst's own construction of politics after 1936. The "mirror stage" essay was first drafted as Lacan's contribution to the Marienbad congress in 1936; introduced as part of a contribution to a volume of the *Encyclopédie française,* edited by Henri Wallon and dedicated to *La vie mentale,* in 1938; subsequently revised and re-presented at the XVI International Congress of Psychoanalysis in Zurich in 1949 (unpublished save for an abstract in the official proceedings, but published in full in the *Revue Française de Psychanalyse*); and again elaborated and extended in a paper read to the British Psycho-Analytical Society in 1951, entitled "Some Reflections on the Ego." The paper was thus delivered in its first form in Hitler's Reich, three years after the seizure of power; in its second iteration, it formed part of a collection edited by the very psychologist to whom Lacan was most indebted for the mirror thesis under cover of a study of the family; its first postwar revision was framed for the neutral territory of Switzerland, but refused by the English Ernest Jones for complete publication; thence no doubt its careful explanatory form—"the mirror stage *pour les enfants anglais*" in London two years later. In all these iterations, the mirror stage itself as model and described procedure changes little enough, but the successive explanatory contexts and adduced conclusions might be read as a veritable gloss on the maturation of psychoanalysis itself as it is forced to confront the unthinkable triumph of what Lacan himself terms "la vie concentrationnaire" in the 1949 iteration of the essay. Which is to say that the stage is staged on a scene of spatial terror, and does not emerge unscathed. Lacan was to restage this terror in an imaginary masquerade described to the first session of his 1962 seminar on "Angoisse."[21] Lacan imagines himself in an animal mask confronting not his audience but a giant praying mantis; not unnaturally, given the propensity of the female of the species to consume the male, he is anxious that the mask be sufficient not to give away his own identity, but also, on looking into "the enigmatic mirror of the ocular globe of the insect," he is equally disturbed not to see his own image but that of the mask. Perhaps equally disturbing would be the thought that through all these iterations of the insect as "other" reflected in the uncertain mirror of self-representation and desire, it is the insects that are, in the end, mistaken for or projected as subjects, thence to become through mimicry the models for the subjects' shelter.

Crickets uncertain of their solitary or gregarious identity; leaf insects disguising themselves from one predator only to submit to another; grasshoppers in panic: all have recently reemerged in digital form, with carefully studied and accurately acted out habits; and whether or not we may attribute the *Antz* wars or *A Bug's Life* to a fin-de-siècle Lacan effect, these movies seem to mirror the question of individuality and identity in the modern crowd implicitly posed by Lacan's 1949–1951 conclusions. In *A Bug's Life* the ants behave according to rule, with reluctant princess and exiled hero subject to the will of the crowd, saved only by the invention of a group of actors masquerading as superheroes and the construction of a huge, birdlike "ark," both props to identities damaged by habit and rote: maverick ants inside a paper bird launched to terrify grasshopper bullies, orchestrated by a traveling circus of masked insects, all perversely countering the agoraphobic swarm and its will to compliance. False and assumed imagos, then, as the only recourse in a world of paranoid, schizophrenic subject identities otherwise bound to the burrows. And, as the credits confirm, with their clips of the film shoot itself, this was a movie made by bugs for bugs. Our only point of entry into this ant heap would be, so to speak, as a post-*Metamorphosis* being, a kind of "monstrous vermin," figured by Kafka as already a kind of architectural construction "as hard as armor plate," with a "vaulted brown belly, sectioned by arch shaped ribs, to whose dome the cover . . . could scarcely cling."[22] This bug, whose scaly body could hardly negotiate its former perspectival environment, was, in a sense, entirely at home in itself; and as we negotiate our ways through the software tunnels of Flick's world, we might have cause to reflect on the relative comfort of the shell-like environments, blobs, and viscous surfaces that are being prepared for our new identities as digital subjects. As Henri Poincaré wrote in 1907,

> We can conceive, living in our world, of thinking beings whose table of distribution would be in four dimensions and who, consequently, would think in hyperspace. It is not certain, however, that such beings, admitting that they are born there, could live there and defend themselves against the thousand dangers with which they would be assailed.[23]

Notes

Introduction

1. Anthony Vidler, *The Architectural Uncanny: Essays in the Modern Unhomely* (Cambridge, Mass.: MIT Press, 1992), p. 225.

2. For a comprehensive summary of these intellectual developments see Stephen Kern, *The Culture of Time and Space, 1880–1918* (Cambridge, Mass.: Harvard University Press, 1983).

3. For a brief but incisive summary of this movement see Mitchell W. Schwarzer, "The Emergence of Architectural Space: August Schmarsow's Theory of *Raumgestaltung*," *Assemblage* 15 (August 1991), pp. 50–61.

4. See Harry Francis Mallgrave and Eleftherios Ikonomou, eds., *Empathy, Form, and Space: Problems in German Aesthetics, 1873–1893* (Santa Monica: Getty Center for the History of Art and the Humanities, 1994). The following summary is heavily indebted to this work, the most comprehensive and useful account of the "rise of space" in architectural history and theory, with full translations and an informative introduction. For Riegl's interpretation and critique of Hildebrand, see Margaret Iversen, *Alois Riegl: Art History and Theory* (Cambridge, Mass.: MIT Press, 1993), especially pp. 71–90.

5. Schwarzer, "The Emergence of Architectural Space," pp. 48–61.

6. Heinrich Wölfflin, *Prolegomena zu einer Psychologie der Architetktur* (Munich: Kgl. Hof- & Universitäts-Buchdruckerei, 1886).

7. Mallgrave and Ikonomou, eds., *Empathy, Form, and Space*, pp. 286–287. From August Schmarsow, "The Essence of Architectural Creation," first delivered as an inaugural address at the University of Leipzig, 8 November 1893. Published as *Das Wesen des architektonischen Schöpfung* (Leipzig: Karl W. Hiersemann, 1894).

8. Ibid., 295–296.

9. See Paul Zucker, "The Paradox of Architectural Theory at the Beginning of the 'Modern Movement,'" *Journal of the Society of Architectural Historians* 10, no. 3 (October 1951), pp. 8–14.

10. Geoffrey Scott, *The Architecture of Humanism* (London: Constable and Company, 1914), pp. 226–228.

11. Alois Riegl, *Die spätrömische Kunstindustrie nach der Funden in Österreich-Ungarn,* 2 vols. (Vienna: K. K. Hof- und Staatsdruckerei, 1901–1923). For a concise account of Riegl's optical history of architecture, see Iversen, *Alois Riegl,* chap. 5, "Late Roman Art and the Emancipation of Space," pp. 71–90.

12. Paul Frankl, *Principles of Architectural History: The Four Phases of Architectural Style, 1420–1900,* trans. and ed. James F. O'Gorman (Cambridge, Mass.: MIT Press, 1968), p. i.

13. Sigfried Giedion, *Space, Time and Architecture: The Growth of a New Tradition* (Cambridge, Mass.: Harvard University Press, 1941).

14. Harry Francis Mallgrave notes that "Schmarsow's proposal was effectively canonized by the Dutch architect Hendrik Berlage in his important lecture of 1904, in which he defined architecture as the 'art of spatial enclosure.'" In Gottfried Semper, *The Four Elements of Architecture and Other Writings,* trans. Harry Francis Mallgrave and Wolfgang Herrmann, introduction by Harry Francis Mallgrave (Cambridge: Cambridge University Press, 1989), p. 42; referring to Berlage, *Gedanken über Stil in der Baukunst* (Leipzig: Julius Zeitler Verlag, 1905), and "Raumkunst und Architektur," *Schweizerische Bauzeitung* 49 (1907).

15. See the excellent discussion of Mies's spatial antecedents in Fritz Neumeyer, *The Artless Word: Mies van der Rohe on the Building Art* (Cambridge, Mass.: MIT Press, 1991), pp. 171–193.

16. R. M. Schindler, "Space Architecture," *Dune Forum* (February 1934), pp. 44–46.

17. Jonathan Crary, *Techniques of the Observer* (Cambridge, Mass.: MIT Press, 1990).

18. Erwin Panofsky, *Perspective as Symbolic Form* (1924–1925), trans. Christopher Wood (Cambridge, Mass.: MIT Press, 1991), p. 31; Hubert Damisch, *The Origin of Perspective,* trans. John Goodman (Cambridge, Mass.: MIT Press, 1994), pp. xiii–xiv.

19. See Damisch, *The Origin of Perspective,* p. 447, where he concludes, "perspective tends toward discourse as toward its own end or reason for being; but it has its origin (or its departure) outside speech, outside that *phonic* element: on that plane where painting is inscribed, where it works and reflects on itself, and where perspective demonstrates it." We might paraphrase this conclusion for architecture as implying that perspective in some way both constitutes the discipline and reflects on it. Thus warped space in this sense would be the very form of thought about and in architecture.

20. Damisch, *The Origin of Perspective,* p. 28.

21. By far the best historical introduction to these questions is Kern, *The Culture of Time and Space.* In the domain of art, Linda Dalrymple Henderson's *The Fourth Dimension and*

Non-Euclidean Geometry in Modern Art (Princeton: Princeton University Press, 1983) is still extremely useful.

22. Among many other works, the following should be cited as exemplary: Henri Lefebvre, *The Production of Space,* trans. Donald Nicholson-Smith (Oxford: Blackwell, 1991), originally published as *La production de l'espace* (Paris: Editions Anthropos, 1974); Michel Foucault, *Discipline and Punish: The Birth of the Prison,* trans. Alan Sheridan (New York: Vintage/Random House, 1979), and especially the provocative and influential article "Of Other Spaces," *Diacritics* (Spring 1986), pp. 22–27, originally "Des espaces autres," *Architecture-Mouvement-Continuité* (October 1984); Gilles Deleuze, *The Fold: Leibniz and the Baroque,* trans. Tom Conley (Minneapolis: University of Minnesota Press, 1993); Paul Virilio, *L'espace critique* (Paris: Christian Bourgeois, 1984); Victor Burgin, *In/Different Spaces: Place and Memory in Visual Culture* (Berkeley: University of California Press, 1996); Bernard Cache, *Earth Moves: The Furnishing of Territories,* trans. Anne Boyman, ed. Michael Speaks (Cambridge, Mass.: MIT Press, 1995); Elizabeth Grosz, *Space, Time and Perversion* (London: Routledge, 1995).

23. Lefebvre, *The Production of Space,* p. 33.

24. See Victor Burgin, *In/Different Spaces,* pp. 27ff. In retrospect, the fundamental criticism of the otherwise incisive contributions of Lefebvre to spatial analysis would be the not-so-hidden presence of the utopian drive toward the citizen's "rights to the city," and the expected imminent advent of a real, as opposed to a virtual, transparency between society and space. Such a vision, which underlay many similar critiques of capitalist space in the 1960s, from Guy Debord to Paul Virilio, is in one sense only the radicalization of the more idealistic "transparencies" attempted by Le Corbusier, Mies van der Rohe, et al.—a replay, so to speak, of the dialectic of Enlightenment, with Lefebvre playing the part of Rousseau/Babeuf versus Le Corbusier as d'Alembert/Robespierre. As Victor Burgin notes, the almost total suppression of the psychoanalytical let alone the psychological paradigm, in a study written between 1968 and 1974, blocks the development of some of Lefebvre's most intriguing asides into the imbricated relations of the mental and social space (whether or not, as Burgin hints, this was more than simply a result of Lefebvre's scorn for psychoanalysis as a bourgeois individualist practice, or a more direct competitiveness with his contemporary Jacques Lacan). Lacan's fault, for Lefebvre (discussion of which is relegated to three cursory footnotes in *The Production of Space*), is not only to have privileged the epistemological priority of language over space—of communication over life—but to have frozen the subject, by way of the mirror stage, into a "rigid form" rather than "leading it towards transcendence in and through a space which is at once practical and symbolic (imaginary)." (Lefebvre, *The Production of Space,* p. 185, note 19.) Lefebvre rejects the "mirror" as a deceitful and dangerous instrument of abstraction that swallows up and holds the body captive on and in its "glacial surface." There is, he contemptuously concludes, "little justification for any systematic generalization from the effects of this particular object, whose role is properly confined within the immediate vicinity of the body." (Ibid., pp. 185–186.)

25. Jacques Lacan, transcript of unpublished seminar "Angoisse," 19 December 1962: "What I wish to say . . . is that the first thing to put forward concerning this structure of anxiety is something that you always forget in the observations where it is revealed; fascinated by the content of the mirror, you forget its limits, and that anxiety is framed." And again, "a mirror does not extend to infinity, a mirror has limits."

26. Ibid., 12 December 1962. It should be noted that the French uses *vide* indiscriminately for "void" and "vacuum." Thus Lacan's "void" is also Pascal's "vacuum."

27. Lacan's French terms "des noeuds, des pleins, des paquets d'ondes" are rich in implication. *Pleins* can mean "solids," but also, with respect to *vides,* "fullnesses." *Paquets* can be packets but also "bundles," and when paired with waves seems to imply a disturbingly *informe* condition.

Horror Vacui

1. Freud had embarked on this "correction" from the 1890s, when he appended notes to the German edition of the *Tuesday Lectures.* Thus, in contradiction to Charcot's thesis that the cause of hysteria, vertigo, and agoraphobia was to be traced to heredity, Freud noted: "The more frequent cause of agoraphobia as well as of most other phobias lies not in heredity but in abnormalities of sexual life." Freud, *The Standard Edition of the Complete Psychological Works of Sigmund Freud,* ed. James Strachey, 24 vols. (London: Hogarth Press, 1953–1974) 1:139. Freud's note appeared in J. M. Charcot, *Poliklinische Vorträge,* vol. 1, trans. Sigmund Freud (Leipzig and Vienna: Deutiche, 1892), p. 224.

2. Sigmund Freud, "Obsessions and Phobias: Their Psychical Mechanism and Their Aetiology," in Freud, *Standard Edition,* 3:74. Originally published in French as "Obsessions et phobies (leur mécanisme psychique et leur étiologie)," *Revue Neurologique,* 3 no. 2 (30 January 1895), pp. 33–38.

3. Gélineau's older contemporary Henri Legrand du Saulle had even tried to establish the etiology of the disease in France as resulting from the siege of Paris itself, a "claustrophobic" experience, followed by a sudden release into "agoraphobic" conditions with the lifting of the German encirclement. See my "Agoraphobia," below in this volume.

4. For a comprehensive summary, see Jean-Pierre Fanton d'Andon, *L'horreur du vide* (Paris: Editions du Centre National de recherche scientifique, 1978).

5. Charles Binet-Sanglé, "La maladie de Blaise Pascal," *Annales médico-psychologiques,* 8th series, 9 (1899), pp. 177–199. For a discussion of the medical obsession with Pascal's obsession, see Murkje Scholtens, *Etudes médico-psychologiques sur Pascal* (Haarlem, 1958).

6. George Saintsbury, "Pascal, Blaise," *The Encyclopedia Britannica,* 11th edition (New York: Encyclopaedia Britannica Company, 1911), p. 879. Gustave Lanson was skeptical of the accident's historicity but still mentioned it in his *Histoire de la littérature française* in 1894: "A

carriage accident, from which he was saved by a miracle near to the Neuilly bridge, is no doubt only a legend; but the natural evolution of his ideas, the impossibility of attaining permanent happiness, the infinite to which he aspired, and finally the insoluble mystery—psychological or theological—of grace led to the definitive crisis: that night of 23 November 1654, a night of ecstasy and joy, where, face to face with his God, Pascal gave himself to him, and for ever." Lanson, *Histoire de la littérature française* (1894, 1909–1912), edited and completed by Paul Tuffrau (Paris: Hachette, 1951), p. 456.

7. Cited in Blaise Pascal, *Oeuvres complètes,* ed. Jean Mesnard, 3 vols. (Bruges: Desclée de Brouwer, 1964ff.), 1:969; quoting from *Lettres de M. B[oileau] sur differens sujets de morale et de piété* (Paris, 1737), 206–207.

8. Pascal, *Oeuvres complètes,* 1:885, "Extrait d'un mémoire sur la vie de M. Pascal."

9. Jean Mesnard in Pascal, *Oeuvres complètes,* 1:968.

10. Condorcet speaks of Pascal's researches into the behavior of fluids and "the study of man" that alleviated his melancholy. The philosopher was, noted Condorcet, "returned ceaselessly into himself by sadness." This melancholy was, Condorcet held, "still more augmented by a peculiar accident. Pascal was riding out with four horses and without postilion, as was then the custom. Passing over the Neuilly Bridge, which had no guard rail, the two first horses fell over. They were already beginning to drag the carriage into the Seine, but happily the traces broke, and Pascal was saved. His imagination, which retained strongly the impressions that he had once received, was troubled for the rest of his life by involuntary terrors. They say that often he imagined that a precipice opened up beside him." Marie Jean Antoine Nicolas de Caritat, marquis de Condorcet, "Eloge de Blaise Pascal," in *Oeuvres de Condorcet* (Paris, 1847), 3:592–593.

11. Pascal's invention was reported by Henri Sauval, *Histoire et recherches des antiquités de la ville de Paris* (Paris, 1724), 1:192–193: here he was credited with conceiving a system of carriages (*carrosses à cinq sols*) following fixed routes according to fixed schedule. Recent biographers have found little documentation for this or the other two anecdotes, but John R. Cole believes that the carriage system might have been thought up by Pascal: Cole, *Pascal: The Man and His Two Loves* (New York: New York University Press, 1995).

12. See my *Transparency and Utopia* (forthcoming), chapter 1, "The Devil's Gaze."

13. Louis-François Lélut, reprinted in his *L'amulette de Pascal, pour servir à l'histoire des hallucinations* (Paris: Baillière, 1846), pp. xvi–372. Lélut, member of the Institute, doctor in chief of the third section of *aliénés,* Hospice de la Salpêtrière, and doctor of the prison for the condemned, was also the author of a pathological study of Socrates (*Du démon de Socrate, spécimen d'une application de la science psychologique à celle de l'histoire* [Paris, 1836]).

14. See Henri Gouhier, *Blaise Pascal commentaires* (Paris: J. Vrin, 1966), pp. 382–387. The "pathological Pascal" survived well into the twentieth century. See René Onfray, *L'abîme de*

Pascal (Alençon, 1923), who argues that the sensation of a void on the left side was the result of migraine headaches, themselves caused by circulatory troubles in the brain, and proved by the fact that, according to Onfray's examination of the manuscripts, Pascal filled the page when he was normal, while leaving blank spaces when he was suffering from anxiety.

15. Edmond and Jules de Goncourt, *Journal. Mémoires de la vie littéraire,* ed. Robert Ricatte, 3 vols. (Paris: Robert Laffont, 1989), 2:35. The doctor Jacques-Joseph Moreau (de Tours) was to publish his *La psychologie morbide* three years later (Paris, 1869).

16. Goncourt and Goncourt, *Journal,* 3:266 (entry of Sunday, 5 May 1889). See Alphonse Daudet, *La douleur,* pp. 27, 32.

17. Goncourt and Goncourt, *Journal,* 3:270 (entry of Thursday, 16 May 1889).

18. Goncourt and Goncourt, *Journal,* 3:510 (entry of Thursday, 18 December 1890). The reference is to Georges Rodenbach's poem "Du silence," later published in his *Le règne du silence* (Paris: Charpentier, 1891), 7:194.

19. Maurice Barrès, *L'angoisse de Pascal* (Paris: Georges Crès, 1918), p. 23.

20. Ibid., pp. 24–26.

21. Ibid., p. 32.

22. Ibid., p. 100.

23. Ibid., p. 118.

24. Ibid., p. 126.

25. Blaise Pascal, "De l'esprit géométrique et de l'art de persuader," in *L'oeuvre de Pascal,* ed. Jacques Chevalier (Paris: Gallimard, Bibliothèque de la Pléiade, 1954), pp. 358–386. This text has been variously dated 1655, 1657, and 1658; recent editors prefer the later dates.

26. Hubert Damisch, *The Origin of Perspective,* trans. John Goodman (Cambridge, Mass.: MIT Press, 1994), pp. 384–385.

27. Pascal, "De l'esprit géométrique," cited in Damisch, *The Origin of Perspective,* pp. 384–385.

Agoraphobia

1. Georg Simmel, "Die Grosstädte und das Geistesleben," *Jahrbuch des Gehestiftung zu Dresden* 9 (1903), pp. 185–206.

2. See Debora L. Silverman, *Art Nouveau in Fin-de-Siècle France: Politics, Psychology, and Style* (Berkeley: University of California Press, 1989), pp. 79ff.

3. See Robert A. Nye, *The Origin of Crowd Psychology in Gustave Le Bon and the Crisis of Modern Democracy in the Third Republic* (London: Sage, 1975).

4. Carl E. Schorske, "The Idea of the City in European Thought," in Oscar Handlin and John Burchard, eds., *The Historian and the City* (Cambridge: MIT Press, 1966), pp. 95–114.

5. Signaled by George and Christiane Crasemann Collins in their translation of Camillo Sitte's *City Planning According to Artistic Principles* (New York: Random House, 1965), reprinted as *Camillo Sitte: The Birth of Modern City Planning* (New York: Rizzoli, 1986). Sitte's interest in agoraphobia was noted by Cornelis van de Ven in *Concerning the Idea of Space: The Rise of a New Fundamental in German Architectural Theory and in the Modern Movements until 1930* (Assen: Van Gorcum, 1974), and more recently in my "Agoraphobia: Spatial Estrangement in Simmel and Kracauer," *New German Critique* 54 (Fall 1991), pp. 31–34, revised and extended in "Psychopathologies of Modern Space: Metropolitan Fear from Agoraphobia to Estrangement," in Michael S. Roth, ed., *Rediscovering History: Culture, Politics, and the Psyche* (Stanford: Stanford University Press, 1994), pp. 11–29. Esther da Costa Meyer, in her article "La donna è mobile," *Assemblage* 28 (1996), usefully extends the discussion to the question of gender, with a consideration of theories after Freud. Van de Ven notes the gloss on Sitte provided by his Belgian translator Camille Martin, who in an added Chapter VII stated: "The ideal street must form a completely enclosed unit. The more one's impressions are confined within it, the more perfect will be its tableau: one feels at ease in a space where the gaze cannot be lost in infinity."

6. Sitte, *City Planning According to Artistic Principles,* p. 45. The German reads: "In jüngster Zeit ist eine eigene nervöse Krankheit constatirt worden: die 'Platzscheu'. Zahlreiche Menschen sollen darunter leiden, d.h. stets eine gewisse Scheu, ein Unbehagen empfinden, wenn sie über einen grossen leeren Platz gehen sollen." (Camillo Sitte, *Der Städte-Bau nach seinen künstlerischen Grundsätzen. Ein Beitrag zur Lösung modernister Fragen des Architektur und monumentalen Plastik unter besonderer Beziehung auf Wien* [Vienna: Carl Graeser, 1889], p. 53.)

7. Ibid. German text: "Als Ergänzung zu dieser medicinischen Beobachtung sie die künstlerische angeschlossen, dass auch aus Stein und Erz geformte Menschen auf ihren monumentalen Sockeln von dieser Krankheit befallen werden, und somit immer lieber (wie schon eingangs erwähnt) einen kleinen alten Platz zum Standquartier wählen als einen leeren grossen. Von welchen Dimensionen müssen auf solchen Riesenplätzen alle Statuen sein? Mindestens doppelte und dreifache Naturgrösse und darüber. Gewisse Feinheiten der Kunst sind da von vornherein unmöglich."

8. Ibid., p. 53. German text: "Die Platzscheu ist eine neueste, modernste Krankheit. Ganz natürlich, denn auf den kleinen alten Plätzen fühlt man sich sehr behaglich, und nur in der Erinnerung schweben sie uns riesengross vor, weil in der Phantasie die Grösse der

künstlerischen Wirkung an die Stelle der wirklichen tritt. Auf unseren modernen Riesen-plätzen mit ihrer gähnenden Leere und erdrückenden Langweile werden auch die Bewohner gemüthlicher Altstädte von der Modernkrankheit der Platzscheu befallen. In der Erin-nerung dagegen schrumpfen sie zusammen, bis wir nur mehr eine sehr kleine Vorstellung als Rest übrig behalten, gewöhnlich noch immer zu gross im Vergleiche zur Nichtigkeit ihrer künstlerischen Wirkung."

9. Ibid., p. 107. Sitte would no doubt have been happy to read the report of a lifelong suf-ferer of this modern disorder some twenty years later who, while managing to outgrow his fear of crowds, nevertheless continued to be adversely affected by spaces and their sur-rounding buildings: "an immense building or a high rocky bluff fills me with dread. How-ever the architecture of the building has much to do with the sort of sensation produced. Ugly architecture greatly intensifies the fear." The anonymous author of this account, writ-ing sixteen years after Sitte's death, had evidently incorporated the lessons of the Viennese planner into his own self-analysis: "I would remark that I have come to wonder," he noted, "if there is real art in many of the so-called 'improvements' in some of our cities, for, judg-ing from the effect they produce on me, they constitute bad art." "Vincent," "Confessions of an Agoraphobic Victim," *American Journal of Psychology* 30 (1919), p. 297.

10. Edmond and Jules de Goncourt, *Journal. Mémoires de la vie littéraire,* ed. Robert Ri-catte, 3 vols. (Paris: Robert Laffort, 1989, 1:145: "the Boulevard de Strasbourg has the air of the major artery of an improvised California."

11. Carl Friedrich Otto Westphal, "Die Agoraphobie, ein neuropathische Erscheinung," *Archiv für Psychiatrie und Nervenkrankheiten* 3 (1871), pp. 138–161. This essay has recently been translated, with an introduction, in *Westphal's "Die Agoraphobie,"* with commentary by Terry J. Knapp and Michael T. Schumacher (Lanham, Md.: University Press of America, 1988). Westphal followed this article with three shorter notes: "Nachtrag zu dem Aufsatze 'Ueber Agoraphobie'," *Archiv für Psychiatrie und Nervenkrankheiten,* 3 (1872), pp. 219–221; "Ueber Platzfurcht. Briefliche Mittheilungen," *Archiv für Psychiatrie und Ner-venkrankheiten* 7 (1877), p. 377; and "Agoraphobie (1885)," in *Carl Westphal's Gesammelte Abhandlungen,* 2 vols. (Berlin: August Hirschwald, 1892), 1:374–387. Dr. E. Cordes replied at length to Westphal's first article in "Die Platzangst (Agoraphobie), Symptom einer Er-schöpfungsparese," *Archiv für Psychiatrie und Nervenkrankheiten* 3 (1872), pp. 521–574.

12. Emile Littré and Ch. Robin, *Dictionnaire de médecine* (Paris: Baillière, 1865), p. 30. These illnesses of space had previously been considered of physiological origin. Thus Dr. Morel of Rouen characterized them under the class "délire émotif," or emotional delirium, which he believed stemmed from disturbances of the nervous system. He described the case of a M. de X of Passy in 1845, who was terrified of imaginary "wells" and "precipices" that he saw everywhere. Morel, "Du délire émotif," *Archives générales de médecine,* vol. 1 (Paris: P. Asselin, 1866), p. 398.

13. Westphal, "Die Agoraphobie," pp. 139–151.

14. E. Gélineau, *De la kénophobie ou peur des espaces (agoraphobie des allemands)* (Paris, 1880), p. 24.

15. Henri Legrand du Saulle, *Etude clinique sur la peur des espaces (agoraphobie, des allemands), névrose émotive* (Paris: V. Adrien Dalahaye, 1878), p. 6. The first part of this memoir appeared in *Gazette des hôpitaux* (October, November, December 1877). Legrand du Saule practiced at the hospital of Bicêtre and was doctor in chief at the Dépôt de la Préfecture.

16. Legrand du Saulle, *Etude clinique sur la peur des espaces,* pp. 6–7.

17. Ibid. The "poetics" of agoraphobia reached a high point in the proto-phenomenological study of Claude-Etienne Bourdin, *Horreur du vide* (Paris: Charles de Lamotte, 1878), who concluded that the primary cause of "peur des espaces" was moral rather than physical.

18. Legrand du Saulle, *Etude clinique sur la peur des espaces,* pp. 7–8.

19. Ibid., p. 9.

20. Ibid., p. 10.

21. Ibid., p. 11. Unlike the other cases cited, this patient was equally unable to support large open spaces in the countryside, experiencing agoraphobic fear when asked to draw maps of the territory for maneuvers. "Il est effrayé à la vue d'une plaine sans fin" (p. 11).

22. Ibid., p. 13.

23. Ibid., p. 23.

24. Emile Littré, *Dictionnaire de la langue française,* 4 vols. and supplement (Paris: Hachette, 1883), *Supplément,* p. 355.

25. Legrand du Saulle, *Etude clinique sur la peur des espaces,* p. 31, noted that his patient, a consumer of large amounts of coffee and a heavy smoker, was terrified in the face of a wide bridge, always feeling as if he were in front of a void. Suppression of coffee and stimulants helped diminish the symptoms.

26. Ibid., pp. 32–33.

27. Dr. Benjamin Ball, *De la claustrophobie. Mémoire lu à la Société Médico-psychologique dans la séance du 28 Juillet, 1879* (Paris: E. Donnand, 1879).

28. Ibid., pp. 5, 6.

29. Georges Gilles de la Tourette, *Les états neurasthéniques* (Paris: J.-B. Baillière, 1898), pp. 15–16.

30. Ibid., pp. 45–46.

31. Ibid., p. 90.

32. Jean-Martin Charcot, *Leçons du mardi à la Salpêtrière, Notes de cours de MM. Blin, Charcot et Colin* (Paris: Centre d'étude et de promotion de la lecture, Les classiques de la psychologie, 1974), p. 104.

33. Ibid., p. 103.

34. William James, *The Principles of Psychology,* 2 vols. (New York: Henry Holt, 1890; rpt., New York: Dover, 1950), 2:421–422.

35. Sigmund Freud, *The Standard Edition of the Complete Psychological Works of Sigmund Freud,* ed. James Strachey, 24 vols. (London: Hogarth Press, 1953–1974) 1:139. See note 1 to "*Horror Vacui,*" above.

36. Fernand Levillain, *La neurasthénie, maladie de Beard* (Paris: A. Maloine, 1891), p. 30.

37. Charles Féré, *La pathologie des émotions* (Paris: F. Alcan, 1892).

38. These examples are drawn from Charles Féré, *The Pathology of the Emotions: Physiological and Clinical Studies,* trans. Robert Park (London: The University Press, 1899), chapter XIV, "Morbid Emotivity," pp. 359–390.

39. Julien Guadet, "André," *L'Architecture* (6 September 1890), p. 430. I am deeply indebted to David Van Zanten for providing this interesting reference to an early case of "architect's agoraphobia." Louis-Jules André (1819–1890), pupil of Le Bas and Huyot, had won the Grand Prix in 1847; Guadet, first studying with Henri Labrouste, had entered André's *atelier* after Labrouste had closed his in 1856. See Donald Drew Egbert, *The Beaux-Arts Tradition in French Architecture,* ed. David Van Zanten (Princeton: Princeton University Press, 1980), pp. 63ff.

40. Guadet, "André," p. 430.

41. Ibid.

42. Marcel Proust, *A la recherche du temps perdu,* 4 vols. (Paris: Bibliothèque de la Pléiade, 1988), 3:1513–1514: "[Note] Pour Sodome II (Balbec)/M. de Charlus entra (dans le salon des Verdurin) avec des mouvements de tête penchée, ses mains ayant l'air de manier un petit sac, caractéristiques chez les dames bourgeoises bien élevées et chez ceux que les Allemands appellent les homosexuels d'une certain agoraphobie, l'agora se trouvant être là l'espace de salon qui sépare la porte du fauteuil où se tient la maîtresse de maison. (Cahier 62, fo. 57 ro.)."

43. Ibid., 3:299; *Sodome et Gomorrhe,* II, ii: "la porte s'ouvrir sur Morel suivi de M. de Charlus. Celui-ci, pour qui dîner chez les Verdurin n'était nullement aller dans le monde, mais

dans un mauvais lieu, était intimidé comme un collégien qui entre pour la première fois dans une maison publique et a mille respects pour la patronne. Aussi le désir habituel qu'avait M. de Charlus de paraître viril et froid fut-il dominé (quand il apparut dans la porte ouverte) par ces idées de politesse traditionnelles qui se réveillent dès que la timidité détruit une attitude factice et fait appel aux ressources de l'inconscient. Quand c'est dans un Charlus, qu'il soit d'ailleurs noble ou bourgeois, qu'agit un tel sentiment de politesse instinctive et atavique envers des inconnus, c'est toujours l'âme d'une parente du sexe féminin, auxiliatrice comme une déesse ou incarnée comme un double qui se charge de l'introduire dans un salon nouveau et de modeler son attitude jusqu'à ce qu'il soit arrivé devant la maîtresse de maison. Tel jeune peintre, élevé par une sainte cousine protestante, entrera la tête oblique et chevrotante, les yeux au ciel, les mains cramponnées à un manchon invisible, dont la forme évoquée et la présence réelle et tutélaire aideront l'artiste intimidé à franchir sans agoraphobie l'espace creusé d'abîmes qui va de l'antichambre au petit salon."

44. Proust, *A la recherche du temps perdu,* 4:271.

45. Sigmund Freud, "Preface and Footnotes to the Translation of Charcot's *Tuesday Lectures," Standard Edition,* 1:139. Allan Compton has provided the most detailed review of Freud's early development in "The Psychoanalytic View of Phobias. Part I: Freud's Theories of Phobias and Anxiety," *Psychoanalytic Quarterly* 61, no. 2 (1992), pp. 206–229. This four-part article comprehensively studies the history and present state of the psychoanalytic study of phobia. See also "Part II: Infantile Phobias," ibid., 61, no. 2 (1992), pp. 230–252; "Part III: Agoraphobia and Other Phobias of Adults," ibid. 61, no. 3 (1992), pp. 400–425; "Part IV: General Theory of Phobias and Anxiety," ibid. 61, no. 3 (1992), pp. 426–446.

46. Josef Breuer and Sigmund Freud, *Studies on Hysteria,* in Freud, *Standard Edition,* 2:112–114.

47. Sigmund Freud, *The Complete Letters of Sigmund Freud to Wilhelm Fliess 1887–1904,* trans. and ed. Jeffrey Moussaieff Masson (Cambridge, Mass.: Harvard University Press, 1985), p. 218.

48. Freud, "The Neuro-Psychoses of Defence" (1894), in *Standard Edition,* 3:57.

49. Guy de Maupassant, "Le signe," in *Contes et nouvelles,* ed. Louis Forestier, 2 vols. (Paris: Gallimard, Bibliothèque de la Pléiade, 1979), 2:729.

50. Freud, *Complete Letters to Fliess,* p. 248. This assertion forms part of the fragment "Draft M. The Architecture of Hysteria," enclosed with a letter to Fliess, 25 May 1897.

51. Ibid., p. 247.

52. Ibid., p. 248.

53. Some of these writings are discussed by Meyer, "La donna è mobile." See also Helene Deutsch, "The Genesis of Agoraphobia," *International Journal of Psychoanalysis* 10 (1929), pp.

51–69; Edoardo Weiss, "Agoraphobia and Its Relation to Hysterical Attacks and to Traumas," *International Journal of Psychoanalysis* 16 (1935), pp. 59–83; Anny Katan, "The Role of 'Displacement' in Agoraphobia" (1937), *International Journal of Psychoanalysis* 32 (1951), pp. 41–50.

54. Freud, *Standard Edition,* 22:84. Helene Deutsch remarks having concluded that the two women patients she described suffered from the "feminine-masochistic tendency": "I do not know whether these cases afford a complete explanation of the problem why agoraphobia occurs only in the street. Of course, these patients must always have a tendency to anxiety, which breaks out under certain conditions associated with the street. Freud holds that these conditions are (a) the loss of the protective shelter of the house and (b) the temptations of the street. Temptation arises when regressive factors have degraded the love-life into prostitution, and this is brought about by the masochistic tendencies so clearly manifested in my patients. Similarly, the street constitutes a special danger to exhibitionistic impulses, and these too were markedly present." (Deutsch, "The Genesis of Agoraphobia," p. 69.)

55. Freud, *Standard Edition,* 10:115.

56. Jacques Lacan, *Le séminaire de Jacques Lacan,* book IV, *La relation d'objet, 1956–1957,* ed. Jacques-Alain Miller (Paris: Editions du Seuil, 1994), pp. 309–327.

57. Ibid., p. 326.

58. Ibid., p. 327.

59. Charles Melman, cited in *La phobie* (Grenoble: La Bibliothèque du Trimestre Psychoanalytique, 1989), pp. 126–127.

60. Wilhelm Worringer, *Abstraction and Empathy: A Contribution to the Psychology of Style,* trans. Michael Bullock (New York: International Universities Press, 1953), p. 15.

61. Ibid., pp. 15–16.

62. Ibid., p. 129.

63. Ibid., p. 15.

64. Wilhelm Worringer, *Form in Gothic,* ed. Sir Herbert Read (London: Alec Tiranti, 1964), pp. 15–19; originally published as *Formprobleme der Gothik* (1912).

65. Ibid., p. 174.

66. Dora Vallier, "Lire Worringer," introduction to Wilhelm Worringer, *Abstraction et Einfühlung,* trans. Emmanuel Martineau (Paris: Editions Klincksieck, 1978), pp. 5–7.
    Other art historians, more convinced of the liberating effect of modern abstraction, and seeing agoraphobia as a cultural condition more appropriate to the age of theology, were to reverse Worringer's thesis. Thus Emil Kaufmann, a convinced supporter of the modern movement, contrasted the new spatial order of the Enlightenment, as demonstrated in the

geometric and abstract plans for Claude-Nicolas Ledoux's ideal city of Chaux, to the medieval, organicist order: "In the irregular towns of the Middle Ages and subsequent epochs, the houses adapted themselves to the natural configuration of the ground, they squatted close to the ground like frightened animals; the result was a bizarrely irregular pattern of streets, pleasing to the eye in its variety. There is in this disposition the reflection of an anxiety that is for the most part the reason for the attachment and the admiration that old towns inspire in us." Emil Kaufmann, *Von Ledoux bis Le Corbusier. Ursprung und Entwicklung der autonomen Architektur* (Vienna and Leipzig: Verlag Dr. Rolf Passer, 1933), p. 17: Kaufmann was, no doubt unwittingly, echoing William James in his linking of agoraphobia to the primitive fear of open space exhibited by animals; he would have agreed with James that such emotion "has no utility in modern man."

67. The Sanatorium Bellevue in Kreuzlingen, Switzerland, was founded by Ludwig Binswanger the elder and taken over by his son Robert in 1880; its direction had passed to Robert's son Ludwig in 1910. Freud mentions to Fliess having read Robert Binswanger's "thick handbook of neurasthenia" in the same letter as he expounds the theory of "anxiety+window" (see notes 47 and 50 above). For an account of Freud's relations with Ludwig, see Ludwig Binswanger, *Sigmund Freud: Reminiscences of a Friendship* (New York and London: Grune & Stratton, 1957); Freud visited the Kreuzlingen sanatorium 25–28 May 1912.

68. Ludwig Binswanger, *Being-in-the-World: Selected Papers,* trans. Jacob Needleman (New York: Basic Books, 1963), p. 318.

69. Ibid., p. 295. This passage is taken from Binswanger's account of the case of Lola Voss, first published in *Das Schweizer Archiv für Neurologie und Psychiatrie* 63 (Zurich, 1949).

70. Ibid., p. 292.

71. See E. H. Gombrich, *Aby Warburg: An Intellectual Biography* (Chicago: University of Chicago Press, 1986).

72. This talk was later published in an abridged version as "A Lecture on Serpent Ritual," *Journal of the Warburg Institute* 2 (1939), 277–292. The full transcript has now been translated with an excellent interpretive essay by Michael P. Steinberg in Aby M. Warburg, *Images from the Region of the Pueblo Indians of North America* (Ithaca: Cornell University Press, 1995).

73. Gombrich, *Aby Warburg,* p. 216.

74. Ibid., p. 281.

75. Ibid., pp. 225–226.

76. Aby Warburg, Journal, 9 September 1929, cited in Gombrich, *Aby Warburg,* p. 302.

77. Gombrich, *Aby Warburg,* p. 258.

1. Sigfried Giedion, *Mechanization Takes Command: A Contribution to Anonymous History* (New York: Oxford University Press, 1948), p. 720.

2. Reviewing a number of studies by urban geographers from David Harvey to Edward Soja, Rosalyn Deutsche pointed to the implications of Janet Wolff's 1985 observation that "the literature of modernity describes the experience of men" for the critique of totalizing concepts of vision that fail to recognize the challenge of "feminist theories of visual space." Rosalyn Deutsche, "On Men in Space," *Artforum* 28, no. 6 (February 1990), p. 22. It is obvious that modernist space, and its late twentieth-century extensions, are for the most part constructed by and for men, but this construction was, and still is, a profoundly problematic one. The apparently serene transparency and all-dominating positivism of modernist urban space was inevitably riddled with the rejection, suppression, anxiety, and phobic fear that its authors were attempting to cure.

3. Ayn Rand, *The Fountainhead* (New York: Signet Books, 1971). We perhaps remember the novel best in its filmed version, directed by King Vidor with Gary Cooper as the genius architect Howard Roark (that it should have made so good a film was perhaps not surprising, given Rand's years in Hollywood scriptwriting after her emigration from Russia in 1925). For our purposes, the book's interest is that Roark was represented as a veritable synthesis of modern architectural "masters," from Frank Lloyd Wright to Le Corbusier with echoes of Raymond Hood, but with the physique of a Leni Riefenstahl Nazi hero-god. Wright's Fallingwater was the obvious model of Roark's August Heller house: "The steel hulk of the Heller house rose into a blue sky. The skeleton was up and the concrete was being poured; the great mats of the terraces hung over the silver sheet of water quivering far below. . . . He looked at the squares of sky delimited by the slender lines of girders and columns, the empty cubes of space he had torn out of the sky" (p. 134). The film also featured Raymond Massey as Gail Wynand, the William Randolph Hearst of New York; Robert Douglas as Elsworth Toohey, the insidiously collectivist architectural critic; Henry Hull as Henry Cameron, a Louis Sullivan figure, forgotten and alcoholic; Patricia Neal as Dominique Francon, daughter of the society architect Guy Francon (who does not appear in the film); and Kent Smith as Peter Keating, the opportunist classmate of Roark. See Andrew Saint, *The Image of the Architect* (New Haven: Yale University Press, 1983), pp. 1–18. The book, even if it caricatures to absurdity the genius architect and the romantic myth of independence, and however deeply it is marked by the didactic message of Rand's anticommunist "objectivism," offers fascinating insights into the vulgar reception of the architectural debates in Europe and the United States during the 1920s.

4. Rand, *The Fountainhead*, p. 15.

5. Ibid., p. 16.

6. Ibid., p. 15.

7. See Le Corbusier, *New World of Space* (New York: Reynal and Hitchcock and The Institute of Contemporary Art, Boston, 1948). Perhaps the best treatment to date of "ineffable space" in Le Corbusier is by Daniel Naegele, "Photographic Illusionism and the 'New World of Space,'" in *Le Corbusier—Painter and Architect* (Aalborg: Nordjylands Kunstmuseum, 1995), pp. 83–117.

8. Le Corbusier, *New World of Space,* p. 66.

9. Ibid., p. 8.

10. Ibid., pp. 7–8.

11. Le Corbusier, *Le voyage d'Orient* (Paris: Les Editions Forces Vives, 1966), p. 173.

12. Ibid., p. 154.

13. Ibid., p. 153.

14. Ibid., p. 158.

15. Sigmund Freud, "A Disturbance of Memory on the Acropolis," in *The Standard Edition of the Complete Psychological Works of Sigmund Freud,* ed. James Strachey, 24 vols. (London: Hogarth Press, 1953–1974), 22:241.

16. Le Corbusier, *Voyage d'Orient,* p. 166.

17. Georg Simmel, "Sociological Aesthetics," in *The Conflict in Modern Culture and Other Essays,* trans. K. Peter Etzkorn (New York: Teachers College Press, 1968), p. 78; this essay was originally published as "Soziologische Aesthetik," *Die Zukunft* 17 (1896), pp. 204–216.

18. Rand, *The Fountainhead,* p. 64.

19. Ibid., p. 243.

20. Ibid., pp. 151, 152.

21. Virginia Woolf, *Mrs. Dalloway* (New York: Harcourt, 1925), pp. 280–281.

22. Le Corbusier, "La rue," *L'Intransigeant* (May 1929), republished in Le Corbusier and Pierre Jeanneret, *Oeuvre complète 1910–1929* (Zurich: Girsberger, 1937), p. 118 (English translation).

23. Ibid., pp. 118–119.

24. Maurice de Fleury, "Les névroses urbains," *Les Cahiers de la République des Lettres* (Paris, 1928), p. 107.

25. Le Corbusier, *New World of Space,* p. 48.

Spaces of Passage

1. See Massimo Cacciari, *Architecture and Nihilism: On the Philosophy of Modern Architecture*, trans. Stephen Sarterelli with an introduction by Patrizia Lombardo (New Haven: Yale University Press, 1993). The first part is a translation of Cacciari's book *Metropolis* (Rome: Officina, 1973). See also Francesco Dal Co, *Figures of Architecture and Thought: German Architecture Culture 1880–1920* (New York: Rizzoli, 1990).

2. "Ueber Arbeitsnachweise," *Frankfurter Zeitung*, 17 June 1930, cited in Karsten Witte, "Introduction to Siegfried Kracauer's 'The Mass Ornament'," *New German Critique* (Spring 1975), 63.

3. See David Frisby, *Fragments of Modernity* (Cambridge, Mass.: MIT Press, 1989), p. 73.

4. Georg Simmel, *Philosophie des Gelds*, ed. David Frisby and Klaus Christian Köhnke (Frankfurt: Suhrkamp, 1989), p. 661. Frisby translates "Berührungsangst" as "agoraphobia" in the English edition, *The Philosophy of Money*, trans. T. Bottomore and D. Frisby (London: Routledge, 1978), p. 474.

5. Simmel, "Soziologie des Raumes," *Jahrbuch für Gesetzgebung, Verwaltung und Volkwirtschaft* 27 (1903), pp. 27–71, cited in Frisby, *Fragments of Modernity*, p. 77.

6. See the last section of his *Soziologie. Untersuchungen über die Formen der Vergesellschaftung* [Sociology: Studies of the Forms of Socialization] (Munich and Leipzig: Duncker und Humblot, 1923), pp. 460–526. This was first published in Leipzig in 1908, under the title *Der Raum und die räumlichen Ordnungen der Gesellschaft* (Space and the Spatial Organization of Society).

7. Georg Simmel, "Soziologie des Raumes" (1903), translated as "The Sociology of Space," in David Frisby and Mike Featherstone, eds., *Simmel on Culture: Selected Writings* (London: Sage Publications, 1997), pp. 137–138.

8. Simmel elaborated this notion by examining the interdependence of spatial exclusivity and spatial nonexclusivity. Some social forms, the state for example, manifested themselves in a unique and localized space that excluded the possibility of other forms inhabiting the same space; other institutions, like the church, for instance, were not so dependent on locational fixity, allowing for the possibility of other churches operating on the same territory. Social elements might then be characterized on a scale from the spatially exclusive to the supraspatial.

9. Georg Simmel, "Metropolis and Mental Life," in Simmel, *On Individuality and Social Forms: Selected Writings*, ed. with an introduction by Donald N. Levine (Chicago: University of Chicago Press, 1971), p. 325; translated from "Die Grossstadt und das Geistesleben," *Die Grossstadt. Jahrbuch der Gehe-Stiftung*, 9 (1903).

10. Simmel, "Metropolis and Mental Life," p. 338.

11. Simmel, "Exkurs über die Soziologie der Sinne," in *Soziologie,* p. 486.

12. Simmel, *The Philosophy of Money,* p. 477.

13. Simmel, "Exkurs über den Fremden," in *Soziologie,* pp. 509–512.

14. There is little scholarship on Kracauer's architecture. For a brief summary of his attitude to urban form, see Tillmann Hess, "Zur Architektur in Kracauer's Stadtbildern (mit einem Exkurs zu Le Corbusier)," in Andreas Volk, ed., *Siegfried Kracauer. Zum Werke des Romanciers, Feuilletonisten, Architekten, Filmwissenschaftlers und Soziologen* (Zurich: Seismo Verlag, 1996), pp. 111–130.

15. Siegfied Kracauer, *Ginster. Von ihm selbst geschrieben* (Berlin: S. Fischer, 1928), reprinted in Kracauer, *Ginster. Georg* (Frankfurt: Suhrkamp, 1979).

16. Kracauer, *Ginster. Georg,* p. 106.

17. Ibid., p. 199.

18. Siegfried Kracauer, "Hotelhalle," in *Der Detektiv-Roman. Ein philosophischer Traktat,* in *Schriften I: Soziologie als Wissenschaft, Der Detektiv-Roman, Die Angestellten* (Frankfurt: Suhrkamp, 1971), pp. 128–137.

19. Ibid., p. 129.

20. Ibid., p. 134.

21. Ibid., p. 135.

22. Ibid., p. 136.

23. Ibid., p. 137.

24. Walter Benjamin, *Gesammelte Schriften,* ed. Rolf Tiedemann and Hermann Schweppenhäuser, 7 vols. (Frankfurt am Main: Suhrkamp Verlag, 1979–1989), 3:196.

25. Ibid., 5:527. Benjamin speaks of "das 'Kolportagephänomen des Raumes'" as the "legendary ground of the Flâneur's experience."

26. Ibid., 5:645–646. Benjamin uses the French words *vertu évocatrice* to describe this sensation.

27. Ibid., 5:646.

28. Jean-Martin Charcot, *Leçons sur l'hystérie virile,* intro. Michèle Ouerd (Paris, 1984), p. 214.

29. Ibid., p. 237.

30. Jean-Martin Charcot, *Charcot the Clinician: The Tuesday Lessons*, trans. Christopher G. Goetz (New York: Raven Press, 1987), p. 31.

31. Ibid., p. 41.

32. Benjamin, *Gesammelte Schriften*, 5:647.

33. Ibid., 5:1054.

34. Ibid., 3:197.

35. Ibid., 5:679.

36. Sigfried Giedion, *Bauen in Frankreich* (Leipzig: Klinkhardt und Biermann, 1928), p. 85; cited in Benjamin, *Passagen-Werk*, 5:533.

37. Benjamin, *Gesammelte Schriften*, 5:514.

38. Siegfried Kracauer, *From Caligari to Hitler: A Psychological History of the German Film* (Princeton: Princeton University Press, 1947), p. 307.

Dead End Street

1. G. W. Leibniz, letter to Jacob Thomasins, 26 September–6 October, 1668, in *Oeuvres de G. W. Leibniz,* ed. Lucy Prenant, vol. 1 (Paris: Aubier Montaigne, 1972), pp. 74–75.

2. Walter Benjamin, "The Work of Art in the Age of Mechanical Reproduction," in *Illuminations,* ed. Hannah Arendt, trans. Harry Zohn (New York: Schocken Books, 1969), p. 239. First published as "Das Kunstwerk im Zeitalter seiner technischen Reproduzierbarkeit," in the *Zeitschrift für Sozialforschung,* no. 5 (1936), and republished in Benjamin, *Gesammelte Schriften,* ed. Rolf Tiedemann and Hermann Schweppenhäuser, 7 vols. (Frankfurt am Main: Suhrkamp Verlag, 1974–1989), vol. 1, and in Benjamin, *Das Kunstwerk im Zeitalter seiner technischen Reproduzierbarkeit. Drei Studien zur Kunstsoziologie* (Frankfurt am Main: Suhrkamp Verlag, 1963).

3. One notable exception is the essay by Gertrud Koch, "Cosmos in Film: On the Concept of Space in Walter Benjamin's 'Work of Art' Essay," *Qui Parle* 5, no. 2 (Berkeley, 1992), pp. 61–72.

4. Siegfried Kracauer, *The Mass Ornament: Weimar Essays,* trans. Thomas Y. Levin (Cambridge, Mass.: Harvard University Press, 1995), p. 323. In German, the essay "Kult der Zerstreuung. Über die Berliner Lichtspielhäuser," originally published in the *Frankfurter Zeitung* of 4 March 1926, was republished in *Das Ornament der Masse. Essays* (Frankfurt am Main: Suhrkamp Verlag, 1963), pp. 311–317.

5. This and the following passages are from Benjamin, "The Work of Art in the Age of Mechanical Reproduction," p. 240. German text in Benjamin, *Das Kunstwerk. Drei Studien,* p. 40.

6. Walter Benjamin, *The Correspondence of Walter Benjamin, 1910–1940,* ed. Gershom Scholem and Theodor W. Adorno, trans. Manfred R. Jacobson and Evelyn M. Jacobson (Chicago: University of Chicago Press, 1994), p. 254. Translation of Benjamin, *Briefe,* 2 vols. (Frankfurt am Main: Suhrkamp Verlag, 1978).

7. Hubert Damisch, "Fenêtre sur rue," in *Skyline. La ville Narcisse* (Paris: Seuil, 1996), p. 51.

8. "But then if I look out of the window and see men crossing the square, as I just happen to have done, I normally say that I see the men themselves, just as I say that I see the wax. Yet do I see any more than hats and coats which could conceal automatons? I *judge* that they are men. And so something which I thought I was seeing with my eyes is in fact grasped solely by the faculty of judgement which is in my mind." René Descartes, *Meditations on First Philosophy,* "Second Meditation," in *The Philosophical Writings of Descartes,* trans. John Cottingham, Robert Stoothoff, and Dugald Murdoch, 3 vols. (Cambridge: Cambridge University Press, 1984), 2:21.

9. Walter Benjamin, "Eduard Fuchs, Collector and Historian," in Benjamin, *One-Way Street, and Other Writings,* trans. Edmund Jephcott and Kingsley Shorter (London Verso, 1979), 363; German text in *Das Kunstwerk. Drei Studien,* 83.

10. Benjamin, letter to Gerhard Scholem, from the Var, 18 September 1926, in Benjamin, *Correspondence,* p. 306.

11. Benjamin, *One-Way Street,* p. 78.

12. Ibid., p. 89.

13. Ibid., p. 59.

14. Samuel Weber, *Mass Mediauras: Form, Technics, Media* (Stanford: Stanford University Press, 1996), pp. 94–95.

15. Heinrich Wölfflin, *Renaissance and Baroque,* trans. Kathryn Simon (Ithaca: Cornell University Press, 1964), p. 38.

16. Ibid., p. 164, n. 2.

17. Heinrich Wölfflin, *Renaissance und Barock. Eine Untersuchung über Wesen und Entstehung des Barockstils in Italien* (1888; Leipzig: Kochler und Amelang, 1986), p. 71.

18. In Harry Francis Mallgrave and Eleftherios Ikonomou, eds., *Empathy, Form, and Space: Problems in German Aesthetics, 1873–1893* (Santa Monica: Getty Center for the History of Art and the Humanities, 1994), p. 170.

19. Jacques Lacan, *Le séminaire de Jacques Lacan,* book XX, *Encore, 1972–1973,* ed. Jacques-Alain Miller (Paris: Editions du Seuil, 1975), p. 105.

20. Daniel Paul Schreber, *Memoirs of My Nervous Illness,* trans. and ed. Ida Macalpine and Richard A. Hunter (London: Wm. Dawson and Sons, 1955), p. 193. Schreber's text was originally published as *Denkwürdigkeiten eines Nervenkranken* (Leipzig: O. Mutze, 1903) and became the subject of Freud's celebrated paper "Psychoanalytic Notes upon an Autobiographical Account of a Case of Paranoia (Dementia Paranoides)," of 1911.

21. Wölfflin, *Renaissance und Barock,* p. 105. This sentiment was echoed in turn by Riegl, Frankl, Giedion, and Walter Benjamin in the first half of the century, and more recently by Bruno Zevi, Paolo Portoghesi, Robert Venturi, and, among other critics, Gilles Deleuze and Jacques Lacan.

22. Ibid.

23. A. E. Brinckmann, *Plastik und Raum. Als Grundformen künstlerischer Gestaltung* (Munich: R. Piper Verlag, 1924), p. 85.

24. Hans Auer, "Moderne Stylfragen," *Allegemeine Bauzeitung* 50 (1885), pp. 19–21, 25–27, quoted in Mallgrave and Ikonomou, eds., *Empathy, Form, and Space,* p. 79.

25. Adolf Göller, "What Is the Cause of Perpetual Style Change in Architecture?" (1887), in Mallgrave and Ikonomou, eds., *Empathy, Form, and Space,* pp. 222–224. First published as "Was ist die Ursache der immerwährenden Stilveränderung in der Architektur?" in Göller, *Zur Aesthetik der Architektur: Vorträge und Studien* (Stuttgart: Konrad Wittwer, 1887), pp. 1–48.

26. Friedrich Nietzsche, *Menschliches, allzumenschliches,* II, section 1, in Nietzsche, *Sämtliche Werke: Kritische Studienausgabe,* ed. Giorgio Colli and Mazzino Montinari, 15 vols. (Munich: Deutscher Taschenbuch Verlag and de Gruyter, 1988), 2:471, as translated by David Britt and cited in Alexandre Kostka and Irving Wohlfarth, eds., *Nietzsche and "An Architecture of Our Minds"* (Los Angeles: Getty Research Institute for the History of Art and the Humanities, 1999), p. 341.

27. Walter Benjamin, *Ursprung des deutschen Trauerspiels* (1928), in Benjamin, *Gesammelte Schriften,* 1:235.

28. Ibid., pp. 234–235.

29. Alois Riegl, *Die Entstehung der Barockkunst in Rom* (Vienna: Anton Schroll, 1908), p. 32.

30. Walter Benjamin, *The Origin of German Tragic Drama,* trans. John Osborne (London: New Left Books, 1977), p. 82.

31. Ibid., p. 92.

32. Ibid. Benjamin is quoting from Herbert Cysarz, *Deutsche Barockdichtung. Renaissance, Barock, Rokoko* (Leipzig: H. Haessel, 1924), p. 108 (fn). The reference to the "panorama" occurs on p. 27 (fn).

33. Benjamin, *The Origin of German Tragic Drama,* p. 92.

34. Ibid., p. 95.

35. Ibid., p. 96.

36. Ibid., p. 97. Benjamin is working from the German translation of Bergson's *Essai sur les données immédiates de la conscience:* Henri Bergson, *Zeit und Freiheit* (Jena: E. Diederichs, 1911), pp. 84–85.

37. Benjamin, *The Origin of German Tragic Drama,* p. 81 (my emphasis).

38. Ibid., p. 91.

39. Ibid., p. 93. Benjamin takes this citation from Georg Philipp Harsdörfer, *Vom Theatrum oder Schawplatz* (Berlin, 1914), p. 6: "stattliche Paläste/und fürstliche Garten-Gebäude/ die Schauplätze [sind]."

40. Benjamin, *The Origin of German Tragic Drama,* p. 92.

41. Cited in ibid., pp. 92–93.

42. Ibid., p. 92.

43. Benjamin, *The Origin of German Tragic Drama,* p. 119. Benjamin quotes from Friedrich Nietzsche, *Die Geburt der Tragödie,* in *Werke,* vol. 1 (Leipzig, 1895), p. 59. Nietzsche draws the picture of the Greek theater, terraced, "rising in concentric arcs," where "each spectator could quite literally survey the entire cultural world around him and imagine himself, in the fullness of seeing, as a chorist. . . . The structure of the Greek theater reminds us of a lonely mountain valley: the architecture of the stage resembles a luminous cloud configuration which the Bacchae behold as they swarm down from the mountaintops." Nietzsche, *The Birth of Tragedy and The Genealogy of Morals,* trans. Francis Golffing (New York: Doubleday, 1956), p. 54.

44. Benjamin, *The Origin of German Tragic Drama,* p. 79.

45. Ibid., p. 119.

46. Ibid., p. 99.

The Explosion of Space

A version of this essay was first published in *Assemblage* 21 (1993), pp. 45–59. An extended version was published in the collection *Film Architecture: Set Designs from Metropolis to Blade Runner,* ed. Dietrich Neumann (New York and Munich: Prestel, 1996), pp. 13–25. See also, in the same collection, Anton Kaes, "Sites of Desire: The Weimar Street Film" (pp. 26–32), and Dietrich Neumann, "Before and after Metropolis" (pp. 33–38). I thank Dietrich Neumann and Thomas Y. Levine for their helpful criticism and suggestions.

1. Dziga Vertov, *Kino-Eye: The Writings of Dziga Vertov,* ed. Annette Michelson, trans. Kevin O'Brien (Berkeley: University of California Press, 1984), p. 17.

2. Le Corbusier, "Esprit de vérité," *Mouvement* 1 (June 1933), pp. 10–13, translated in Richard Abel, *French Film Theory and Criticism: A History/Anthology,* 2 vols. (Princeton: Princeton University Press, 1988), 2:111–113.

3. Georges Méliès, "Les vues cinématographiques" (1907), in Marcel L'Herbier, ed., *Intelligence du cinématographe* (Paris: Editions Coréa, 1946), pp. 179–187; Eric Rohmer, "Cinema, the Art of Space" (1948), in Eric Rohmer, *The Taste for Beauty,* trans. Carol Volk (Cambridge: Cambridge University Press, 1989), pp. 19–29.

4. The best discussion of the architectural contribution to set design, in the context of the expressionist twenties, is still Lotte H. Eisner's *L'écran démoniaque* (Paris: Eric Losfeld, 1965).

5. Robert Mallet-Stevens, "Le cinéma et les arts: L'architecture," *Les Cahiers du Mois-Cinéma* (1925), in L'Herbier, ed., *Intelligence du cinématographe,* p. 288.

6. Abel Gance, "Qu'est-ce que le cinématographe? Un sixième art," *Ciné-Journal,* no. 195 (9 March 1912), in L'Herbier, ed., *Intelligence du cinématographe,* p. 92.

7. Elie Faure, "De la cinéplastique," *L'arbre d'Eden* (Paris: Editions Crès et Cie, 1922), in L'Herbier, ed., *Intelligence du cinématographe,* p. 268.

8. Ibid.

9. Ibid., p. 275.

10. Ibid., p. 276.

11. Ibid., p. 278.

12. Herman G. Scheffauer, "The Vivifying of Space," *Freeman* (24 November–1 December 1920), reprinted in Lewis Jacobs, ed., *Introduction to the Art of the Movies* (New York: Noonday Press, 1960), p. 77. See also Scheffauer, "Cubism on the Screen," *New York Times* (28 November 1920), and "Motion Picture Architecture," *New York Times* (5 December 1920). The essay "The Vivifying of Space" was reprinted in Scheffauer's collection of essays *The New Vision in the German Arts* (New York: B. W. Huebsch, 1924). I am indebted to Dietrich Neumann for pointing out Scheffauer's considerable reliance on, if not plagiarism of, Heinrich de Fries, whose article "Raumgestaltung im Film" was published in *Wasmuths Monatshefte für Baukunst,* nos. 1–2 (1920–1921), pp. 63–75. A partial translation is in Neumann, ed., *Film Architecture,* pp. 183–185.

13. Scheffauer, "The Vivifying of Space," p. 78.

14. Ibid., p. 79.

15. Ibid., pp. 79–81.

Scheffauer's analysis was echoed by the art critic Rudolf Kurtz in *Expressionismus und Film* (Berlin, 1926), p. 123: "Perpendicular lines tense towards the diagonal, houses exhibit crooked, angular outlines, planes shift in rhomboidal fashion, the lines of force of normal architecture, expressed in perpendiculars and horizontals, are transmogrified into a chaos of broken forms. . . . A movement begins, leaves its natural course, is intercepted by another, led on, distorted again, and broken. All this is steeped in a magic play of light, unchaining brightness and blackness, building up, dividing, emphasizing, destroying." (As cited in Siegbert Solomon Prawer, *Caligari's Children: The Film as Tale of Terror* [New York: Da Capo Press, 1988], p. 189.)

16. Scheffauer, "The Vivifying of Space," p. 82.

17. Ibid., p. 83.

18. Ibid., p. 84.

19. Erwin Panofsky, *Perspective as Symbolic Form,* trans. Christopher S. Wood (New York: Zone Books, 1991), p. 154. Panofsky's essay "Die Perspektive als 'symbolische Form'" was first published in the *Vorträge der Bibliothek Warburg* for 1924–1925 (Leipzig and Berlin, 1927), pp. 258–330.

20. Ernst Bloch, "Building in Empty Spaces," in *The Utopian Function of Art and Literature: Selected Essays,* trans. Jack Zipes and Frank Mecklenburg (Cambridge, Mass.: MIT Press, 1988), p. 196. Originally published as "Die Bebauung des Hohlraums," in *Das Prinzip Hoffnung* (Frankfurt am Main: Suhrkamp, 1959). Bloch here refers directly to Panofsky's essay.

21. Kurtz, *Expressionismus und Film,* p. 54, cited in Prawer, *Caligari's Children,* p. 189.

22. Hugo Münsterberg, *Film: A Psychological Study* (1916; New York: Dover, 1969). For a general study of his theory see Donald L. Fredericksen, *The Aesthetic of Isolation in Film Theory: Hugo Münsterberg* (New York: Arno Press, 1977).

23. Münsterberg, cited in Gerald Mast and Marshall Cohen, eds., *Film Theory and Criticism: Introductory Readings,* 3d ed. (New York: Oxford University Press, 1985), p. 332.

24. Louis Aragon, "Du décor," *Le Film* 131 (16 September 1918), 8–10, translated in Abel, *French Film Theory and Criticism,* 1:165, 166.

25. Erwin Panofsky, "Style and Medium in the Motion Pictures," originally published in *Princeton University. Department of Art and Archeology. Bulletin* (June 1936), pp. 5–15; revised version in *Critique* 1, no. 3 (January–February 1947), pp. 5–28, reprinted in Panofsky, *Three Essays on Style,* ed. Irving Lavin (Cambridge, Mass.: MIT Press, 1995), p. 122.

Metropolitan Montage

1. Siegfried Kracauer, *Theory of Film: The Redemption of Physical Reality* (New York: Oxford University Press, 1960), p. 72.

2. Ibid., p. 218.

3. Ibid., p. 232.

4. Marcel Carné, "Quand le cinéma descendra-t-il dans la rue?" *Cinémagazine* 13 (November 1933), translated in Richard Abel, *French Film Theory and Criticism: A History/Anthology,* 2 vols. (Princeton: Princeton University Press, 1988), 2:127–129.

5. Kracauer, *Theory of Film,* p. xi.

6. Ibid., p. 52. Kracauer elaborated (p. 62): "The affinity of film for haphazard contingencies is most strikingly demonstrated by its unwavering susceptibility to the 'street'—a term designed to cover not only the street, particularly the city street, in the literal sense, but also its various extensions, such as railway stations, dance and assembly halls, bars, hotel lobbies, airports, etc. . . . Within the present context the street, which has already been characterized as a center of fleeting impressions, is of interest as a region where the accidental prevails over the providential, and happenings in the nature of unexpected incidents are all but the rule. . . . There have been only few cinematic films that would not include glimpses of a street, not to mention the many films in which some street figures among the protagonists."

7. Ibid., p. 62.

8. Ibid., p. 65.

9. Ibid., p. 207.

10. Ibid., p. 17.

11. Ibid.

12. Walter Benjamin, "The Work of Art in the Age of Mechanical Reproduction" (1935), translated in Gerald Mast and Marshall Cohen, eds., *Film Theory and Criticism: Introductory Readings,* 3d ed. (New York: Oxford University Press, 1985), pp. 689–690.

13. Walter Benjamin, *Das Passagen-Werk,* in *Gesammelte Schriften,* ed. Rolf Tiedemann and Hermann Schweppenhäuser, 7 vols. (Frankfurt am Main: Suhrkamp Verlag, 1974–1989), 5:135.

14. See Gertrud Koch, "Cosmos in Film: On the Concept of Space in Walter Benjamin's 'Work of Art' Essay," *Qui Parle* 5, no. 2 (Berkeley, 1992), pp. 61–72. Koch analyzes the spatial metaphors of the "Work of Art" essay in terms of their application to Benjamin's concept of the film medium as propelled by the collapse in distance between the camera, the

director, and the audience. For Koch, the "unconscious optics" of the camera is a result of its status as a subject, a kind of "demiurge" that "builds a new world out of the rubble of the old one." Ibid., p. 70.

15. Benjamin, *Gesammelte Schriften,* 5:527.

16. Kracauer, *Theory of Film,* p. 170.

17. Sergei Eisenstein, *Nonindifferent Nature,* trans. Herbert Marshall (Cambridge: Cambridge University Press, 1987), p. 122.

18. See ibid., pp. 123–154. For a discussion of Eisenstein's filmic interpretation of Piranesi in the context of the European avant-garde, see Manfredo Tafuri, *The Sphere and the Labyrinth,* trans. Pellegrino d'Acierno and Robert Connolly (Cambridge, Mass.: MIT Press, 1990), pp. 55–64.

19. Eisenstein, *Nonindifferent Nature,* p. 140.

20. See ibid., pp. 159–165, an analysis along the same lines as the discussion of Piranesi in Nikolai Gogol's, "On the Architecture of Our Time," published in 1831.

21. Sergei Eisenstein, "Montage and Architecture," in *Selected Works,* vol. 2, *Towards a Theory of Montage,* ed. Michael Glenny and Richard Taylor, trans. Michael Glenny (London: BFI Publishing, 1991), pp. 59, 60.

22. Auguste Choisy, *Histoire de l'architecture* (Paris: E. Rouveyre, 1899), vol. 1, p. 413.

23. Eisenstein, *Selected Works,* 2:60.

24. Le Corbusier, *Vers une architecture* (Paris: Vincent Fréal et Cie, 1923), p. 31.

25. Robert Mallet-Stevens, "Le cinéma et les arts: L'architecture" (1925), in Marcel L'Herbier, ed., *Intelligence du cinématographe* (Paris: Editions Coréa, 1946), p. 289.

26. Ibid., 290.

27. Ibid., 288.

X Marks the Spot

1. Anon., *X Marks the Spot: Chicago Gang Wars in Pictures* (Chicago: Spot Publishing Co., 1930). The context for the enormous popularity of pulp presentations of gangsterdom and the "invention" of gangster mythology is well described in David E. Ruth, *Inventing the Public Enemy: The Gangster in American Culture, 1918–1934* (Chicago: University of Chicago Press, 1996), especially pp. 118–143.

2. Georges Bataille, *Oeuvres complètes,* vol 1, *Premiers écrits 1922–1940* (Paris: Gallimard, 1973), p. 256. This article was first published in *Documents,* no. 7 (1930), pp. 437–438.

3. Georges Didi-Huberman, *La ressemblance informe ou le gai savoir visuel selon Georges Bataille* (Paris: Macula, 1995), p. 154.

4. Georges Bataille, "L'obélisque," in *Oeuvres complètes,* 1:502.

5. Jacques Lacan, "Seminar on 'The Purloined Letter,'" trans. Jeffrey Mehlman, in Glenn W. Most and William W. Stowe, ed., *The Poetics of Murder* (New York: Harcourt Brace Jovanovich, 1983), pp. 21–54; translation of "Le séminaire sur 'La Lettre volée'" (1956), in Jacques Lacan, *Ecrits I* (Paris: Editions du Seuil, 1966).

6. Edgar Allan Poe, "The Purloined Letter," in *The Complete Tales and Poems* (New York: Modern Library, 1938), p. 212.

7. Lacan, "Seminar on 'The Purloined Letter,'" p. 33.

8. *"Basic Course Unit Guide: Crime Scene Search Technique,"* State of California, Commission on Peace Officer Standards and Training, 1985, pp. 43.4–43.7.

9. Poe, "The Purloined Letter," p. 208.

10. Ibid., p. 219.

11. Lacan, *Ecrits I,* p. 24.

12. Fredric Jameson, "On Raymond Chandler," in Most and Stowe, eds., *The Poetics of Murder,* p. 127.

13. Ibid., p. 144.

14. Ibid., p. 138.

15. Cited without reference in ibid., p. 128.

16. See Denis Hollier, *La prise de la Concorde. Essais sur Georges Bataille* (Paris: Gallimard, 1974); English translation as *Against Architecture: The Writings of Georges Bataille,* trans. Betsy Wing (Cambridge, Mass.: MIT Press, 1989).

17. Translated in Georges Bataille, "Space," in Robert Lebel and Isabelle Waldberg, eds., *Encyclopaedia Acephalica* (London: Atlas Press, 1995), p. 75.

18. Ibid., p. 77.

19. See Yve-Alain Bois and Rosalind Krauss, "A User's Guide to Entropy," *October* 78 (Fall 1996), pp. 55–56. Bois sees Bataille as working against architecture as an anthropomorphic image of man, but retreating before the implications of this attack. Here I would simply point to the insidious powers of "space" in Bataille's construction, and its consequent undermining of man's institutions and bodies. Perhaps the point is somewhere in between: that for Bataille "space," properly *un*defined, was inevitably going to undo man's work with little need of help from the critic.

Home Alone

1. See William Gibson, *Burning Chrome* (New York: Ace Books, 1986), pp. 8ff.

2. Georg Simmel, *On Individuality and Social Forms,* ed. D. Levine (Chicago: University of Chicago Press, 1971), p. 143.

3. Citations are from Vito Acconci's typescript explanations.

Full House

1. See Luigi Moretti, "Strutture e sequenze di spazi," *Spazio. Rassegna delle arti e dell'architettura,* no. 7 (December 1952/April 1953), pp. 9–18.

2. David Thistlewood, "Losing Details, Winning Monuments," review of *Rachel Whiteread: Shedding Life,* Tate Gallery, Liverpool, *Times Literary Supplement* (18 October 1996), p. 20.

Deep Space/Repressed Memory

1. Mike Kelley, "Repressed Architectural Memory Replaced with Psychic Reality," *Architecture New York* 15 (1996), p. 39.

2. Ibid., pp. 38, 39.

3. "Mike Kelley Interviewed by Kim Colin and Mark Skiles, 4 August 1995," *Offramp* 1, no. 6 (1996), p. 96.

4. Sigmund Freud, "Screen Memories" (1899), in Freud, *Early Psychoanalytic Writings,* ed. Philip Rieff (New York: Collier Books, 1963), p. 230.

5. Ibid., p. 232.

6. Walter Benjamin, "The Work of Art in the Age of Mechanical Reproduction," in *Illuminations,* ed. Hannah Arendt, trans. Harry Zohn (New York: Schocken Books, 1969), p. 239.

7. Kelley, "Repressed Architectural Memory," p. 38.

8. "Mike Kelley Interviewed," p. 91.

9. Ibid., p. 90.

10. Freud, "Screen Memories," p. 243.

11. Ibid., p. 250.

12. Ibid., p. 247.

13. Ibid., p. 245.

14. "Mike Kelley Interviewed," p. 87.

15. Kelley, "Repressed Architectural Memory," p. 38.

16. "Mike Kelley Interviewed," p. 89.

17. Ibid., p. 96.

18. Benjamin, "The Work of Art in the Age of Mechanical Reproduction," pp. 236–237.

19. Kelley, "Repressed Architectural Memory," p. 39.

20. Jacques Lacan, "Le stade du miroir," in *Ecrits I* (Paris: Editions du Seuil, 1966), p. 94 (my translation).

21. Ibid.

22. William Gibson, *Idoru* (New York: G. P. Putnam's Sons, 1996).

23. William Gibson, *Neuromancer* (New York: Ace Books, 1984), p. 51.

24. Ibid., p. 5.

25. Ibid., p. 52.

26. Ibid., p. 25.

Terminal Transfer

See Martha Rosler, *Rights of Passage* (Belgium and New York, 1997) and *In the Place of the Public: Observations of a Frequent Flyer* (Frankfurt: Museum für Moderne Kunst, 1998), for the collected photographs that are the subject of this essay.

1. See Edward Dimendberg, "The Will to Motorization: Cinema, Highways, and Modernity," *October* 73 (Summer 1995), pp. 90–137. *Plunder Road* was directed by Hubert Cornfield and released by Twentieth Century Fox in 1957.

2. Kevin Lynch, *The Image of the City* (Cambridge, Mass.: MIT Press, 1960).

3. Automotive Safety Foundation, *Driver Needs in Freeway Signing* (Washington, December 1958).

4. Lynch, *The Image of the City*, p. 125; he cites Pierre Jaccard, *Le sens de la direction et l'orientation lointaine chez l'homme* (Paris: Payot, 1932), H. A. Witkin, "Orientation in Space," *Research Reviews*, Office of Naval Research (December 1949), and A. Binet, "Reverse Illusions of Orientation," *Psychological Review* 1, no. 4 (July 1894), pp. 337–350.

5. Lynch, *The Image of the City*, p. 125.

6. Ibid., pp. 29, 31–32.

7. "In the Place of the Public," Jay Gourney Modern Art, New York, October–November 1993.

8. Richard Neutra, "Terminals? Transfer?," *Architectural Record* 68 (August 1930), p. 104.

9. Le Corbusier, *Oeuvre complète,* vol. 4 (Zurich: Boesinger, 1946), p. 199.

10. United States Department of Commerce, *Airport Terminal Buildings* (Washington, April 1953), p. 11.

11. "The Concrete Bird Stands Free," *Architectural Forum* 113 (December 1960), pp. 114–115.

12. Lionel Brett, "Arrival and Departure," *Architectural Review* 118, no. 703 (July 1955), p. 5.

13. Michael Brawne, "Airport Passenger Buildings," *Architectural Review* 132 (November 1962), p. 348.

14. Quoted in Martha Rosler, "In the Place of the Public: Observations of a Frequent Flyer," *Assemblage* 25 (1995), p. 61.

15. Siegfried Kracauer, "On Employment Agencies: The Construction of a Space," trans. David Frisby, in Neil Leach, ed., *Rethinking Architecture: A Reader in Cultural Theory* (London and New York: Routledge, 1997), pp. 59–64. Published in German as "Über Arbeitsnachweise: Konstruktion eines Raumes," in Kracauer, *Schriften,* vol. 5.2, ed. Inka Mülder-Bach (Frankfurt am Main: Suhrkamp Verlag, 1990), pp. 185–192.

16. Kracauer, "On Employment Agencies," p. 59.

17. Ibid., p. 62.

18. *American Airport Designs* (New York: Taylor, Rogers, Bliss for the Lehigh Portland Cement Co., 1930), p. 11.

19. Stephen Spender, *Collected Poems 1928–1985* (London: Faber and Faber, 1985), pp. 41–42. Spender evokes the atmosphere of a terminal in other poems of the era, in "The Pylons" and especially in "Unemployed" and "In Railway Halls," both seemingly echoing Kracauer's sentiments. Spender writes in "In Railway Halls" (p. 51):

> In railway halls, on pavements near the traffic,
> They beg, their eyes made big by empty staring
> And only measuring Time, like the blank clock . . .
> Time merely drives these lives which do not live
> As tides push rotten stuff along the shore.

Angelus Novus

1. Coop Himmelblau, *The Power of the City* (Vienna: Georg Büchner, 1988), p. 95.

2. Ibid., p. 93.

3. Ibid., p. 95.

Beyond Baroque

With affectionate homage to "Beyond Baroque," one of the liveliest sites of performance, readings, and intellectual interchange in Venice, California.

1. Richard Neutra, *Wie baut Amerika?* (Stuttgart: J. Hoffman, 1927), p. 69, cited in Emil Kaufmann, *Von Ledoux bis Le Corbusier* (Vienna: Rolf Passer, 1933), p. 62.

2. Sigfried Giedion, *Space, Time and Architecture: The Growth of a New Tradition* (Cambridge: Harvard University Press, 1941), p. 416.

3. Ibid.

4. Ibid.

5. See Linda Dalrymple Henderson, *The Fourth Dimension and Non-Euclidian Geometry in Modern Art* (Princeton: Princeton University Press, 1983).

6. Gilles Deleuze, *The Fold: Leibniz and the Baroque,* trans. Tom Conley (Minneapolis: University of Minnesota Press, 1993), p. 19.

Death Cube "K"

1. Gilles Deleuze and Félix Guattari, *Kafka: Toward a Minor Literature,* trans. Dana Polan (Minneapolis: University of Minnesota Press, 1986), pp. 75–76.

2. William Gibson, *Idoru* (New York: G. P. Putnam's Sons, 1996), p. 3.

3. Immanuel Kant, *Anthropology from a Pragmatic Point of View,* trans. Mary J. Gregor (The Hague: Martinus Nijhoff, 1974) 54, 4, cited in Jean-François Lyotard, *The Inhuman: Reflections on Time,* trans. Geoffrey Bennington and Rachel Bowlby (Stanford: Stanford University Press, 1991), p. 182.

4. Franz Kafka, *The Diaries of Franz Kafka, 1914–1923,* ed. Max Brod, 2 vols. (New York: Schocken Books, 1949), 1:33.

5. Walter Benjamin, letter to Gershom Scholem, 12 June 1938, in *The Correspondence of Walter Benjamin, 1910–1940,* ed. Gershom Scholem and Theodor W. Adorno, trans.

Manfred R. Jacobson and Evelyn M. Jacobson (Chicago: University of Chicago Press, 1994), p. 563.

6. Eddington, cited in ibid., p. 564.

7. Benjamin, letter to Scholem, in *Correspondence,* p. 564.

8. Deleuze and Guattari, *Kafka,* pp. 72–77. This essay was first published as *Kafka: Pour une littérature mineure* (Paris: Editions de Minuit, 1975).

9. Franz Kafka, "The Great Wall of China," in *The Complete Stories,* ed. Nahum N. Glatzer (New York: Schocken Books, 1971), pp. 238–239.

10. Franz Kafka, *The Trial,* trans. Willa and Edwin Muir (New York: Schocken Books, 1992), p. 141.

11. Deleuze and Guattari, *Kafka,* pp. 75–76.

12. Robin Evans, "Mies van der Rohe's Paradoxical Symmetries," in *Translations from Drawing to Building and Other Essays* (London: Architectural Association, 1997), p. 269.

13. Colin Rowe, "La Tourette," in *The Mathematics of the Ideal Villa and Other Essays* (Cambridge: MIT Press, 1976), p. 196, citing Le Corbusier, *Vers une architecture* (Paris, 1958), p. 150.

14. Rowe, "La Tourette," p. 197.

15. Javier Navarro de Zuvillaga, "Kafka's Concept of Space," *Architectural Association Quarterly* 7, no. 1 (January/March 1975), p. 22.

16. Ibid.

17. All citations from Morphosis are from a preliminary draft of *Morphosis: Building and Projects 1993–1997* (New York: Rizzoli, 1999), Appendix 11, pp. 1–35.

18. Siegfried Kracauer, "Franz Kafka: On His Posthumous Works," in *The Mass Ornament: Weimar Essays,* trans. Thomas Y. Levin (Cambridge: Harvard University Press, 1995), p. 268.

19. See Bernard Cache, *Earth Moves: The Furnishing of Territories* (Cambridge, Mass.: MIT Press, 1995).

Skin and Bones

1. Gilles Deleuze, *The Fold: Leibniz and the Baroque,* trans. Tom Conley (Minneapolis: University of Minnesota Press, 1993), p. 4.

2. Ibid.

3. The long-delayed publication of Bernard Cache's *Terre Meuble,* written in 1983 and signaled by Deleuze in 1988 as *L'ameublement du territoire* (literally "The Furnishing of the Territory"), as the English-language *Earth Moves* has simply reinforced a movement, summarized already in Greg Lynn's edited volume *Folding in Architecture* (London: Academy Editions, 1993), that has rapidly overcome the last such speed-driven neo-avant-garde, deconstructivism.

4. Gottfried Wilhelm Leibniz, *Die Philosophischen Schriften,* 7 vols., ed. G. J. Gerhardt (Berlin: Weidmannsche, 1882), 5:131. See also G. W. Leibniz, *New Essays on Human Understanding,* trans. and ed. Peter Remnant and Jonathan Bennett (Cambridge: Cambridge University Press, 1981), pp. 144–145.

5. See Jonathan Crary, *Techniques of the Observer: On Vision and Modernity in the Nineteenth Century* (Cambridge: MIT Press, 1990), pp. 25–66, for a detailed exposition of the camera obscura principle and its role in representation.

6. Leibniz, *New Essays,* pp. 144–145.

7. Leibniz, *Philosophischen Schriften,* 5:131.

8. Leibniz, *New Essays,* preface, p. 60.

9. Marcel Jean, "L'architecture allégorique," *Art,* special number of *L'Architecture d'Aujourd'hui* (1946), pp. 24–27.

10. Marcel Jean, in *Cahiers d'Art* (June 1936).

11. Jean, "L'architecture allégorique," p. 24.

12. See Greg Lynn, *Folds, Bodies and Blobs: Collected Essays* (Brussels: La Lettre Volée, 1998), especially "Multiplicitous and Inorganic Bodies," pp. 33–61.

13. Victor Hugo, *Les misérables,* trans. Norman Denny (Harmondsworth, Middlesex: Penguin Books, 1976), pp. 822–823.

14. Ibid., p. 826.

15. Ibid., p. 825.

16. Deleuze, *The Fold,* p. 28.

17. Ibid.

18. Ibid., pp. 34, 35.

19. Ibid., pp. 136–137.

20. The following projects are illustrated and explained in Greg Lynn, *Animate Form* (New York: Princeton Architectural Press, 1999).

21. Deleuze, *The Fold,* p. 137.

22. Ibid., p. 136.

23. Ibid., p. 137.

Building in Empty Spaces

See Andreas Huyssen's incisive analysis "The Voids of Berlin," *Critical Inquiry* 24 (Autumn 1997), for a comprehensive treatment of the "void" in Berlin's spatial and ideological history.

1. Here I am suggesting that while Libeskind's void is, as Huyssen suggests (ibid., p. 79), certainly "fractured" and signifying of history, it is also and fundamentally a void without space, a void constructed to be perceived by the body and its senses without sight, as if in a visual vacuum, so to speak.

2. Ernst Bloch, "Berlin as Viewed from the Landscape," in *Literary Essays* (Stanford: Stanford University Press, 1998), p. 362.

3. Ibid., p. 370.

4. Ibid., p. 365.

5. See Daniel Libeskind, "Symbol and Interpretation," in *Radix-Matrix: Architecture and Writings* (Munich: Prestel, 1997), pp. 152–154.

Planets, Comets, Dinosaurs (and Bugs)

This essay was first delivered as a talk to the Department of Architecture, University of California, Berkeley, in the fall of 1997, and in revised form to the "Architecture and Identity" symposium organized by the students in the History of Architecture and Urban Studies program at Cornell University in the spring of 1998.

1. Sigmund Freud, "Findings, Ideas, Problems," in *The Standard Edition of the Complete Psychological Works of Sigmund Freud,* ed. James Strachey, 24 vols. (London: Hogarth Press, 1953–1974), 23:299.

2. W. J. T. Mitchell, *The Last Dinosaur Book* (Chicago: University of Chicago Press, 1998), a study that usefully summarizes the place of dinosaurs in Western cultural history from the late eighteenth century to the present.

3. Jacques Lacan, "Le stade du miroir comme formateur de la fonction du Je telle qu'elle nous est révélée dans l'expérience psychanalytique. Communication faite au XVIe congrès international de psychanalyse, à Zürich, le 17 juillet 1949," in *Ecrits I* (Paris: Editions du Seuil, 1966), pp. 89–97. Translated in *Ecrits: A Selection,* trans. Alan Sheridan (New York:

W. W. Norton, 1977), pp. 1–7. As Sheridan notes, the first version of this essay, "Le stade du miroir," was delivered at the International Psychoanalytical Congress in Marienbad, August 1936. The revised version of 1949 was first published in the *Revue française de psychanalyse,* no. 4 (October–December 1949), pp. 449–455.

4. William Gibson, *Neuromancer* (New York: Berekeley Publishing Group, 1984), p. 52.

5. Lutz Niethammer, *Posthistoire: Has History Come to an End?,* trans. Patrick Camiller (London: Verso, 1992).

6. Peter Dodge, *A Documentary Study of Hendrik de Man, Socialist Critic of Marxism* (Princeton: Princeton University Press, 1979), p. 346.

7. Gianni Vattimo, *The End of Modernity: Nihilism and Hermeneutics in Post-modern Culture,* trans. Jon R. Snyder (Baltimore: Johns Hopkins University Press, 1991), p. 7.

8. Ibid., p. 11.

9. Robert Smithson and Mel Bochner, "The Domain of the Great Bear," *Art Voices* (Fall 1966), reprinted in Jack Flam, ed., *Robert Smithson: The Collected Writings* (Berkeley: University of California Press, 1996), pp. 26–27.

10. Flam, ed., *Robert Smithson,* p. 32.

11. Ibid., p. 15.

12. "Interstellar Flit," undated typescript (c. 1961–1963), Smithson Papers, reel 3834, frame 645, quoted in Robert A. Sobieszek, *Robert Smithson: Photo Works,* exh. cat. (Los Angeles: Los Angeles County Museum of Art; Albuquerque: University of New Mexico Press, 1993), p. 19.

13. Flam, ed., *Robert Smithson,* p. 13.

14. Ibid., p. 14.

15. Ibid.

16. Michel Foucault, "Of Other Spaces," *Diacritics* (Spring 1986), p. 24. In this construction of the mirror *as* a topos, both utopia and heterotopia, Foucault is playing on, but diverging from, the Lacanian version of the mirror that acts as a staging ground for the reflected subject. Foucault's mirror is thus a place in itself, which leads to the possibility (and danger) of the classification of actual spaces as heterotopias. Hence the fascination of architects with Foucault's notion, and the literal application of "heterotopic" ideas to buildings and projects that followed in the 1980s.

17. Flam, ed., *Robert Smithson,* pp. 143–153.

18. Ibid., pp. 150–151.

19. Mitchell, *The Last Dinosaur Book,* p. 208.

20. R. Chauvin, "Notes sur la physiologie comparée des orthoptères," *Bulletin de la Société Entomologique de France* (1941, no. 10), pp. 153–154.

21. Lacan, transcript of unpublished seminar, "Angoisse," 14 November 1962.

22. Franz Kafka, *The Metamorphosis,* trans. and ed. Stanley Corngold (New York: W. W. Norton, 1996), p. 3.

23. Henri Poincaré, "La relativité de l'espace," *L'Année Psychologique* 13 (1907), p. 16.

Index of Names